OUT OF THIN AIR

Praise for Out Of Thin Air

'Through reading this book you will come to understand that the heart and soul of running are to be found in Ethiopia. I welcome everyone to experience the Ethiopian love of running, and to come and have the same life-altering experience that Michael had. Running is life!'

Haile Gebrselassie, Olympic gold medal winner
and World Champion

'*Out Of Thin Air* is full of wonderful insights and lessons from a world where the ability to run is viewed as something almost mysterious and magical. With his understated writing style, Crawley gently pulls back the layers on one of the world's most incredible sporting cultures, revealing a powerful simplicity at its core.

This is an honest portrait of Ethiopian running that doesn't shy away from the difficulties of the life there, or the hardships and insurmountable obstacles most of the runners face in their quest to find success, and the book can leave you feeling a little sad, as well as inspired. But more than anything, after reading it you will look at the great runners of Ethiopia a little differently the next time you see them streaking away majestically at the front of a major race.'

Adharanand Finn, author of *Running with the Kenyans*

'A deep dive into the rich and complex culture that produces some of the fastest runners the world has ever seen. Michael Crawley's perceptive portrait will force you to re-examine your assumptions about why those who dream even the biggest dreams sometimes succeed.'

Alex Hutchinson, author of *Endure*

OUT OF THIN AIR

Running wisdom and magic from above the clouds in Ethiopia

MICHAEL CRAWLEY

BLOOMSBURY SPORT
LONDON · OXFORD · NEW YORK · NEW DELHI · SYDNEY

BLOOMSBURY SPORT
Bloomsbury Publishing Plc
50 Bedford Square, London, WC1B 3DP, UK

BLOOMSBURY, BLOOMSBURY SPORT and the Diana logo are
trademarks of Bloomsbury Publishing Plc

First published in Great Britain 2020

A catalogue record for this book is available from the British Library

Library of Congress Cataloguing-in-Publication data has been applied for

ISBN: HB: 978-1-4729-7532-4; TPB: 978-1-4729-7533-1;
eBook: 978-1-4729-7531-7

2 4 6 8 10 9 7 5 3 1

Typeset in Adobe Garamond Pro by Deanta Global Publishing Services, Chennai, India
Printed and bound in Great Britain by CPI Group (UK) Ltd, Croydon CR0 4YY

To find out more about our authors and books visit www.bloomsbury.com
and sign up for our newsletters

For Roslyn and Maddy

A Note on Times and Shoes

Most of the training and racing described in this book took place between 2015 and 2016, which is not all that long ago in the grand scheme of things. However, given the developments in footwear technology since then, in marathon-running terms it seems almost like a different era. A brief note on running times therefore seems appropriate. For the uninitiated, the recording of times in this book follows the convention of listing hours, minutes and seconds separated by a full stop. So 2.01.39 means two hours, one minute and 39 seconds.

Much of the focus in the athletics press in the last couple of years has been on shoes rather than athletes, with the perception being that people are now running significantly faster than before. This feeling was shared in Ethiopia, where excitement (and anxiety) about the potential of shoe technology was widespread. If you look at the rankings, though, the difference in speed at the top level of the sport isn't that big. The 50th ranked male marathon runner in 2015 ran 2.07.57, compared with 2.06.22 in 2019. The difference was around two minutes for women, from 2.23.30 for 50th in the rankings in 2015 to 2.25.42 in 2019. An improvement of a minute and 30 seconds to two minutes does suggest that shoes have distorted performances to an extent, but perhaps not in the astronomical way some commentators suggest.

That 50th ranked time – around two hours and eight minutes for men, and two hours 25 minutes for women – is the sort of time the athletes I knew had in mind when they talked about 'changing their lives' through the sport. In 2015 it was the kind of time that would be likely to net a contract with Nike or Adidas. To put that in perspective, in parkrun terms that's a little over eight consecutive parkruns in 15.10 for men, or 17.15 for women.

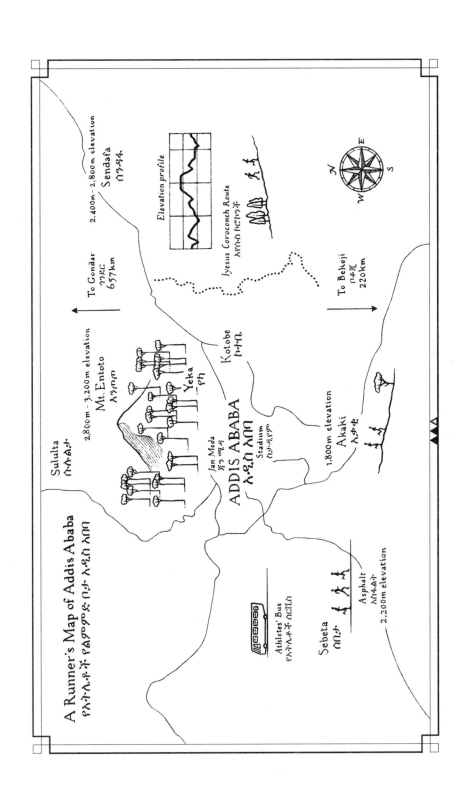

CONTENTS

1

SPECIAL AIR

When my alarm goes off at 4.40 a.m. I have already been awake for six or seven minutes. The familiar wail has already crackled from the church's speakers, our dog has been barking at hyenas all night and I always find it difficult to sleep knowing I have to be up so early. I'm already wearing my running shorts and I stumble into the rest of my kit, laid out the night before to make things as simple as possible at this hour. Five minutes later Hailye and Fasil knock on my door. Hoods up against the cold, we head down to the team bus. 'Are you tired?' I ask Fasil in Amharic. 'I am not tired!' he exclaims, grinning. It is extremely rare for Fasil to admit to being tired. The number of people in the pitch-black street surprises me. The Amharic word for dawn is *goh* and people tend to start their day as though this has been shouted, loudly, in their ear. Already men stride purposefully through the dust and groups of people wait for the minibuses that head for the town centre. These minibuses start around 4 a.m. and the familiar shout of the potential destinations, '*Piazza, Arat Kilo!*' can already be heard. A kid in a faded Arsenal shirt leans out of the door of one of them and tries out his English. 'Where are you go?' he says. 'Entoto,' I tell him, as he vanishes into the darkness.

When I board the Moyo Sports team bus it is already full of dozing athletes. In hooded training tops or draped with traditional cotton *shammas*, they look like an incongruous mixture of monks and boxers, all trying to catch a few more minutes' sleep before training. Hailye, assistant coach and sub-agent, monitors his phone constantly, telling the driver where to pick up the athletes. They wait at the dark roadside for the bus alongside the casual labourers waiting for their own rides and quietly preparing themselves for their own form of toil.

In the faint glow of predawn the occasional runner flashes past, taking the opportunity to train on the roads before they become too busy. Caught in a haze of headlight and exhaust fume they are momentary ghosts who quickly disappear again into the darkness. The bus winds its way uphill past settlements still in darkness. As we drive, dawn gradually breaks, revealing a dashboard cluttered with Christian iconography and two windscreen stickers. On the left is a white dove, on the right an overly bulbous Nike swoosh. The road turns from tarmac to cobbles and finally to a dirt path as we work our way up the switchbacks to the starting point of the run, finally stopping when the path threatens to become too narrow to drive along. No-one moves apart from coach Meseret in the front seat, who resets his three stopwatches and makes last-minute notes on a sheet of paper scrawled with numbers. Finally, he turns round in his seat and orders people off the bus.

It is now 6 a.m. I stand outside the bus, watching my breath turn to mist and rise towards the mountain, further obscuring the half-dark path we're about to run up. I shake my legs nervously and try to taste the increased thinness of the air. The bus has taken over an hour to wind its way up here and we are now a good few hundred metres higher than where I've been living in Addis Ababa at 2500 metres above sea level. I'd received a text from Hailye a few weeks earlier when I'd been planning my time here. 'I would advise you especially not to miss Entoto,' it said. 'It is the secret for Haile Gebrselassie to fly to victory in Berlin with an outstanding performance.' This 'secret' turns out not to be a particularly well kept one in Addis, though. Many of the runners in the forest I've been training in for the past couple of weeks have already spoken in hushed tones about the mountain, which has a mythical quality to it. 'This place is 3800 metres,' Meseret tells me. 'You can check on the internet!' I'm not convinced it's quite *that* high, I tell him. I don't want to believe him, anyway. Surely we're not the equivalent of almost halfway up Everest and planning on running uphill?

In the end the exact altitude isn't all that important. The *belief* in the altitude is, though. Running up here isn't going to do your lung capacity any harm, but it may well be even better for a young runner's capacity to dream. The air up here is 'special,' Aseffa tells me as he stretches his back after our bus journey. Powerfully built for a runner, Aseffa's nickname is 'Biretu', which Hailye translates as 'Iron Man'. Teklemariam, whose receding hairline is put down to his brain power by the other runners, adds, 'It is good for haemoglobin.' Seeing my surprise that this is part of his relatively limited English vocabulary he adds, 'You know haemoglobin?' Not personally, I reply. 'You just run *very* slowly,' he tells me. 'The air is *special*.'

Entoto is over three times higher than the highest point in England. It is the sort of altitude at which you get a headache as soon as you start running and at which, it turns out, I start to lose the feeling in my fingers. It is where Emperor Menelik II founded Addis Ababa at the end of the 19th century. It is cold up here and before long Menelik's wife insisted they moved the palace into the valley, where it was a little warmer and there were hot springs. The mountain is planted with eucalyptus trees imported from Australia and it is therefore known as 'the lung of Addis Ababa', but it doesn't feel like there's much oxygen up here. 'It will put some kind of pressure on your respiration system I think,' coach Meseret tells me. He wears a sky-blue, knee-length Adidas jacket, his hood up with the drawstrings fastened tightly under his chin to keep out the cold. 'Just breathe in,' he says, taking a full-body breath in, standing on his tiptoes, 'and out,' he says, releasing the air forcefully from his lungs. 'And in… And out.' He pats me on the shoulder affectionately.

There is a marked air of reluctance emanating from the bus when we arrive. It takes a good few minutes for sapling limbs to unfurl themselves from cramped seats and a sleepy trepidation has replaced the usual joviality of the training group. The Ethiopians, clearly, share a little of my fear of the mountain. For the main group, the coach tells me, the training session is 70 minutes at a pace of 3.50 per kilometre followed by 12 flat-out hill sprints of 200 metres. 'But I don't think you need hill reps today,' he adds, turning to me. I tell him I think he's probably right. 'Just do 90 minutes easy,' he says. 'Well, you know, easy but hard,' he adds as he walks away. This is exactly the kind of cryptic statement I could do without hearing on a semi-dark roadside, halfway up a mountain and only partially acclimatised to the altitude. I'm relieved when Teklemariam tells me that he will run with me instead of the main group.

Our bus, its windows fogged with the condensed breath of 60 of the most effective lungs on the planet, sits on the edge of a clearing surrounded by forest. Teklemariam tells me to follow him and starts to amble very slowly in the direction of the forest, behind the others. I feel better once we start running, reassured by the familiar feeling of my body starting to wake up, muscles warming at a slightly faster rate than the air around them. This may be the highest run I've ever attempted, but the feeling of getting going on a morning run is always the same, providing some comfort in an alien environment. My limbs loosen, open out and gradually tune in to the easy tempo set by Teklemariam. I feel immediately light-headed, though, and my lungs are working seriously hard even at a slow pace. Meseret is right about it putting pressure on my 'respiration system'. I'm suddenly very aware of the muscles required to draw in and expel air, the mechanics of breathing. This is usually such an unconscious process that it takes me by surprise. I feel like my body is struggling to monitor the lack of oxygen and then registering it, causing me to focus on really filling my lungs, as coach Meseret described.

The sun has started to flicker through the eucalyptus trees that line our route and the only sound is the rhythmic patter of shoe on trail. Gradually the silence of the bus journey gives way to the playful chatter of an Ethiopian morning run and I know that as long as the main group just ahead of us are still talking, the run can't be too serious. But then the vague path we are following keeps going up, with two hills in quick succession lasting 10 minutes each. The trees start to look unnatural. They stand too proud, ruler-straightened. Then they start to thin out, revealing a bare, lunar landscape – an Ethiopian Ventoux.

My mind starts to wander, the lack of oxygen up here preventing any particularly coherent thoughts, and the trail starts to remind me of Hamsterley Forest near where I grew up in Durham. I imagine the forest in an enormous bell jar, starved of oxygen. The path, which at first seemed to rise and fall at the whim of the mountain's undulations, seems to take more capricious routes up the slope. And as my legs fatigue, the amount of oxygen reaching them decreases with the thinning air.

The runners ahead of me depart from the group in twos and threes. An unspoken decision to increase the pace is reached, heads go down, and gaps increase. This happens imperceptibly at first, then alarmingly quickly. Suddenly I'm struggling like I have never struggled before on a run. I have only been at altitude for a week. My lungs can't deal with this and my legs don't know how to respond to the sudden cut-off of fuel. I focus on just lifting my legs, on getting to the top of each false summit. Finally, on not walking. Rather than opening out to take in the view, my perspective dwindles to the patch of ground beneath my feet as I try to will my legs to keep going. My attention shrinks to the sensations within my own body, which are notoriously difficult to describe.

I think of Olympic marathon fourth-place finisher and *Sports Illustrated* journalist Kenny Moore's reluctance to use the word 'pain' when writing about running. 'It's not the pain of a burning stovetop,' he wrote. 'It feels like weakness. It feels like weight that can't be borne, panic that can't be controlled.' It feels, I think, like I need to stop. My thoughts lose their coherence completely and I start making vague word associations. As I labour up a steep hill I find myself intoning, 'Camber, clamber, caper, scarper, scamper.' As my breathing becomes increasingly ragged, the panic that starts to well up in my lungs takes me back to my earliest running memory. My hands are on my nine-year-old knees as I try to suck air while apologising to my dad for slowing him down, his hand on my shoulder telling me it's OK, that he is just happy that we are running together. Afterwards, when I'm calmer, the feeling that running had hurt, but that it had mined something deeper within me than the other sports I played.

Finally, Teklemariam ambles back to reassure me that we have 'only 200 metres more' to run. Every few hundred metres I ask him how far we have to run *now*. Each time he responds, 'I told you, 200 metres.' He thinks the joke gets funnier. It doesn't. By now I am crawling along, eyes stinging, sweating pure salt and wishing I had the breath to argue with him. And then I stumble around a corner and there is the bus and I can stop. Two minutes later, Teklemariam has already regained his charm. Like the great Haile Gebrselassie, his grin is infectious. It is not quite 7.30 a.m. and I have already run 13 miles. The sun has risen above Addis, and we are back in time to watch the main group hurtle up and down a steep incline on their post-run hill reps. I have already remembered why I love this.

I stand with Meseret at the top of the hill, at 3500 metres, overlooking rolling farmland. *Tukuls*, round, dirt-walled farmsteads, and circular piles of golden straw dot the hillside. As the group race up the incline, Meseret shouts '*Na! Na!* – 'Come! Come!' – willing them to get to him faster. They race every rep, with Tsedat winning most of them. He is exactly five feet tall (1.52m) and his little legs whirl powerfully underneath him. After the seventh repetition Hunegnaw, who is coming back from injury, doubles over and retches. 'They're going to kill me,' he tells Meseret. 'Jog, jog, get down the hill!' Meseret responds. There is no sympathy during the session, but afterwards, as everyone relaxes on the grass, Meseret puts an arm around him and reassures him that he's coming back into shape. 'I know, I know,' Hunegnaw replies with a weak laugh. He ran 59.39 for a half marathon a couple of years ago and finished eighth at the World Athletics Cross Country

7

Championships. He knows if he can put a few months of training together he will be in a position to challenge the best in the world. But here pedigree means very little and there are hundreds of others in a position to challenge him now, including the 20 in our group this morning.

As we sit on the grass, other runners emerge from the forest and meander around the field before returning into the trees. Some run in pairs, others in large groups, single-file trains of 15 or more. No-one runs alone. 'There are a lot of runners up here,' I comment. Meseret nods. 'There are 5000 at least in Addis Ababa,' he says. 'They start as a big flock of birds, but eventually the flock will melt away to nearly nothing. Only a few can become successful. From the few hundred you have seen this morning you will be able to count the successful ones on your fingers.' He surveys the group running a diagonal across the field, their legs perfectly in time. 'And what does it take to find that success?' I ask. 'The successful ones,' he replies, 'are the ones who watch with their eyes and think with their minds before they move their legs. The ones who run on emotion only can't make it.' This strikes me as a curious response and I realise I was expecting one of the usual running clichés about hard work or giving 110 per cent. I write it down in my notebook, the first of 12 that I will fill in my time in Ethiopia.

People joke around in the sun and Hunegnaw and another runner wander off to buy weak local beer, *tella*, from one of the farms. Another surprise: coach Meseret condones this as an excellent source of carbohydrates. A man with a briefcase runs clumsily down the slope and one of the runners says something in Amharic, the only word of which I catch is *jibb*, hyena. Everyone bursts out laughing and I ask Hailye what they said. 'It is a kind of proverb,' he tells me. 'The fastest hyena gets the antennae,' he says, holding his fingers above his head. 'Horns, you mean,' I say. 'Yes, the horns. Because they have gone too quickly, they catch up with the head and the others get the good meat. It means you should not hurry.' This seems like a curious proverb for a professional athlete, whose livelihood is dependent upon moving quickly, to subscribe to. No-one is hurrying to get back from training today, though; our bus driver is asleep on the grass in the sun.

The contrast between pre-training trepidation and post-training joviality couldn't be more marked, and I realise I've gone through more emotions in the last two hours than I would in some weeks. At the beginning of 15 months in Ethiopia it occurs to me that running and anthropology both allow you to do a similar thing: to live a whole other life. As an anthropologist I immerse myself deeply into the rhythms and complications of life in Addis Ababa, and as a runner, because every run contains its own range of emotions, and because serious distance-running training has its own unique challenges, each approach to a race is akin to a journey or an adventure.

Forty years or so ago the sociologist Max Weber wrote that, 'Disenchantment is the distinctive injury of modernity.' Many of us in the West, he writes, believe that 'There are no mysterious incalculable forces that come into play, but rather that one can, in principle, master all things by calculation.' This is even more true today than when he wrote it. We run with heart-rate monitors and GPS watches at a carefully planned pace. We upload the GPS data about our running to apps like Strava, and joke that it 'doesn't count' if it is not uploaded, catalogued and compared to others. Sports scientists test our top athletes in order to determine their physiological parameters. We feel that we know our limits. Ethiopia appeals to me because here the runners believe that 'mysterious incalculable forces' have a huge part to play in their success. Why else would they travel for hours at a time, three days a week, in order to run somewhere like Entoto? To get up at 4 a.m. to travel somewhere with hallowed ground and 'special' air makes running more pilgrimage than recreation.

Ethiopia is a place where I have been told that energy is controlled by angels and demons, and where witch doctors can help you to acquire another runner's power. It is a place where an anonymous runner in the forest told me, miming an imaginary scoreboard and with a completely straight face, that he had dreamt that he would run 25.32 for 10,000m – almost a full minute faster than the world record. It is a place where they tell me that the air at Entoto will transform me into a 2.08 marathon runner. It is a place, in short, of magic and madness, where dreaming is still very much alive.

Transcendent as the performances of especially gifted Ethiopian and Kenyan athletes are, distance running is a sport in which it is still seemingly acceptable for commentators to refer to them collectively as 'the East Africans' or even just as 'the Africans'. I once sat through an hour of BBC commentary on the 2016 Great Scottish Run in which Moses Kipsiro, a Ugandan with a name, was referred to throughout simply as 'the Kenyan' as he raced against Scottish runner Callum Hawkins. Given that the race was in Glasgow, where Kipsiro had recently won the 5000m and 10,000m double in the Commonwealth Games, I found this even more striking than usual. Think about it for a second. In what other sport would this not be met with outrage? If Didier Drogba was referred to simply as 'the West African' or Novak Djokovic (who is Serbian) as 'the Croat'? It is also notable that in Ethiopia the naming convention is for a child to have one given name, which is then followed by their father's name and sometimes also by their grandfather's name. This means that when commentators refer to the great Ethiopian runner Kenenisa Bekele as 'Bekele' they are actually referring to his father, which Ethiopians watching races find confusing. In respect of this, throughout this book I try to use given or first names as much as possible.

Part of the reason for this, I think, is the mystique of distance running. The popular image of the 'loneliness of the long-distance runner' encourages the presentation of introverted personas, of athletes who fly in, astound us with scarcely comprehensible feats of speed and endurance, and then vanish again into thin air, back into the forests of Entoto. That is why I decided to call this book *Out of Thin Air*, to play on the two different meanings of the phrase. We know little about the lives and beliefs of some of the most talented athletes in the world, and the feats they accomplish therefore seem to spring almost from nowhere. This explains why *The Unknown Runner* was still considered an appropriate title for a film about Geoffrey Kamworor, in spite of the fact that he was already World Junior Cross Country champion and is now the half marathon world record holder.

The second reason is because we usually explain long-distance running success as being a direct result of a set of deterministic factors that are out of the control of the athletes who possess them, chief among which is altitude. We assume that the performances of elite Ethiopian, Kenyan and Ugandan runners are produced almost directly 'out of thin air'. Others seek answers in particular genetic traits. The Athlome Project, for instance, an international consortium of scientists working on exercise genetics and genomics, attempts to discover the 'genetic variants associated with elite athletic performance'. The project's director, Yannis Pitsiladis, has written numerous articles based on the premise that it is likely there is some genetic component to elite athletic performance, but has conceded that as yet none has been found.

The assumption of some sort of genetic or altitude-derived advantage comes down to 'nature'. Runners from Ethiopia and Kenya are seen as 'naturally gifted,' and this extends to the way in which people talk about poverty. The implication is that growing up in rural poverty necessitates a more 'natural' way of life. This is characterised in media portrayals as working on the land as a child and running long distances to and from school barefoot, with these activities seen as naturally producing champion runners. We come to believe that running for Africans is something they take to easily, without thought or consideration. I am an anthropologist, not a scientist, and I do not seek to disprove these theories. However, I think it is important to point out the effects that talking about long-distance running in this way has. The tendency to describe African runners as 'effortless' or as 'born to run' masks the years of preparation and sacrifice that have gone into creating this illusion. It fails to recognise the running expertise that is specifically Ethiopian, or Kenyan or Ugandan. And it fails to acknowledge the institutional support, in fact far superior to that of the UK, offered to Ethiopian runners. I was convinced that there was a more nuanced set of cultural influences of Ethiopian running success at play and it was these factors I wanted to explore more during my time in Addis.

To refer to 'East African' distance running is to conflate runners from quite different cultures, many of whom are from different ethnic groups, who speak a variety of languages and whose religious beliefs shape their running in particular ways. Most of the books on running in the region are about Kenya, where it is possible to speak English, and where there are a number of comfortable hotels set up to cater for journalists and Western runners. When we speak of 'East African' running, then, we are actually primarily talking about Kenyan running. I was drawn to Ethiopia partly for this reason and partly because I was fascinated by Ethiopian exceptionalism: Ethiopia was the first nation to adopt Christianity, the only African country with its own alphabet and the only one to outwit European colonialism.

Since Abebe Bikila's surprise, bare-footed victory in the 1960 Olympic marathon, Ethiopian men have won twice the number of marathon gold medals as Kenya. They occupy six of the top ten spots on the all-time marathon lists. They have won five Olympic 10,000m titles since 1980 to Kenya's one, in spite of boycotting the event twice. Ethiopian men and women hold all four 5000m and 10,000m world records. Since Mo Farah started winning global titles on the track, he has only been beaten twice in major championships over 5000m and 10,000m – both times by Ethiopian runners.

As Meseret and I look out over the field at Entoto we can see representatives of all levels of Ethiopian running. In one corner of the field, six Toyota Hilux – the car of choice for the top runners, they cost around $100,000 to import – are parked in formation, as if this were an open-air showroom. The pedigree of the athletes who zigzag in and out of the trees is revealed by clothing; from those in the new-season Adidas and Nike kit or the bright yellow jackets of the Ethiopian national team to those in ragged shorts and plastic sandals. Often, though, they are running together. I pick out one group, who zigzag left and right across the field, the route chosen by the runner at the front who is, Meseret tells me, a 2.05 marathon runner. In fact, he describes him as having run *ka amist* or 'and five' and I have already noticed that when people list marathon times here they just give the minutes, not the hours – running slower than three hours is unheard of. At the back, though, struggling to stay in touch, is a teenager who looks like he's just wandered over from one of the nearby farms. The train of runners meanders around the field, the leader turning almost 180 degrees every minute or so and the rest following like a shoal of fish. 'Why do they zigzag like that, Meseret?' I ask. 'I don't know,' he replies. 'They learn that from each other, No-one is telling them to run like that.' This too surprises me. A coach admitting that the athletes learn from each other, not from him? I wonder whether they also run like this to allow the slower runners, the farm kids intrigued by the brightly coloured jackets, to stay in touch and learn the trade too.

Another group on the field is going through a seemingly interminable set of drills. They swing their arms high before turning and jogging back towards us, before making controlled circles in front of themselves with both hands. 'What is this drill for?' I ask Hailye. 'It is just for relaxation,' he says. 'They are pretending to sow seeds for harvest.' I have, needless to say, never seen this particular exercise before. They go through a series of different motions, exaggerating each running movement in isolation, like pianists going through their scales, before finally shaking hands with each other and sitting down on the grass. Many of the exercises look vaguely familiar, but I realise that they remind me less of any warm-up I've ever seen than of the Ethiopian music videos I've watched in bars and restaurants here. The runners shake their shoulders and stamp on the ground in unison with a rhythm reminiscent of a distinctive dance style called *esketsa*, which means shoulder dancing, which involves vigorous shuddering of the shoulders and forceful exhalations of breath.

There are at least 200 runners on this field alone. I will be here for 15 months, conducting anthropological fieldwork on the culture of Ethiopian long-distance running. Of those on the field who haven't already 'made it', some of the runners in front of me will give up before I finish my fieldwork, disheartened by injury or lack of improvement. A few will change their lives for ever. This book follows the fortunes of a group of elite long-distance runners as they attempt to hit the big time – and my attempts both to keep up with them, and to understand things like zigzag running and dancing as warm-up a little better.

Far from the Western obsession with 'marginal gains' and the sports scientists trying to explain athletic success in the lab, my experience living and running in Ethiopia unveiled to me a far more intuitive, creative and adventurous approach to the sport. Coverage of the various two-hour marathon projects, the most recent of which saw Eliud Kipchoge of Kenya running 1.59.40 for the distance in Vienna, has cast Western scientists as the 'experts' on East African running, focusing on innovations such as carbon fibre-plated shoes and aerodynamic running formations. As I was told by one young Ethiopian runner, though, 'A scientist does not know time, a doctor does not run.' We think of global sport at the top level as being dominated by sports science and laboratory testing, but even some scientists acknowledge that a simple running race can measure physical traits better than any lab test. To an Ethiopian runner, there is no more objective test than a simple race from A to B and the best way to learn about running is to run – a lot.

My time in Ethiopia confirmed to me that high performance and enjoyment of running are not mutually exclusive. That by becoming more in tune with our bodies, with others, with our environments and by following our intuition, we can still achieve without sacrificing what drew us to the sport in the first place. That there's an alternative to the soul-sapping tech and science-obsessed training methodology which dominates global sports programmes and which has filtered down to the general public. Read on to find out what we can all learn about running from people who retain a healthy scepticism for sports science and a pride in an expertise developed through experience. My time in Ethiopia helped me discover and adopt alternative ways of thinking about sports psychology from people who have never heard of sports psychology, and for whom the secrets of running are far too enigmatic and mysterious to be distilled in a test tube.

Why do Ethiopian runners get up at 3 a.m. to run up and down a hill? How does going out looking for hyenas make you a better runner? And how can embracing a creative and 'dangerous' approach to running make it less boring and more of an adventure? Follow me, if you will, into the forest.

2

I COULD HAVE BEEN A *MESINKO* PLAYER

I arrive in Ethiopia at two o'clock in the morning on 14 September, 2015 and from where I'm standing at the baggage carousel I can see not one but two adverts featuring Haile Gebrselassie, Ethiopia's best-known runner and probably the most famous Ethiopian outside of Ethiopia. He is selling two forms of lubricant, one for Total and the other for Johnnie Walker. The slogans: 'Make your Engine an Athlete of the Road' and 'Just Keep Going. Keep Walking'. Given that I am here to study the links between long-distance running and ideas about progress, forward movement and 'development' these seem fitting. The woman at the Visa on Arrival desk is half asleep, but perks up when I use one of my few newly acquired Amharic phrases to tell her I am a runner.

Once I have collected my bag – containing for the most part a jumbled array of notebooks and running shoes – I open the screenshot of instructions for how to get to my friend Dr Benoit Gaudin's house. Benoit works at Addis Ababa University and we had met a few months previously at a conference he organised called East African Running: The Social Science Perspective. He has kindly offered to host me for the first few weeks of my fieldwork while I find my feet. The last few days have been a bit hectic as my partner and I packed up our flats in Edinburgh before starting fieldwork. A fellow anthropologist, Roslyn will be spending the year in Somerset studying equine therapy for autistic children. We will both, therefore, be doing much of our fieldwork in actual fields. I hadn't had time to look too carefully at Benoit's email, and reading it as I walk out of the airport and into the night to find a taxi I start to wish I had.

The email reads as follows: 'Tell the taxi driver to take you to the German Embassy, then turn right and head up the hill. When the tarmac road runs out, turn left on to the cobbles. The driver won't want to take you up there, so you might have to insist. Then take a right, then a left, then a right and stop at the yellow gate. Don't get out of the car until the guard opens the gate, there are hyenas around here at night.' There is very little traffic at this time, and we drive quickly past brightly painted corrugated iron shops and the odd bar lit by neon strip lights. To my surprise we also pass several groups of runners, running single file in groups of two or three. They appear in the glare of the headlights for a moment and then disappear like apparitions, and I wonder why on earth people would want to train at this time of night.

After 20 minutes or so the driver announces that we have reached the German Embassy and I point up the hill. I have, at least, learned the phrases for turning left and right – *wada gra* and *wada ken* – and I hope he won't require more detailed instructions. He doesn't seem too keen on the cobblestones – I will soon learn that the runners aren't either – but at least we move up the hill slowly enough for me to peer out into the darkness and try to make out the colour of the gates. Eventually we trundle up to a large yellow door and I ask the driver to stop. He beeps his horn, which is startlingly loud in the quiet of night, and 30 seconds later the guard, holding a torch, opens the gate. He escorts me to my room – a hut outside that used to be occupied by another guard – while deftly fending off the attentions of his dog.

Benoit pads on to the terrace to welcome me before going back to bed, and I climb into my sleeping bag in my little room and wait for sleep. I can already feel the altitude – every couple of minutes my body seems to sense it and I take a big deep breath. My sleep is patchy and light, disturbed by the thin air and sudden eruptions of barking from the neighbourhood dogs who can smell the hyenas that creep into the city at night. The room only has a tiny window and is completely pitch black, and I wake a couple of times wondering where I am.

Being an anthropologist is to try to be a good storyteller of other people's stories. To do this requires a long-term commitment to the place and the people whose stories you want to tell. In my case this will mean, as far as possible, living in close proximity with the runners whose lives I want to understand, and a commitment to eating with them, relaxing with them after running, and above all suffering alongside them in training. Ethnography is the method of research and writing on which anthropology defines itself. It comes from the Latin terms for 'culture' and 'writing', and is perhaps best translated as 'writing the people'. To do this relies upon a method called 'participant observation' (anthropologist James Clifford has brilliantly called it 'deep hanging out'), which consists essentially of spending lots of time with people, observing them, talking to them and building relationships of trust with them.

Loïc Wacquant, the French sociologist who spent years writing about boxing in the ghetto in Chicago, notes that to do this kind of research well in the context of sport we should think more in terms of 'observant participation' than 'participant observation'. In other words, there is more to be learned in the ring itself than from the sidelines. In practice, though, I am aware that this is going to be a challenge. As the anthropologist Michael Jackson muses, to both observe and participate simultaneously is tantamount to being asked to stand in a river and watch from the bank at the same time or, in my case, to be both running with the group and watching from the team bus. On top of this, I am nowhere near as fast as they are. My best time for a half marathon is 66 minutes, while the athletes in the group I will be training with are between four and eight minutes faster.

However, for Tim Ingold, who conducted his early research on tracking and hunting practices with the Skolts, a Sámi people of northern Finland, the distinction between observing and participating is a false one. 'To observe,' he writes, 'means to watch what is going on around and about, and of course to listen and feel as well. To participate means to do so from within the current of activity in which you carry on a life alongside and together with [the people] that capture your attention.' I am hoping, on the morning of my second day in Ethiopia, to find some people to run with. I want to be swept up in the 'current of activity' as quickly as possible.

I know vaguely that the forest is up the hill, so at 6 a.m. I start a slow walk up the cobbles from the house. Everyone else seems to be heading in the other direction with a great deal of urgency, pounding down the hill with schoolbooks or briefcase in hand. The few of us who are heading upwards are moving a lot more slowly. Most wear white *shammas* and are clearly heading to church, but a couple wear tracksuits like I do. At least I know I am going the right way.

As we approach the church we walk past, and in some cases almost trip over, people in various poses of prayer. Only a small proportion of Orthodox Christians in Ethiopia consider themselves pure enough to actually *enter* a church due to a variety of dietary and purity taboos. They therefore stand with their foreheads to the trees in the courtyard or clutch the railings that run round the outside. Much like the churchgoers, the runners come up here to be elevated above the hustle and bustle of city life. I remember a fragment of an interview filmed in this forest with Haile Gebrselassie. 'My work up here is hard,' he told the journalist, 'but it is nothing compared with what some of the people down there have to endure.' I am here to try to get a sense for what life is like for those people who have decided to reject the struggle of daily life in the city in favour of a different form of toil in the hills and forests.

The cobbled road ends at the church, and gives way to stubbled grass and the beginning of the eucalyptus forest that stretches for many kilometres to the north, but the hill continues steeply up as far as I can see into the trees. I stop to catch my breath before starting to run. I estimate my pulse with my finger to my wrist and it is at almost one hundred just from the walk up here. I begin to run straight up the hill, keeping to a faint trail, but my breathing is almost immediately ragged and erratic in the thin air, and I find myself turning to run across the hillside rather than grinding to a halt on the slope. After a minute or two I spot the runners I'd noticed on the way up, now at the head of a group of six or seven. The leader of this single-file line, who wears bright purple tights and a red jacket, gestures to the line behind him as he crosses my path and shouts, 'Come on!' in English.

I had anticipated it taking a little while before I found people to run with, so I am pleasantly surprised to find that it has taken all of five minutes. I turn and join in at the back of the group, behind a young runner in a well-worn Adidas tracksuit. I find myself following his foot placement, trying to avoid the bigger tufts of stubbled grass, and I enjoy slipping into the rhythm of the group, who are thankfully not running particularly fast. We make our way up the slope gradually by running long, switch-back diagonals on the camber of the hillside. This means that we never have to run up the steepest sections, but also that we are constantly at an angle. As we get towards the top of the hill I nevertheless start to struggle with the incline and let a few metres open up between myself and the runner in front. This gap grows gradually larger as we head towards the top of the hill, and I decide that on my first run here I should probably take it easy and go at my own pace, so I let the group go and continue running straight when they make their next zigzag turn.

Before I know it, the line of runners comes up alongside me and I am grabbed by the wrist and guided back to my place at the back of the queue. 'We run together,' the runner closest to me says in English. I resign myself to following the group, and the purple tight-clad pied piper at the front, as best as I can. Whenever we pass a big stone or a prominent tree root on the trail the runner at the front of the group clicks his fingers behind his back in warning, which is mirrored by the runner behind him and so on down the line to me. This series of clicks is the only communication between us until we pass a runner heading in the other direction. He has an unusually stooped running style and the leader of our group says something to him that makes the rest of the line laugh. 'What did he say?' I ask the runner in front of me, whose name I later learn is

Tilahun. 'He said, "Have you lost something?"' Tilahun replies, before mimicking an exaggerated stoop, 'Because he always runs like this!'

By now we have reached more open ground at the top of the hill, and we run across farmers' fields and through more widely spaced eucalyptus trees. As the landscape opens out so too do the strides of the runners ahead of me, and I find I am losing more ground with each zigzag that we run and having to turn earlier in order to catch up. I also find I am really enjoying myself, having not done much running with a group in a long time. As the line passes me going in the other direction, I receive a series of encouragements. The runners shout, '*Ayzoh!*' to me as they run past. This is a term that means something along the lines of 'take heart' or 'keep your head up' and is a term as much of sympathy as encouragement. It is a phrase that will turn out to be among the most heard in my whole time in Ethiopia as I struggle to keep up with people.

Having wound up the pace to almost a sprint, with gaps starting to appear in what had been the almost military precision of the line of runners, the run abruptly comes to a halt. Exactly one hour has passed. We regroup and start to jog very slowly back down the hill to the church, where we form a circle to do some stretching. Tilahun has questions for me. After asking me where I am from and why I am here and what time I can run for 10 kilometres he asks, 'Why did you want to run alone?' I explain that I was tired, that I didn't want to hold them up and that I wanted to run at my own pace.

'Training alone is just for health,' is his response. 'To be changed you have to run with others. You need to adapt to their pace, not run your own.' This is something that will be hammered into me over the subsequent months. Running alone – like eating alone or even just sitting alone – is seen as deeply antisocial and borderline suspicious in Ethiopia. As we stretch – still following the guidance of the runner who had led the run up the hill, who we copy – a couple of slightly overweight Americans in shorts, t-shirts and running shoes walk past us up the hill. 'They are visitors I think,' he says. 'They run for health and for the good air, but we run for results. We are always thinking about how to modify our time.' He clutches his forehead in mock anguish. 'How can I modify? How can I modify? So that's why sometimes we run until we collapse.' He bursts out laughing. 'If you just run for health, no worries!'

It is not yet 8 a.m. when we walk slowly down the hill, but the sun is getting warm. Tilahun asks me where I will train tomorrow. 'I'll just come back here I think. This forest seems nice,' I reply. He frowns and shakes his head. 'You have to make the most of different places. The environment is very educated.' He tells me he is going to Entoto to run slowly and benefit from the 'special air' on the mountain, adding that in order to be successful it is important to adapt to different places around the city and their different air conditions, and to make the most of the various surfaces and gradients available to run on.

'Athletics is one thing you must do with others,' he reiterates. 'And you have to use the environment. You have to go up and down,' he adds, gesturing back up the hill. 'If you stay here and train with us and use all of the different places around Addis Ababa you will be successful.' As we part ways we arrange to meet again in a couple of days. To me an hour of running is still just an hour of running. I don't mind too much where it happens and I don't feel like getting up at 5 a.m. to trek across the city just yet. As I walk home, though, I think about what he said about working with the environment and with other people, themes that will become increasingly important as my time in Ethiopia goes on.

* * *

I fall into a routine for the first few weeks that begins with walking up into the forest at 6 a.m. to run with Tilahun or one of the other runners I've met. This is a source of some confusion at first because 6 a.m. is referred to as 'twelve o'clock' in Ethiopia, 7 a.m. as 'one o'clock'. Measuring the day from 6 a.m. was customary in biblical times and is still how most Ethiopians measure time today. Being on the equator it makes a lot of sense to start counting with the break of dawn and as a runner it seems intuitive to measure time this way too – you start to value time in terms of the first opportunity to run in daylight. This is not Ethiopia's only temporal idiosyncrasy. The Ethiopian year has a 13th month – *Pagume* – and the calendar starts in September rather than January. The Ethiopian calendar is also between seven and eight years behind our own timeline, because Orthodox Christians disagree about the year of Jesus' birth. It is not only the runners who seem to have a different relationship to time.

Having returned from training, the rest of the morning is spent making notes and reading, usually with Benoit's cat Cléophée, who has had the extreme good fortune of trading the life of a Parisian housecat for a large territory in a country with some of the most diverse bird life on the planet, asleep on my lap. I find that running and writing is a combination that works quite well for me. Norman Mailer, reflecting on attempting to jog with Muhammad Ali, thought that they were incompatible, asking, 'Who wanted the brilliance of the mind discharged through the ankles?' I find, though, that the pleasant fatigue that follows running makes me more likely to settle and focus on writing rather than succumb to other distractions. In the afternoon I take a couple of 'taxis', 12-seater Toyota minibuses with around 20 people crammed into them, to Arat Kilo on the other side of the city for Amharic lessons in a café with Mimmi Demissie.

These lessons quickly turn into endurance tests in their own right. My good friend Diego Malara, an anthropologist who spent two years studying Ethiopian Orthodox Christianity here, recommended Mimmi to me. If I ask for a break in the lesson she says, 'Diego would do two hours straight, then smoke five cigarettes, then we would do another two hours. You have to try harder.' I try my best to concentrate for three hours, fuelled by endless cups of coffee poured from the traditional *jabenna* pot of the circulating waitress, before retracing my steps back to Benoit's by taxi. Amharic is a beautiful-sounding language with an attractive alphabet consisting of 33 characters that can each be written in seven different ways. It is also grammatically complex, with sentence constructions that pack an awful lot of meaning into individual words. Through the addition of a prefix and a suffix and something called an infix – an extra bit of meaning snuck into the middle – a phrase that is several words in English can be rendered in one in Amharic. In Ethiopia the most common greeting is '*Tena yistiligne*' – literally 'May he [God] give you health on my behalf.' *Tena* means health, whilst *Yistiligne* in this simple greeting takes seven words to convey in English. I often leave these lessons with a headache.

Back at Benoit's I hope that his wife Valerie and children Solal and Flore are in the mood for speaking English to spare myself – and them – from having to resort to my rusty and at this stage over-caffeinated French. I am beginning to find that my brain only has room for one foreign language and that Amharic words work their way into my French, although Benoit seems happy to converse in Franharic as well. Benoit and I then retire to his terrace, which must have about the best view in Addis, for a St George's beer – usually referred to as Giorgis – and a lengthy discussion of running and social science.

While there is often a romanticised view of runners from Ethiopia and Kenya – of children striding to school barefoot across high-altitude plateaus and of people 'running away from poverty' – Benoit is keen to emphasise that it is not the poorest of the poor who become runners in Ethiopia.

'The runners have to have some sort of support from their family,' he tells me, 'and they need to have the time and energy to train.' This is something that is brought home to me on one walk back from the forest with Tilahun. We are joined by a portly man swinging a briefcase on his way to work, who (conveniently for me) asks Tilahun what it takes to be a runner. Tilahun ticks off the ingredients for running success as he sees them on his fingers. First, you need *gize* – time. For running, but mostly for *ireft* – rest between training sessions. Second, you need good quality food in sufficient quantities to sustain training. And third, you need *ya sport masariya*. This is translated either as 'sports materials' or 'facilities': running shoes and running kit, but also the bus fare to access preferable training locations around the city. You have to be able to access the beneficial training environments Tilahun spoke about the subject on my first morning run and this could be an insurmountable expense for some.

Far from the media portrayal of East African athletes – of success *because* of a lack of shoes and *because* of hardship – these requirements actually represent a significant barrier to entry. They also represent a very significant investment and sacrifice – of education, of working opportunities and even of marriage. At this early stage of my research I didn't fully understand this, though. 'I guess it's not the end of the world if it doesn't work out for someone like Tilahun,' I say to Benoit. 'He can always go back to the farm.' Benoit shakes his head. 'No. How do you find a wife if you're 25 and a loser? The runners believe that they have something inside of them, so if they fail what does that mean?'

This idea of having something inside of you, a latent potential that needs only to be unleashed, is something that I have a faint notion of from reading a classic study of the Amhara, the ethnic group of the runners I would be living and training with. Most of the top runners in Ethiopia are from the Amhara or Oromia regions, with a smaller number from Tigray in the north. Because of the way training groups are formed from personal connections, though, the group I trained in were almost all Amhara. In *Wax and Gold*, Donald Levine writes of the Amhara notion of *idil*, which translates roughly as 'chance'. Amhara Orthodox Christians believe their *idil* to be a kind of interior state of being about which only God has truly privileged knowledge. This means they believe that if they work hard and virtuously, they may be rewarded with performances that are truly transcendent and spectacular. It also means that Ethiopian runners wear their ambition lightly. Even if they might privately have a fairly self-aggrandising view of their own possibilities, to express this would be incompatible with the kind of virtuous life that must be lived in order to be rewarded. Not wanting to express pride in personal achievements explains why when confronted with a microphone in a post-race interview and the question, 'How do you feel after winning the race?' even the more famous and well-travelled Ethiopian athletes will often seem reticent.

I found very early on in my time in Ethiopia that while both male and female athletes at first seemed shy and reluctant to talk about themselves, this was more pronounced with the female runners. Because it was seen as culturally inappropriate for me to interview female athletes, and because I didn't want to make people feel uncomfortable, my focus was on male runners for my research and for this book. The very title of Levine's book alludes to the problem of direct expression of your feelings. *Wax and Gold* is a form of Amhara poetry in which each line of text contains two meanings – the superficial or 'wax' meaning, named for the mould used when casting objects in gold, and the 'gold' meaning lying beneath, which must be prised out with skill. I remember thinking as I read up on this in Edinburgh before my trip that it could complicate the process of conducting and understanding interviews. It would also make it hard to talk to runners directly about their aspirations.

The belief in *idil* – that is, the belief that if you act in a certain way anyone may be raised to a position of greatness – also means that there is little in the way of belief in innate athletic talent or genetic ability in Ethiopia. Tilahun talks about only needing to 'modify' his times. He adds, 'I have two legs, you know, just like the others,' before patting them as if to reassure himself. When he tells me at one point that if I stay in Ethiopia for a year and do everything right I could run a 2.08 marathon I laugh, but I don't think he is joking.

Throughout my time in Ethiopia, in fact, I never heard anyone mention 'talent' or 'natural ability'. Runners use the word *lememed* to refer to training as a runner, which literally means 'adaptation' or getting used to something. Runners are either good at managing the process of adaptation or they are not. A good runner is most likely to be described as *gobez,* which means some kind of combination of cleverness and cunning, denoting an ability to plan and manage their training well. As Meseret frequently puts it to the runners, 'You can be changed.' The implication here is a strong belief in the inherent malleability of bodies provided that runners conduct themselves in a certain way. I am often told how bad I am at managing this process of adaptation, insisting as I do on writing during the day, walking around to do interviews and otherwise refusing to allow my body to 'adapt' to the training load. One implication of this belief is that an inability to 'adapt' is often seen as the problem of the individual, as a moral failing of some kind or simply a result of not 'working' hard enough. It is never ascribed merely to not having the 'natural talent' to do so, which is how I (and I suspect most sports scientists) would explain my inability to run a marathon in 2.08.

Tilahun started running because he happened to catch a fragment of radio commentary on Kenenisa Bekele's winning run at the 2009 World Athletics Championships in Berlin. 'He's from a village not far from mine,' he explains, 'so I thought, if he can do it, why can't I?' Some people start running because they realise they are good at it at school. Some because they hear about it on the radio or watch a big race on television. And some start because – to quote Forrest Gump – they just 'felt like running'.

* * *

The next afternoon I go to meet Hailye, the sub-agent of Moyo Sports management, the professional group of athletes I have arranged to train with while I'm here. The group are represented by Malcolm Anderson, an 'athlete representative' (more often referred to as a 'manager' in Ethiopia) who is based in Edinburgh on the rare occasions he is not flying around the world to races. I was extremely lucky to meet Malcolm, whose route to working in athletics came via a stint of teaching PE and English in the Kenyan Highlands, and an MSc in African Studies at Oxford, where he wrote his thesis on the history of Kenyan athletics. The role of the athlete representative is to help athletes plan their racing schedules, and negotiate the terms of their entry into races abroad and contracts with sponsors, for which they charge a standard commission of 15 per cent on all earnings.

Many of the runners I meet in the forest talk about their desire to get to the level of working with a manager and it is sometimes assumed that this might be a role I could fulfil for people. The management system, as it is usually called, sits above a lively and well-funded club structure. While many runners rely on their clubs for a consistent source of income, they rely on the networks of a well-connected manager to arrange the potentially far more lucrative races abroad. Malcolm pays for the bus which transports the 30 or so runners in the group to training three mornings a week, as well as the salaries of Hailye and coach Meseret. Hailye's main day-to-day job consists of attending training with the athletes, providing feedback to Malcolm and helping runners submit visa applications, the logistics of which are perhaps the biggest challenge of the whole enterprise.

Hailye and I meet in Hirut Café in Kotebe, a suburb of Addis about five kilometres from the city centre, and sit on a balcony on the first floor overlooking the main road out of the city to the East. Cars, huge red and yellow buses, and lorries jostle for position on the too-narrow road, and the pedestrians on the pavement step over hawkers who have laid their goods out perilously close to the traffic. Car horns sound and exhaust fumes waft up to where we are sitting. Hailye gestures up the hill behind us and tells me, 'This is athlete village. There are so many athletes here. Thousands of athletes.' It strikes me that this is very different from Iten, the Kenyan town that has become known for its runners, and from the image of rural 'simplicity' many people connect with East African running. Below us is a scene of hustle and we are still very much in the heart of Ethiopia's sprawling capital city.

In fact, while almost all of the best runners in Ethiopia live in Kotebe, Hailye doesn't think it is an ideal place to train. 'For training the rural areas are better,' he tells me, 'but here you get opportunities.' For those who want to race abroad it is vital to train in a group like Moyo Sports, which means living in Addis. Kotebe does have the advantage of being on the edge of the Yeka Sub-City Forest, but the forest is steep and uneven, and the routes are littered with stones and tree roots. The community of runners who live in Kotebe do so out of a kind of compromise, then, perched on the periphery of the global running industry.

Hailye is a remarkable character. He taught himself English while working as a night guard, spending a big proportion of his monthly salary on lessons and then practising phrases in the mirror to keep himself awake at night. After attending college in Debre Birhan, a hundred kilometres or so from Addis, he graduated with a degree in sociology and social anthropology from Addis Ababa University. He agreed to translate at a meeting between Malcolm and one of the first Ethiopian athletes he started working with, and his encyclopedic self-taught knowledge of athletics stems from that meeting. Contracts between managers and athletes are only

12 months long, a rule set by the world governing body. It is therefore a fickle world that is full of intrigue, with athletes switching managers frequently. To do his job effectively requires tirelessly working to cultivate and maintain the trust of the athletes in the group.

Hailye introduces me to Fasil, his roommate, who started running in Kotebe only a year previously. He trains with the Moyo Sports group, but has not yet reached the level of signing a contract with Malcolm or applying for a passport to travel abroad. Fasil retains the physicality of someone who has worked 12-hour days hauling stones around, the muscles in his arms roped with veins. He tells me how he got started in the sport as we share a meal of *tibes firfir*. This dish, which consists of leftover *injera* – Ethiopia's sour pancake-like bread made from a grain called *teff* – mixed with spicy red meat, is utterly delicious. Hailye refers to it as 'peasant food', because it is traditionally a way of using up leftover *injera*, and it reminds me a bit of *migas*, the Andalusian leftover bread and chorizo dish, which is also a favourite of mine. Perhaps the food prepared by people used to working long days in the fields just suits runners. We scoop up handfuls as Fasil talks.

'I didn't start running until I was 19,' Fasil begins. 'No-one knew about running as a way of making money in the part of Gondar where I grew up, a whole day and night's bus journey from here. I only found out about it when I moved here. Life is expensive in Addis. I was told before I moved here that the city would "clean my face and my pockets," and when I came here I had to work really hard. I was working as a labourer most of the day and then as a guard at night, out patrolling the streets. I met Hailye because I was working on his compound, digging the foundations. I became curious about running when I saw Hailye and others going to the forest and I asked them what they were doing. Even then, I thought, it is probably too late for me, I won't be able to catch up with them. After a year of working all day and most of the night, I began to try to think if there was another way to make a living. I learned to play the *mesinko* in Gondar and I thought maybe I could make money as a minstrel, singing songs around the city.'

A *mesinko*, Hailye explains, is a single-stringed lute used by traditional *azmari* singers, whose brand of improvised ribaldry I would later experience over gourds of honey wine. It wasn't a vocation Hailye himself particularly approved of and he had, in fact, suggested Fasil try running instead. 'I went down to Mercato,' Fasil continues, referencing the biggest open-air market in Africa, 'to buy a *mesinko*. And I was walking around the alleyways and I came across a shop selling running shoes, and I thought, "I might as well try some on." So I put them on and jumped up and down, and they were so bouncy I felt like I could run for ever. So I spent all the money I had on the shoes and I had to run all the way back to Kotebe, because I had nothing left for the taxi fare.'

After translating this last bit for me, Hailye adds in English, 'You see, this is why I wanted you to meet Fasil. He's a bit different.' But Fasil has already launched into the next bit of the story. 'So anyway,' he says, 'the next day I put on my new shoes, and I walked up to the forest and I just started following the first group of runners I saw.' That sounds familiar, I think. 'And I was just concentrating on keeping up with the guy in front and making sure he didn't get away, and before long we'd ended up on a big plateau with open farmland all around us, and I suddenly realised I didn't know where I was anymore.' Hailye is laughing. 'They'd run all the way to Sululta in the north,' he says. 'Many, many kilometres away. He must have joined in with professionals who were 20 kilometres into an out-and-back 40-kilometre run.'

'Anyway, I was getting a little bit tired at this point,' Fasil continues matter-of-factly. 'But luckily I met a girl who invited me in for some milk and honey on their farm.' Here he laughs and turns to Hailye, who raises his eyebrows. 'She gave me the money for the bus back here. Then the next day I just went back to the forest and did the same thing again, but I was careful to watch where we were going this time.'

I ask him about his upbringing, and whether he thinks that prepared him to make a good start as a runner. 'I think growing up in the countryside makes you strong,' he begins. 'You don't see successful runners who grew up in the city. My parents both died when I was four and I went to live with my uncle. His children went to school while I tended the cows and I was often outside with the herd 16 hours a day. That was tough, because it can get really cold in Gondar. I left there when I was 16 and did various different things. I even worked taking cows to the market in Sudan, walking for days and guarding them from cattle raiders, but that was a dangerous job.' He shows me the scars on his wrists from an unsuccessful cattle-guarding excursion, which led to him being left tied to a tree for two days, and I realise that the lightheartedness of the story about his first run comes from comparison to his previous experiences.

'In Addis life is more expensive, and that is how I ended up working as a labourer in the day and a guard at night. I am so pleased Hailye encouraged me to start running. Running is hard, but when I compare it to what I did before, it is easy. If you are working like I was before, you will break your back, but you will still change nothing. With running you have a chance to change your life.' This is something I will hear again and again when I ask my running friends why they run. 'To change my life.' Deciding to become a runner means to reorder many aspects of your life in a way that will make this possible and runners therefore often define themselves against other young men trying to make a living in the city.

This is brought home to me with some force one Sunday a couple of weeks later. I have got used to the routine of the Moyo Sports group now, which consists of six days of training – three hard days on which we travel somewhere specific on the team bus, interspersed with three 'easy' days – and a rest day on a Sunday. Fasil and I have been at Abere's house near the forest, which he invited us to for a vast salad of avocado, lettuce, tomatoes and chillies doused in salt and vinegar. Abere and Fasil are both from near Gondar in northern Ethiopia. Abere was driving a *bajaj* – a kind of motorised rickshaw – when he started his training. He had so little money that when his first manager arranged a race abroad, in Morocco, he ran in a pair of jelly sandals. Somehow he still managed to run 61 minutes for a half marathon. In his second race, in France, he had a pair of Adidas racing flats, but elected to run in the jelly shoes anyway, because he was more used to them. I don't know if there is an official world record for a half marathon in sandals, but if there is it is almost certainly minutes slower than Abere ran.

We have spent several hours lounging around, watching Ethiopian pop music videos on a small television surrounded by trophies. The videos are all shot in the Gondar region, the footage alternating between farmers in traditional Orthodox Christian dress dancing in fields of swaying *teff* and young men in the city posing by the dual carriageway.

After several hours, Abere accompanies us back towards the road. As we walk through the middle of a group of young men playing football, one of them says something to Abere and he responds angrily. The three of us are dressed recognisably as runners; we all wear running shoes, Fasil wears a purple Nike hooded top and Abere the yellow Adidas tracksuit provided to all runners under contract with the brand the year before. We are quickly surrounded by the men and, after Abere shoves his way past one of them, a young man in a faded Arsenal shirt, sleeves cut off to reveal tattooed biceps, throws a lump of concrete at him. It misses his head by inches. I am taken completely by surprise by the sudden escalation of the confrontation. Fasil, who still sometimes works as a night guard, has one of our assailants on the floor pretty rapidly, but there are seven of them. Just in time, an old man in a *shamma* intervenes, standing between us and them, and eventually succeeding in diffusing the situation.

'They are just people who have already lost hope,' he tells us when they have left. 'Why were you arguing with them?' As Fasil and I walk back through the forest he paints a picture of running as an alternative way of living to that of the young men. 'Guys like that have no plan of living,' he says. 'They wanted to hurt us so they could go to jail and eat the government's *injera*. They have no goals, no hope. But Abere is a man with goals. If he runs and gets money, and builds a hotel, people will benefit from it.' 'So runners are hard workers?' I ask. 'Athletes are good people, they work hard, they think about their country. Those other guys, their only work is fighting.'

Groups of young men like this are ubiquitous in Addis Ababa. At the intersection of streets near where I live with Benoit there are always five or six of a revolving cast of around 20 men. They sit in different places depending on the time of day, moving with the shade, and chew *khat*, smoke cigarettes and occasionally kick a ball about or do some press-ups. All have a level of education, but, they tell me on numerous occasions, there is 'no work'. Hailye disagrees. 'There is work,' he tells me, when Fasil and I return home. 'But they think they are too good for the kind of work Fasil does.' Hailye condemns the kind of idleness described above – hanging around in the street to pass the time – in strong moral terms, telling me on several occasions that he thinks the Ethiopian government should 'collect up' people like this and force them to work 'breaking stones or something.'

For runners to be successful they have to accept a very different approach to day-to-day life, defined by patience and delayed gratification. This is usually compared to the other forms of work that would be available to them, which is referred to as *gulbet sera*, literally 'energy work'. These kinds of work, as Fasil put it, break your back but change nothing. You have to work for 12 hours just in order to eat for the day and you become locked in a cycle of 'work, eat, work, eat'. With running you have to accept a lifestyle that could become boring, and which means you have to withdraw from many aspects of social life, but it means that you have hope of one day making a life-changing amount of money. It allows lots of people to approach life with a hopeful outlook. Before Aseffa from the running group runs a race, for instance, he has already allocated the prize money to various projects in his imagination – $3000 to marry his girlfriend Teje, $7000 for the plot of land near Asella – making his dreams of success as concrete as possible.

I realise that I have started my own running journey in Ethiopia in the same way as Fasil and countless others, by going to the forest and 'following the feet' of the other runners there, and I decide to try to run with him and the other Moyo runners as much as I can over the next few weeks. But it is also very clear to me how different my own experiences as a runner have been, which is a reminder that I have to avoid the bias of my own views on running while I am in Ethiopia. My research into Ethiopian running brings together my two main interests – travel and running – in a way that allows me to spend a great deal of time over a total period of four years reading, writing and spending time in Ethiopia doing both. Travelling and running are borne of a similar itchy feet impulse, I think: running is like travelling from home.

They are, though, as my long-suffering coach in the UK Max Coleby has spent the best part of 15 years pointing out, in tension with one another, especially if your aim is to see how good you can get at running. I was ranked seventh in the UK as a junior 5000m runner, having made my way from last place with eight laps to go to sixth place at the UK Championships in Bedford in 2006. That I got as heavily into running as I did is largely down to the coincidence of growing up a few doors away from Max and his wife Julie. Max ran a 2.14 marathon in the late eighties, back when that performance was only good enough for the 12th and final place on Gateshead Harriers' road relays-winning team, and Julie was a 2.35 marathon runner who once finished seventh in the London marathon. They lent me running books from their large collection, and Max told stories about training in Durham with Brendan Foster and Charlie Spedding. I was hooked on the running culture of the north-east of England long before I was interested in studying the running culture of highland Ethiopia.

I ran 15.02 for 5000m aged 18 and that race was probably the biggest indicator of my potential I had had up to that point. And then I walked off the track and almost immediately on to a train to go Interrailing around Europe, and set about throwing that potential away. I did a bit of running the following year and then more or less nothing for three years while I spent my time studying, drinking and travelling to India, South America and China during the summers.

On the occasions when I had tried to start running again I had given up as a result of back injury problems, but for a long time I didn't really miss it that much. And then, for some reason, I started running again in the most unlikely of circumstances. I moved to Paris at the end of 2010 to start the Erasmus year of my French and English Literature degree at the Sorbonne. In characteristic fashion I arrived about three days before term started with nowhere to live and no idea about the complex bureaucratic demands of renting in Paris, where you are required to have a dossier detailing previous addresses and character references and various other things. I met up with a friend of mine from Edinburgh, Marc, in a hostel, where we searched online for less formal accommodation. What we eventually found was definitely that.

More out of curiosity than anything we replied to an advert on Craigslist offering cheap accommodation, paid for in cash, somewhere called the Territory in the south of Paris near Montparnasse. We didn't have much to go on apart from a *New York Times* piece from a series entitled 'Notes From the Underground', in which the journalist wrote that the place had been described variously as 'a youth hostel, an art studio, a dreamscape and a favela – to which one could add, on first impression, a firetrap, a serial-killer lair and Willy Wonka's chocolate factory'. Run by Sergio Ostroverhy, a Russian artist, at the time the Territory apparently received up to 150 emails a day from people like Marc and I looking for cheap accommodation.

'It is not me who chooses,' Sergio told us from a partially collapsed sofa somewhere within the warren of rooms. 'It is the Territory.' This was word for word the same thing he had said to the *New York Times* reporter, but out of some combination of curiosity and desperation we took the rooms when he offered them to us, even though the sloped ceiling in my room appeared to be made of MDF and the window was some green plastic sheeting duct-taped to the walls.

Some of the tenants were also assistants of Sergio's, tasked with mixing paint and sometimes with literally chaining him to his latest painting to ensure that he worked. The rest of us were a combination of students and writers, but there was also a dancer training at the conservatoire and an actor training in physical theatre. As the cold Parisian winter started to bite, the reality of staying somewhere with one outdoor shower between 15 people began to set in, but the sense of community outweighed that and we all stayed there in spite of the constantly proliferating set of rules. Because he wasn't strictly speaking allowed to have tenants, we had to pretend to outsiders that we were artists and carry A3 portfolios with us whenever we entered or exited the building. For the same reason we were also not allowed keys, so we had to use a walkie-talkie that was hidden in the bushes to contact someone inside who would let us in. The kitchen had an old black and white TV that was hooked up to a security camera inside so that people could check who you were. It was the bohemian dream meets *1984*.

One night shortly after a new Englishman called Louis had moved in, we got talking about running for some reason and Louis revealed that he had been a pretty good runner himself at school, finishing in the '90-somethings' in the English Schools' Cross

Country. He was now in Paris to learn French as part of a kind of modern-day Grand Tour and, as he put it, to 'try to be as pretentious as possible.' He barely ran anymore. When we looked into it, we found that by sheer coincidence we had run in the same race, the 2005 Senior Boys race in Norwich, and finished in 92nd and 99th position, all of four seconds apart. We decided to go for a run, before realising that this was actually going to be quite a challenge logistically.

For our first outing we decided to start from the launderette, where we could leave our clothes and portfolios, and try to run to the Eiffel Tower and back before the washing machines finished. This was less romantic than it sounds, and involved a lot of road crossings and dodging tourists, and we eventually found a quieter bike path that headed out of the city and across the *périphérique*. A weekly outing became bi-weekly and then I found my back wasn't hurting anymore and I wanted to run, badly, for the first time in three years. I started trying to sneak out without Sergio noticing, stashing my portfolio in a gap in the fence near the house and running in trousers so that I conformed to the 'looking like an artist' stipulation. When I grew tired of this I decided to run in shorts, only to find that when I returned and used the intercom to try to get back in, it was Sergio who responded, his nasal voice crackling over the intercom.

'You can't come in,' he said.

'But I live here,' I pointed out.

'You can't run. Artists don't run.'

'This one does,' I responded, exasperated.

'I'll send Marc out with some trousers,' he said and hung up.

I hadn't anticipated the house rules being more than a quirky inconvenience, a funny story to tell when I returned home. Now, though, I wanted to start training properly again in the least likely of environments. I started heading out really early to run along the bike paths and I joined a club in the *banlieu* where a lot of strong second-generation Moroccan and Algerian immigrants trained. I recaptured the sense of order that running had given me when I ran competitively as a junior athlete and rediscovered the pleasure of a simple thing done well every day. Back in Edinburgh I joined a club again – Corstorphine AC – and set about getting back to the level I had been at.

I would still struggle to explain exactly what it was that made me love the sport so much, though. It seems telling that Haruki Murakami borrows his title from Raymond Carver's *What We Talk About When We Talk About Love* for his book of musings on running and writing. Like love, there is something that evades capture in writing. Even those who have been running for decades will tend to shrug knowingly when asked why they do it, as though this can only be understood by the initiated. If pressed for a reason – and also for a reason why so many people are now signing up for Ironman Triathlons and ultra races in the West – I would say it comes down to a resistance to comfort. 'If you flatter yourself that you are altogether comfortable,' Herman Melville wrote, 'and have been for a long time, then you cannot be said to be comfortable anymore.' Running has an attraction much like that described by Roger Deakin in his book about wild swimming, in that it allows us to 'regain a sense of what is old and wild', to get off the beaten track and 'break free of the official versions of things.'

By the time I arrive in Ethiopia five years later I have got back to a reasonable level, running under 50 minutes for 10 miles and competing on the road and cross-country for Scotland. I am curious to see what 15 months of running in Ethiopia can do for my own running, but I am under no illusions about making dramatic improvements. I am there as a researcher and a writer first, and as a runner second, which means that my experience is clearly very different from those with whom I train, whose main motivation is to 'change their lives' for the better. If I am going to learn about Ethiopian running effectively, I will have to try to unlearn the assumptions I have spent 15 years acquiring, and learn by doing and by 'following feet'.

Intrigued by Fasil's insistence that all of the top runners in Ethiopia share a farming background involving hard work in the fields, a few months after I arrive in Ethiopia I decide to head to the heart of the Oromo countryside to visit a small town called Bekoji. How has a small town of 17,000 inhabitants produced the first ever African woman to win an Olympic gold medal (Derartu Tulu), the first ever African woman to win the Olympic marathon (Fatuma Roba), and the holders of the women's 5000m (Tirunesh Dibaba), and the men's 5000m and 10,000m (Kenenisa Bekele) world records?

3

FOLLOWING EACH OTHER'S FEET

The football club stickers on the bus windscreen are layered several thick, indicating either a succession of drivers or one particularly fickle one. For now, this bus supports Manchester United and the Virgin Mary in equal measure. There are two stickers representing each, stuck at the driver's eye level. Young men the same age and build as the runners I've spent my time with hustle around the bus trying desperately to sell biscuits through the open windows, or they try to earn a one-*birr* commission (the *birr* is the unit of currency in Ethiopia) for delivering passengers, often in a rough, uncompromising manner, to the drivers. That's how I end up on this battered old bus to Bekoji. I've been told to try to get on one of the newer – and slightly safer – buses, but I'm being fiercely guarded by the driver. Finding passengers is a competitive business.

We wait for an hour and 15 minutes for the bus to fill with the requisite number of people, chickens, sacks of cement and vats of homebrewed beer. The runners constantly reiterate the importance of patience and I am given ample opportunity to train mine here. When the bus finally pulls out of Kality bus station in the outskirts of Addis we wind slowly and unexpectedly *downhill* at first, and the temperature rises as the altitude falls. This is also an opportunity to practice endurance. Many Ethiopians believe that flowing air, regardless of the temperature, is a source of illness. At 32 degrees they still refuse to crack a window. The air is a heady mixture of wood smoke, sweat, chicken and homebrew vodka, and my Amharic isn't good enough to point out the flaw in this particular health belief in a country heavily affected by tuberculosis. I sweat it out for a couple of hours before we eventually, blissfully, start our climb up to Bekoji at 3000m above sea level.

As we drive we move into true Oromo farmland and signs in Amharic script give way to signs in Afan Oromo. This is written using the Roman alphabet, but has its own spelling, with a liberal addition of vowels. 'Hotel My Family' becomes *Hoteelaa Maay Faamiilee* and we pass a sign for *Farniicher* with a drawing of a plush chair below it. We also drive past the Noble and Trustworthy House PLC, the painted-out windows of which make it look neither. As traffic thins, the bus driver has to be increasingly aware of oxen and sheep on the road, as well as the bold shepherd boys ready to throw stones at vehicles they deem to be driving recklessly. The farmland is a vibrant green here, punctuated with *tukuls*, the mud-walled, thatch-roofed farmsteads. Eagles soar overhead and I see a number of iridescent blue birds flash by the windows of the bus, which blares traditional music and gradually fills with more and more people. They sit on each other's laps or stoop in the aisle, updating each other on local gossip.

When I finally step out of the bus four hours later I get my first taste of the 'special' Bekoji air, and can taste its thinness in the back of my throat and a slight lightness in my head. I check into the Wabee Hotel and explain that I am here to run. Lewte (whose name means 'Progress') checks me in and tells me that the hotel was built by his sister after she won the Dubai marathon. His brother, also a runner, went to a race in the UK four years ago and never returned, he says. He doesn't know which city he lives in now. 'And are you a runner?' I ask him. He looks at me quizzically. 'Of course,' he says. Stupid question. I ask him whether perhaps he might be going for a run in the morning. 'Yes. We can leave at 6 a.m.,' he says. I've been here five minutes and I've already arranged training. This is easier than I thought.

* * *

At 5.55 a.m. the next morning there is a knock on my door. As usual, running is the one thing people are on time for. Receptionist Lewte's friend Alemu joins us at the gate. He is here on holiday from the Oromia Police Club in Addis and as we walk along the road I ask him about the political unrest. The Oromo youth demonstrations were sparked by proposals in the new Addis Ababa city masterplan to seize farmland to cope with the city's expansion, but the anger is deeper than that. When Feyisa Lilesa finished second in the 2016 Olympic marathon in Rio, he did so with his arms crossed over his head, in the gesture used by the protesters. When a UK pundit made an 'M' sign over his head in a post-race interview and said, 'We call this the Mobot. What do you call your sign?' Lilesa responded, 'We call it, "Stop killing my people."' The protests were also against government killings of civilians, mass arrests and the political marginalisation of opposition groups.

'I am with the protesters,' Alemu tells me. Feyisa Lilesa is a hero. He crosses his arms above his head in the sign of peaceful self-protection intended to draw attention to the disproportionate and one-sided use of force by the government against protesters. 'But you're a policeman,' I point out. Like many of the running clubs which pay athletes a salary to train and compete, Alemu's is funded by the government. His employers are the ones who have been shooting people. He looks offended. 'I am a runner,' he says. He will only have to get involved in the violence if it gets 'really bad' and he believes in the protesters' cause. Bekoji is in the heartland of Oromian farming country, Ethiopia's breadbasket. The region is the largest in Ethiopia, both in terms of size and population, but the people feel excluded from Ethiopian politics. Symbols of this exclusion, like foreign factories built on farmland seized by the government, have been attacked and burned in recent weeks, and parts of Oromia have begun withholding food deliveries that were destined for Tigrai, the region where the majority of Ethiopia's politicians come from. The political atmosphere remains tense, but at 6 a.m. Bekoji couldn't be more peaceful.

We hitch a lift up the road in a *bajaj*, the vehicle similar to a motorised rickshaw, giving a carriage drawn by an especially skittish looking horse a wide berth. When we arrive at the edge of a forest, the driver waves away our attempts to pay. Green farmland stretches as far as the eye can see. We start running between widely spaced trees, skipping lightly over tree roots and frequently cutting back on ourselves. Alemu leads the way, taking little thoughtful steps across the ground. He clicks his fingers to warn us about every stone and stick on the ground. The change in altitude registers as a slight headache and an almost immediate heaviness in my legs.

After a couple of miles we gradually speed up, moving on to softer, wetter grass, which sticks up in clumps and tufts, and on which Alemu places his feet even more carefully. We seem to spend most of the rest of the run on a steep camber, which makes me far more aware than usual of the work my hips and the muscles along the outside of my shins are doing. When the camber gets too steep Alemu uses a series of quick-dancing short steps to move further up the slope, like a cross-country skier on a tight turn. I am struggling with the extra altitude – Alemu says we are at 3500m – and these extra bursts of effort are hard to summon. When I ask him afterwards he says he ran on the slopes in this way because I'd just come from Addis, and because it was an 'easy' day. 'Easy' days are usually slow but always long in Ethiopia. It's rare to run for less than an hour and 10 minutes in the mornings. We'd been winding around ponderously today, but tomorrow we'll go straight ahead, he says with an ominous, exaggerated point of his finger.

Tentatively we work our way down the steep slope back to the dry forest where we started, with eucalyptus trees spaced evenly about a metre apart. Here Alemu starts to ramp up the pace, first to just under four minutes per kilometre and then to not far off three minutes, carving lines through the trees before sticking his arms out to indicate a turn like a footballer peeling off to celebrate a goal, then accelerating again, his feet quick and dexterous between the tree roots. I can't run that fast at this altitude, so I cut back a couple of trees early every time he turns. At this he frowns and makes a beckoning motion with his hand, urging me to catch up and run close behind him by clicking his finger and pointing at his own heels.

When we finally stop we jog for a few minutes on the side of the road before running a series of fast strides to get back to town. The kids (and many of the adults) stare open-mouthed at me as I run past and I hear, '*Ya sportenna farenj*' ('Oh, a sporting foreigner!'). Eventually we stop to stretch. Alemu leads these, which includes one where we have to stand on one leg and perform a series of movements without returning the other leg to the floor: an exercise in balance more than an exercise in stretching. Balance is extremely important on this terrain. You only have to watch the athletes take corners without breaking stride to see that; their centre of gravity low as they whip themselves round tree trunks.

Watch old videos of Kenenisa Bekele running the World Cross Country Championships for a master class in this; he won ten titles *in a row* and seemed to be able to accelerate through corners in the later stages of races in a way that defied physics. At his best, Kenenisa is as close to unbeatable as any distance runner who has ever lived and I can't see his world records for 5000m (12.37) or 10,000m (26.17) ever being beaten. I remember watching him in Edinburgh in 2008 when his shoe came off six minutes into the race. He came to a complete stop and calmly took his time putting it on again before catching up with the leaders in the space of three minutes. It looked like he was operating in a different space-time continuum to everyone else. After stretching, Alemu indicates a pile of logs saying, 'According to science we should sit and take ten minutes rest.' I don't know how scientific that is, but I am more than happy to have a sit-down. To rush training seems sacrilegious here. You have to be patient and do things properly.

When we eventually saunter back to the hotel we sit down in the restaurant. I notice that while my shoes are waterlogged and caked with mud, Alemu's look as if he's been running on a treadmill. Somehow he has avoided all the wet ground and I – even though

50

I was following him – have failed to. The waiter meanders over, in crisp white shirt, smart trousers and, I notice, running shoes. 'How far did you run?' he asks. 'An hour,' I reply. '*Tinish*,' he says dismissively, turning away. 'It is little.' I ask him for a coffee and he refuses to bring me one, telling me it's not good to drink coffee on an empty stomach. People always seem to think they know best here, telling me to zip up my jacket or what I can and can't eat. As far as all things running are concerned, though, I'm willing to defer to their obviously superior expertise.

* * *

The following morning Alemu and Lewte arrive at the door of my room even earlier. I have slept quite poorly because of the increase in altitude, my body faintly aware that something has changed. They don't knock immediately, but I can hear religious music blaring from Lewte's phone. I am about to say something along the lines of 'Won't people be sleeping?' but then I remember that this is Ethiopia – 6 a.m. is practically mid-morning. We walk up the road from the guesthouse, our breath turning to mist in the morning air.

I'm not sure why, but Lewte and Alemu are full of beans today, and Alemu's policeman's march is hard to keep up with. We start running on the verge of the road, on a muddy camber, before turning on to a rutted dirt track, following the furrowed tracks of horse-drawn carts, and avoiding the stones and puddles as best we can. When I imagined the 'nice field' they described yesterday it was flat and dry. This one is a vivid green of long thick grass, but I am told we are running 'easy' again today. Wattled ibis browse in the grass, pausing to glance at us if we get too close. We zigzag across dramatically sloping and saturated fields, the dew-heavy grass holding on to our feet. 'This… isn't… easy,' I manage between inhalations. It feels like we are running on an enormous, energy-sapping sponge. Every now and then we run into clumps of bemused oxen, and Alemu flaps his arms like a big skinny bird to scatter them as Lewte and I dodge the horns of those turning to get out of his way. The shepherd kids just stare open-mouthed at the struggling *farenj*.

When Ethiopians describe the weather as 'heavy' they are referring both to the air, which is an effort to breathe, and the ground, which saps your energy from below. 'Heavy' is also a good description of my whole body today. The air feels thick rather than thin, like I can't force it into my lungs. I always expect to be gasping for air at this sort of altitude, but in fact it feels like my brain intervenes before it gets to that point. It's as though it senses the potential danger of running hard this high up and enforces a pace limit of five minutes per kilometre.

I find myself, once again, envying Alemu, his feet dancing so easily over the turf. The problem is that being less skilled at placing your feet is sort of an exponential problem. If you stumble into a puddle and end up with a shoe full of water, you double the weight on your foot, which makes you so tired that you're more likely to make another mistake. Sooner or later my feet are so wet and heavy that I don't even *try* to find the dry ground. Alemu's shoes, meanwhile, still look like he's been running on the treadmill.

Eventually we work our way to a dirt farm track for the last 10 minutes of the run and I start to ask Alemu why we couldn't have just done the whole run here. Then I remember who the experts are. This heavy ground, I tell myself, is where Kenenisa Bekele cut his teeth before going on to become the greatest distance runner of all time. The first time he went to sea level, swapped his heavy shoes for spikes and ran on comparatively firm ground, he must have felt about ready to take off.

We work our way back to what Alemu refers to as 'Sentayehu's forest' and suddenly we are running in the midst of a hundred or so brightly coloured tracksuits. Coach Sentayehu Eshetu is why I am here. Sentayehu grew up in Harar, a walled city over 500 kilometres from Bejoki with a very different culture, and was a footballer in his youth. He came to Bekoji as a primary school teacher, but noticed that some of his students seemed to have an aptitude for running. His coaching practice developed intuitively and he began to run daily training sessions. His first protégé, Derartu Tulu, became Africa's first female Olympic gold medallist, winning the 10,000m in Barcelona in 1992. She went on to become president of the Ethiopian Athletics Federation (EAF). Since that early success, Sentayehu has discovered Kenenisa Bekele, the world record holder in the 5000m and 10,000m, and the female runner Tirunesh Dibaba, nicknamed the Baby-faced Destroyer, who has won eight world track titles. Both Kenenisa and Tirunesh continue to compete 20 years after they made their international debuts, with Kenenisa coming within two seconds of breaking the world record at the Berlin marathon in 2019 when he ran 2.01.41.

If we measure coaches according to how many global titles the athletes they have nurtured have won, Sentayehu only has one man who might be able to compete with him: Brother Colm O'Connell at St Patrick's High School in Iten, Kenya. Both enjoy a devoted following in their small towns and both have created a culture of distance running more or less single-handedly.

Sentayehu's athletes are doing perfectly synchronised exercises in long lines. This is 'rest time', according to Alemu – a short break at the end of the season – but it doesn't seem to stop the athletes turning up in their droves. Five of them decide to join us and we cut through the trees and accelerate out of the corners in a smooth line. The run has gradually speeded up as usual and by now I'm struggling to stay with them.

After an hour and seven minutes Alemu abruptly stops. 'I thought we were doing an hour and ten minutes,' I say, surprised. In Addis the runners are obsessive about running for exactly the time they planned. He looks at his watch, nods, and then takes off, making the familiar 'get in my slipstream' gesture of pointing to his heels. He seems to be saying, 'If you want another three minutes, I'm going to make you work for them,' as he accelerates round a loop of mud-walled houses, dodging kids and donkeys. I glance at my watch: a blistering 3.10 minutes per kilometre pace. I wish I'd kept my mouth shut. For the last few hundred metres I try as hard as I can to stay close to Alemu and 'follow his feet'. Every time I drop a couple of metres behind he seems to sense it and turns, frowning, to click his fingers and point at his heels. After an extraordinarily long three minutes we stop. I am knackered and sit down on a big stone.

Sentayehu's athletes look me over with curiosity. When I sit down a guy who is leading a small stretching circle shakes his head, beckoning that I should get up. 'It's no good sitting down,' he says. 'You have to stretch.' He's right of course. Runners here are always irritatingly and unflinchingly right – and righteous – when it comes to doing training 'properly'. I join in. After 10 seconds in each stretching position he makes a sharp clap of his hands to indicate that we should change position. The stretching session has a ritualistic, rhythmic feeling; when he claps his hands the runners all move effortlessly to the next stretch in a sequence they must have done hundreds of times. I have to watch him intently and I am a second behind with every change of position.

* * *

In the afternoon Alemu returns to take me to meet coach Sentayehu. As we walk he tells me a bit more about his own running. He was born 50 kilometres away from Bekoji and moved here in order to train in 2009. He heard about Kenenisa winning the Olympic 10,000m on the radio and 'simply' decided to move to Bekoji because he'd heard it was a good place to run. I ask him why he thinks athletes from Bekoji have been so successful and he puts it down to diet. 'They eat barley and honey, and drink milk,' he tells me. He is unconvinced by the idea that running ability comes from having to run to school, pointing out that Kenenisa lived in the town's main square, a stone's throw from the school. He does say that most are used to working hard on the farm from a young age, though. 'They are strong before they start to run,' he says.

We meet Sentayehu outside the house Kenenisa Bekele and Tirunesh Dibaba helped him to build at the corner of the forest, but he doesn't invite us in. 'I want to show you my other home,' he says with a chuckle, gesturing towards the forest that slopes away from us. A stocky figure in his fifties, he wears a yellow national team jacket with green sleeves and a faded red Adidas cap. Even though we are just going for a walk, a whistle hangs around his neck, as if he is prepared in case any coaching opportunities present themselves in the forest. Clasping his hands behind his back, he sets off at a leisurely, ruminative pace. 'So you are Mo Farah's countryman?' he asks. 'I am,' I confirm. 'Mo Farah is difficult,' Alemu interjects. Sentayehu nods. 'Mo Farah is running with a system,' he says, referring to Farah's trademark tactic of getting to the front of a race in the last couple of laps and then refusing to give up the inside lane. 'Our athletes are running only with energy.' He tells me that Ethiopian athletes used to run as a team when Kenenisa and Haile Gebrselassie were at their best. 'The race would be open for a while and then suddenly there would be a green flood at the front, and no-one would get past,' he says, smiling. The Ethiopian team would have decided in advance who was the strongest and the other two runners would run in support of their leader. Now, he says, is a time for individualism. No-one wants to run as a team.

'What about your athletes?' I ask him.

'I teach them to read each other,' he says, 'to learn each other's pace, their strengths and weaknesses. After a few years they know the stride of every other runner here intimately.'

'So it's about teamwork?' I ask.

'Exactly. You know, I don't really believe in talent. Ethiopia does not have a problem with finding athletes, we have a problem of creating unity.'

He tells me he thinks the national team should have to live and train together for 'at least' four months before a big competition for the sake of 'integration'. He points to the forest, a long slope with widely spread trees giving way to a jumpable river with a grassy, tree stump-stubbled field on the other side. 'If you watch the athletes run around here, they know it so well that they can run in single file and they *know* when the runner at the front will make a turn. It is seamless.' I've often felt this running in a group here. At the end of the run this morning I felt like the only fish in the shoal getting it wrong, or the only Englishman at a ceilidh. 'You can't get used to being left behind,' he says, because 'being left behind is a training adaptation, just like any other adaptation.' You have to learn to 'follow the feet' of the person in front. If you get used to leaving a two-metre gap, you will do it in a race and that's no good.

Ethiopian runners spend much of their time developing a sense of rhythm and timing. The endless drills I watch every morning are a testament to this. Close your eyes and you hear a foot being planted firmly on the ground, a light scuff, a foot again, an on-beat, off-beat rhythm. It sounds like one person. Open your eyes and a line of 12 runners is doing the same exercise in perfect time with each other. 'Following someone's feet' means more than just keeping up with them; it literally means mimicking their stride, placing your right foot when they place theirs, your left when they do, moulding your stride to their cadence perfectly. I have a loping running action hard-wired from over a decade of practice. I'm nearly six feet (1.83m) tall and trying to run in time with others is not something I've ever been taught to do – or even heard of – at running clubs in England, Scotland or France. It is almost impossible to unlearn your own stride and when people tell me to 'follow their feet' like this I feel like I'm stumbling forward with halting, staccato strides. Watch a group of Ethiopian runners train, though, and they are usually in perfect sync with each other, the same efficient, clipped stride having been developed through countless hours of drills.

I ask Sentayehu to talk me through an average training week for one of his athletes. First, he says, there is always a long, gradual warm-up for 30 or 40 minutes. On Monday they run long hills. He points to the bottom corner of the forest and indicates a route that starts steeply, before climbing at a gentle gradient all the way round the edge of the forest. You can see the route, now he mentions it, etched into the ground by thousands of feet. 'The hill is exactly 400 metres long,' he tells me. So that's where Tirunesh Dibaba got the long-hill session that people talked about in Addis from, I think. He tells me he works on the principle that 40 minutes of continuous work is about right for young athletes. 'So they go up and down for 40 minutes, and then they stop,' he says. Then they stretch for at least 20 minutes, because 'without stretching you will change nothing.'

The next day they do *fartlek*. This is my favourite – and only – Swedish word. It means 'speed play' and essentially stretches of fast running are mixed with spells of slower running. It is popular in Ethiopia, travelling there in the 1960s with Abebe Bikila's Swedish coach Onni Niskanen. This session has 'lots of speed,' Sentayehu says. Again, after a long warm-up they run for 40 minutes. He is keen to stress that in both of these sessions there is no rest, only varying degrees of intensity. 'If you work hard enough,' he says, a twinkle in his eye, '40 minutes is enough.' On Wednesday he says he has started to allow them to run on asphalt. This has only become possible very recently, he says, because 'the Chinese decided to build us a road from Asella.' Even now, they only do this once a fortnight, he says. 'It's like running on stone.' Again, they run for 40 minutes, often one hard 40-minute effort. He follows them on his motorbike, monitoring their progress according to the kilometre markers at the side of the road. 'I wait by the markers,' he says mischievously, then I shout, 'You are late! You have to go faster.'

This is another recent innovation. Both the road and the motorbike only arrived a year ago.

On Thursday they train on soft ground again. They run on a big field, for the usual continuous 40 minutes. 'They might do diagonals, or laps or *fartlek*,' he says, 'something to keep them interested.' On Friday they run a long, easy one hour and 20 minutes, which should have 'plenty of ups and downs but no hills,' Sentayehu says cryptically. He adds that he uses this run as an opportunity to test the runners' ability to lead and take the responsibility of choosing an appropriate route.

Learning to lead is important because of the beliefs the runners share about energy. To 'follow someone's feet' is to share their rhythm and to feed off their energy, and leading or pacemaking is therefore often described by the runners in Addis as 'bearing someone else's burden'. The runners are expected to learn to share their energy and to improve together. There is a phrase in Amharic which describes the importance of this kind of teamwork. 'When many threads come together, they can tie up a lion.' Training is not an individualistic, survival-of-the-fittest pursuit, but rather a communal endeavour. This is why Sentayehu is so disappointed by Ethiopians' recent performances, where the 'green flood' of teamwork has repeatedly failed to materialise at recent major championships. He puts this down to the sheer competition for races that engulfs athletes once they go to Addis Ababa and the individualism that is fostered by large sums of prize money. 'Get the green flood back,' he says with a chuckle, 'and we will say "ciao" to Mo Farah and the Kenyans.'

The runners Sentayehu coaches are at the beginning of their athletic journeys, with many of them under the age of 15. If they progress they will move to one of the government-sponsored training centres or to clubs in Addis Ababa, as Alemu has done. Because the athletes are young, in Bekoji they only train five times a week. On Saturdays they do a warm-up and some drills on their own if they want to, but on Sundays they always take a complete day of rest. 'But they shouldn't switch off,' coach adds. 'They should be thinking always about how to improve for the next week.' This is an important part of his coaching philosophy. He says that the athletes train as a group, but his feedback is individual. He says the worst thing a coach can do is end training abruptly with a swift debrief. 'With my athletes,' he says, 'we sit for 20 minutes after training. Running is a social activity. Then the athletes come to me individually and ask me, "What was my fault today? How can I improve?" I try to give them something to think about after every run.' Much of becoming a runner here is about developing mental strength and resilience. It is also – once again – about patience. Runners could try to accelerate their progress by running more than five times a week, but Sentayehu prefers a gradual, measured approach.

I ask him what was special about Kenenisa and he rolls up the newspaper in his hand, peering through it at me to mimic Kenenisa gazing into the future. 'Kenenisa was incredibly focused,' he says. 'He knew what he wanted. When he was 13 he told me he was going to be World and Olympic champion.' Kenenisa was from one of the poorer families; their only income besides a small patch of farmland came from making horsehair whips for cattle. I imagine him sitting there, at 13, winding the hair for the whips and plotting his route to the top of the sport. 'And Kenenisa had the green flood,' Sentayehu reminds me, with fellow runner Sileshi Sihine helping him to many of his global titles and earning the nickname 'Mr Silver' in the process for the number of times he finished second.

When I talk to Alemu's friends they tell me that they would be like Kenenisa if only they had better shoes and 'facilities'. The increased interest in the town from outsiders has brought with it an influx of second-hand running shoe donations, which has in turn sparked a fledgling belief in having the right gear. Sentayehu sees this as something that allows the athletes to make excuses. No matter that Kenenisa didn't get his first pair of shoes until he went to his first training camp. In spite of this, it is still easy to see Bekoji as a purer, more organic athletic environment, though. It seems like the youngsters who turn up to train with Sentayehu every morning do so for the love of the sport and most of them say they are motivated by wanting to represent Ethiopia.

When I ask Sentayehu whether he thinks we'll ever see another Kenenisa, he wrinkles his nose. 'Kenenisa was special,' he repeats. He was more driven than any other athlete he's come across before or since. And he worries about the changes to runners' motivation. 'If Kenenisa began training now, even, maybe he would not be as successful,' he says. When Kenenisa started, all he knew about was athletics; he had only a vague notion of the money to be made from the sport and he didn't have any of the 'technologies' – TV and mobile phones, but also smart watches and expensive running shoes – that distract the runners of today, even in Bekoji. 'Maybe now they will come from another high-altitude place,' he tells me, 'somewhere they know less about athletics.' This seems a curious conclusion to come to, but in a way it makes sense. Much of Ethiopia's success has come in spite of a lack of facilities and in spite of a lack of officially certified coaching staff. It has grown organically in Bekoji under the guidance of an extraordinary coach. It may be more difficult to find another coach like Sentayehu than to find another champion runner. Before I leave he grabs me by the arm to give me a last piece of advice. 'And one other thing,' he says. '<u>Alcohol is forbidden. And girlfriends and boyfriends are not needed! Zero</u>. You have to write this in your book and it has to be underlined.' Promise fulfilled, coach.

4

SO GOOD, SO FAR

The perceived benefits of training in Addis are often less a case of *what* you do as *where* you do it. The runners I know are constantly weighing the value of various places: the 'heaviness' of the air at Entoto mountain against the expanses of grassland in Sendafa where the 'kilometres come easily'; the chill of the forest against the heat of Akaki, some 800 metres lower. The runner does their best to situate themselves within the pull of these environmental forces in the way that will best enrich their 'condition'.

Conversations on the relative merits of different places can spiral on for hours and athletes will frequently travel across the city to sleep over with a friend in order to train in a specific place the next day. I wake up one Saturday morning to find Teklemariam – who lives 15 kilometres away in Legetafo – vigorously washing his face at the outdoor tap in our compound. 'What are you doing here?' I ask him, bleary-eyed at 5.45 a.m. He explains that he and Hailye have 'planned' a session of hill reps and that he'd arrived last night and shared Hailye's bed. 'I came for the hill,' he says, before adding, reverentially, 'It is Tirunesh's hill,' and explaining that it is where Tirunesh Dibaba (women's Olympic 5000m and 10,000m champion) used to train.

Places are often imbued with importance because of the people who train or once trained there. Entoto, for instance, is associated with Haile Gebrselassie, who I am told by numerous people used to run there every morning at 5.30 a.m. Others are significant for particular air qualities. One area of the Yeka sub-city forest is referred to as Boston, a marathon renowned for being cold, because it feels colder than other parts of the forest and because people often train there when they prepare for the Boston marathon. The word 'condition' in English is used both to describe a physical and mental state of preparedness and the 'air conditions' of particular places, indicating the strength of the perceived link between the two things.

When runners ask, '*Condition yet alle?*' ('Where is condition?') they are referring at once to the mysterious and fickle nature of 'condition' as a physical property *and* to its environmental location, or rather the *combination of environments* that will lead to them making the improvements they need to make. Many of the conversations between coach and athletes on the bus after training centre around the optimum combination of places and surfaces for the week's training depending on the time of the year. If there are no races we sometimes run at 'high altitude' or 'cold' places three times: in Sendafa, Entoto and Sululta, for instance. This is because race-specific fast running is less important. I find these weeks exhausting; sometimes we don't drop below 2700 metres above sea level for three consecutive hard sessions.

More often a combination is sought. We usually train at high altitude on Monday, lower altitude (or a 'hot place') on Wednesday for 'speed' training. and then alternate on Fridays between Sebeta (at a mere 2200 metres) and Sendafa (at 2600 metres and above). Alongside the concerns about place is a consideration of surfaces, and the optimum combination of 'hard' (asphalt and 'rough road') and 'soft' (grass and forest) to make sure legs are used to sustaining the impact required to race, but that their energy isn't 'burned up' by too much running on hard ground. On one occasion while we are discussing the distribution of training sessions, one of the runners who is returning from injury raises his hand and suggests we train at Akaki (renowned for being 'hot') twice that week. Hailye laughs and turns to me. 'He only wants to go there because he's fat,' he says. 'No-one else needs Akaki twice.' Again, choice of place is emphasised as the most efficient way of losing weight.

To get our group of 30 or so athletes, most of whom live in Kotebe, but some of whom also live in various places along the road between Kotebe and Sendafa, or even on the other side of the city, to training every morning is a serious logistical enterprise, which Hailye co-ordinates from his seat at the front of our team bus. An impressive feat of engineering, the bus we hire three mornings a week is called a *Qit Qit*. Constructed from the chassis of an Isuzu truck, with a locally manufactured body made partially from disused oil drums, the bus is the definition of ramshackle. It is also, in my experience at least, completely indestructible and follows us on runs on even the roughest and hilliest terrain.

The bus is driven by the balding and portly Birhanu, who to my great surprise is still, at the age of at least 50, capable of hurtling out of the bus with an armful of water bottles and delivering them to the runners at a pace of 20 kilometres an hour. Birhanu speaks pretty good English and is a source of endless sociological musings ('I bet they don't do that in your country... This is the Amhara way of ploughing'), as well as a running commentary on how each of the runners looks during a particular session. Our bus conductor Tadesse's main job is to organise and deliver the water bottles to the runners every five kilometres, and then to prevent members of the public from trying to get on to the bus on the way back into town. After a few months he reveals to me that he had given running a go for about a year, but stopped to work for Birhanu when he ran out of money. 'Besides,' he tells me, 'I could only run 30.05 for 10 kilometres.' This is perhaps the moment I realise the extent of the gulf between me and the other runners on the bus. Even the conductor is two seconds quicker than me over 10 kilometres, and he ran his PB at 2400 metres above sea level – and then decided running wasn't worth pursuing seriously.

Several months into my time in Ethiopia my own running is still a source of curiosity to the Moyo Sports athletes. They know that I've run for Great Britain, because I use the bag for training (it has an excellent compartment for isolating dirty shoes and kit), but given how difficult it is to make the Ethiopian national team they are confused by how far behind them I usually am in training. That I am doing research for a PhD has been explained to them clearly, but it doesn't really account for why I am putting myself through all the 5 a.m. starts and two-hour runs when I am clearly not in a position to make decent money from the sport. I am quizzed about the job market in the UK and asked about the kinds of jobs that are available. When I say that yes, I probably could get a job in a bank if I wanted to, their confusion rises further. What *was* I thinking, struggling through all those runs and then hiding away to write on my own when I could be at home with my family?

There is a level of respect to be gained purely by virtue of continuing to show up, but I am seen as a strange figure for a while. It helps when my partner Roslyn comes out to visit. We get to spend some time together and visit places like Bishoftu and Harar (where we feed wild hyenas by hand), and the runners can see that I *do*, in fact, have a life that doesn't revolve entirely around hanging about and asking them weird questions. Roslyn comes running on Entoto and it is great to have her perspective on things as an anthropologist less steeped in the world of running. As the weeks go on, the athletes themselves start to pick up on the kinds of things I am interested in and I can tell that they sometimes ask each other questions that are actually for my benefit. A couple of weeks after Abere receives his prize money from a race, for instance, Fasil asks him, 'Abere, what changed for you when you got that money, in terms of your living standards and social life?' Hailye bursts out laughing: 'Fasil becomes the interviewer!' he says.

By this stage I have more or less got used to the early starts and the long bus journeys, and my favourite bus journeys are the ones that end with *coroconch*. This Amharic term is usually translated to me as 'rough road' and basically describes an uneven gravel and mud trail. *Coroconch* is wonderfully onomatopoeic, sounding, to me at least, almost exactly like a runner's shoe striking and then leaving a gravelly trail. The road the runners call Iyesus is my favourite place to run in Ethiopia and probably, if I acclimatise for a few weeks, the world. To get to the head of the road is about a 40-minute drive from Kotebe, after which we pull off the asphalt road and bump and lurch on to the rough track. Named for the church at which it starts (Iyesus – Jesus), the road is an epically undulating dirt track that is almost wide enough for two vehicles, but which, thankfully, rarely needs to be. The road winds its way all the way to Bishoftu, over 50 kilometres away, across farmland that stretches to the horizon on either side, with small roadside villages every few kilometres. There is now an asphalt road to Bishoftu, so apart from very occasional public buses, which can be heard from at least a mile away with their constantly blaring sing-song horns, the only motorised vehicles on the trail are the buses of the various management groups and athletics clubs.

More common are small horse-drawn wagons, pulled by horses elaborately decorated in Oromo style with brightly coloured tassels and pom-poms, or men draped in *shammas* riding alone or in groups. On the many occasions when I'm unable to keep up with the group, I often still have company. A man on horseback will appear alongside me and, having inquired *'Selam naw?'* will act as a silent escort for a few kilometres. Or, in marked contrast, a small group of children will run alongside me – usually managing to keep up for an improbable amount of time – shouting 'China!' At first I was surprised by this, but Hailye points out that the only foreigners most of the kids have seen are Chinese construction workers working on installing telephone masts or road works.

Planted with wheat and *teff*, the fields to each side of the road are a constantly shifting hue of greens and yellows. Like on the asphalt road, white posts mark each kilometre along the trail, and coach Meseret trusts these far more than he trusts the Garmin watches owned by a few of the athletes. 'Even if they aren't exactly a kilometre apart, they don't move from one week to the next,' he reasons. 'And the important thing is that we can compare.' *Coroconch* is one of the four key surfaces in the Ethiopian runner's repertoire, starting with the forest and the track, and then moving towards *coroconch* and eventually asphalt as the runner 'adapts' to the load of training. It requires a specific kind of strength that is different from that of running in the forest or on the roads.

Hailye explains this to me on the bus on the way to Iyesus one morning. 'It takes your energy,' is how he puts it. 'With every step you take it pulls you back, so you have to work harder.' Overhearing us, Meseret chips in. 'It creates a kind of soreness, pulling on the hamstrings,' he says. I've definitely noticed this on previous occasions. The day after a hard *coroconch* run I will often feel like I do after running on snow for the first time in a while. 'It is very different from asphalt,' Hailye says. '*Coroconch* requires power and that's why Fasil is so good on *coroconch*.' Fasil, nicknamed *Korma* (bull) is far more muscular than most of the other runners, who joke that both of their legs could fit into one of his. 'Fasil eats *coroconch* for breakfast,' Hailye adds. I find it fascinating that he is able to run with the group on even their hardest runs here, only to be minutes behind when we run on the roads. Today is to be a relatively steady run for the group, so I am keen to see if I can keep up for a while.

Meseret tells us that he wants us to average around 3.48 per kilometre for 35 kilometres, but is happy for us to start slowly and build into the run. I know that on these hills, at this altitude, I will struggle to run that fast, but I also know that the group are liable to start at more like 4.15 per kilometre and end up at closer to 3.15, so I figure I can run with them for a fair few kilometres. The trail is basically a series of long uphills lasting between two and four kilometres, alternating with a series of long downhills where you lose all of the elevation you gained before you hit the start of the next long climb. Because the trail cuts through open farmland you can see each hill coming a long way off, the trail snaking its way in switchbacks across the hillside ahead.

As expected, we do start off nice and steadily, barely running under 4.30 for the first kilometre. I am very conscious of my foot strike running on *coroconch*. Learning to run in time with the others is still a challenge for me, especially with my long, loping stride that contrasts with the more staccato rhythm of someone like Tsedat. If learning to run in time with other people, stride for stride, is the 'first thing a runner learns' here then it is hardly surprising that it's taking me a long time to unlearn my own stride, honed as it has been over at least a decade. It does kind of ruin the coro*conch*, coro*conch*, coro*conch* rhythm of our footsteps – what Oliver Sacks would call our 'kinetic melody' – when I can't keep time, though, and I try my best to follow Fasil's feet in front of me closely.

The mood in the group is good today and people chat as we run along in these early stages. 'You will lead today,' Tsedat jokes, pointing for me to go to the front of the group, who, unlike in the forest, are running two abreast. I figure I don't get many chances to do this so I do run at the front for a few kilometres, alongside Mekuant Ayenew, who would go on to win the Beijing marathon later in the year. Mekuant is utterly serene at this pace and still breathes through his nose. He runs with his hands out in front of him slightly, like a cartoon character creeping into a room might, and runs so lightly on the ground that it is hard for me to tune into his footsteps. I take advantage of our two-abreast running formation to ask Mekuant a few questions in my faltering Amharic.

He tells me that he started running when he saw someone training in the small town he comes from near Gondar in the north of Ethiopia. He came fourth in a race in his district and from there had the opportunity to travel to a race further away. It was the first time he had travelled more than a few kilometres from home and it was the excitement of this that captured his attention: at that point he had no idea that there was money to be made through running. I ask him about the most important attributes of a runner, and the words he uses are 'respect' and 'patience'. It took years of training before he was good enough to travel abroad to race (he has since run 15 marathons) and by that time he was an addict. 'I am unable to eat without running now,' he says. 'My body needs this.'

He may have already had some impressive international results to his name, including second place in Hannover marathon, but Mekuant was proudest of winning a race most people would never have heard of. Earlier in the year he won the Hawassa marathon for his club, Commercial Bank of Ethiopia (known just as Bank). He won a tiny fraction of the money he won in races abroad, but he came away with more confidence than any other race has given him. 'At those kinds of races you get young guys pushing way beyond their limits and dropping out at 10 kilometres, so it's fast from the start. And on top of that it is at altitude and it is hot and you have maybe a 150 top runners, way more than in a race abroad.' He is looking forward to his next opportunity to show what he can do abroad.

Running on this shifting gravel surface means that you have to try to stay on your toes as much as possible in order to avoid losing too much ground, so a lot of my focus is on the way in which I am running. I try to run lightly like Mekuant, avoiding disturbing the ground too much. After a while I slip back into the group, not wanting them to be held up by humouring the *farenj*. After three or four kilometres we are already running the pace Meseret prescribed of 3.48 per kilometre and I feel pretty good. The dawn light is still soft and the chill is slowly starting to lift. Black kites – rare in Europe but like pigeons here – glide above us and we negotiate our way around a pack of donkeys laden with jerry cans as the runners joke with their owner.

The bus drives ahead to meet us at five-kilometre intervals as usual. When we reach our 10th white post in the road Meseret jumps out of the bus and runs alongside me with my water bottle as Tadesse and Birhanu chase after the others. He is surprised to see me still with the group. '*Gobez*, Mike!' he says. 'Today you will finish with them!' The bus, though, is parked at the bottom of a three-kilometre long hill, a series of energy-sapping switchbacks that will take us up to 2800m above sea level.

We hit the hill and the group keep going at exactly the same pace. I need to be careful if I am going to get through this run. We are running 20 kilometres in one direction and then 15 kilometres back, and Meseret has designed it this way so that we have to run most of the way back uphill. I really want to finish the 35 kilometres today, so I have told Birhanu not to wait and give me the temptation of getting on the bus after 25 or 30 kilometres. But this is a tactic that I know could backfire. I don't want to end up stranded or in the humiliating position of Birhanu having to drive back and scrape me off the roadside.

I let the group go and settle into a pace I know I can cope with for a long time – four minutes per kilometre. This has the advantage of being both a nice round number and, for some reason, the default pace my legs seem to return to on this kind of run. If I can keep it up I'll cover 35 kilometres in around 2.20, which I'll be pretty happy with in the circumstances. But I know I'll need to resist the temptation to try to go quicker, which is difficult in such inspiring surroundings and when other groups of runners are liable to blow past you like you're standing still.

After a few minutes of settling into my rhythm another team bus sweeps past me, engulfing me momentarily in a cloud of dust. This, I have come to realise, is usually a precursor for a lesson in running humility. Sure enough I hear the coro*conch*, coro*conch*, coro*conch* of 25 pairs of feet and the Demadonna group, managed by the Italian Gianni Demadonna, run past me, or rather around me, a runner on each side so that I am momentarily part of the group. Guye Adola, who I have got to know pretty well as a regular of Hirut Café in Kotebe, is attempting his first 40-kilometre training run as he prepares for his marathon debut in Berlin. '*Selam naw, Guye?*' I manage as he passes. 'So good so far,' he replies in English, a slippage that also seems like a perfect description of the run we are embarked upon.

For a minute or so I am literally eating their dust. The first thing I always do when getting back from a *coroconch* run is to brush my teeth – the dry earth that gets kicked up coats them with a muddy beige powder. I settle back into my rhythm and try to remind myself that, in spite of appearances to the contrary, I am running OK. It is starting to warm up a bit now, the mist that covered the fields is lifting and the only sound I can hear for a while is my own feet disturbing the ground. I wave to a farmer who is fixing the cactus hedge around his farmstead and he waves back, clearly a bit bemused by my cheeriness.

After another kilometre or so of running – and without the usual precursor of a bus – I hear footsteps again. At first they sound like the echo of my own, but before I know it I've got company. 'Good morning!' shouts my new companion, in English. 'Good morning,' I respond. '*Selam naw?*' He certainly seems quite happy, a big smile on his face as he cruises along in an old pair of Adidas racing flats. 'I am fine,' he replies.

'Are you fine?'

'I think so,' I tell him. He pats my shoulder.

'We'll run together,' he says. 'Why are you alone?'

'*Ba kelel pace mahed alebign,*' I reply. 'I need to run easy.'

'No problem!' he laughs. 'I've not trained for two months.'

'It doesn't seem that way,' I point out. He barely seems to be breathing.

'That is true. But I'm a crazy man,' he offers by way of explanation. 'Any pace you want, you just tell me and I will go.'

He explains that he has some experience in this department. He paced Haile Gebrselassie to both of his marathon world records in Berlin in 2007 and 2008. 'I was paid quite a lot of money to pace Haile,' he tells me before joking that today he will make an exception and pace me for free.

'What pace do you want then?' he asks.

'Four minutes per kilometre,' I tell him.

'Perfect,' he says. 'This is a nice pace, just keep…' He motions a gentle pawing of the ground with his hands.

We run along in silence for a while and I let him dictate the pace before glancing at his wrist to see he has no watch. 'No GPS?' I ask.

'It is in here,' he says, tapping his temple. 'I'm 36 and I have been running for 19 years, so now it is easy to know.'

A couple of minutes later my watch beeps and '4.00' shows up on the screen. 'What does it say?' he asks. 'Four minutes exactly,' I tell him.

'Of course,' he says, 'Haile always said, "In one second you can win a million dollars and in one second you can lose a million dollars."'

This is a story I have heard a few times from coach Meseret, who tells the athletes that, 'You have to know the value of one second!' Haile Gebrselassie once missed out on a one million dollar bonus, offered for breaking the world record for ten kilometres in Dubai by a mere second, and has talked about the importance of absolutely perfect pacing since then. Meseret is constantly reiterating the importance of running at the pace he asks them to in training and no faster, cautioning that running with too much 'emotion' is not good for the group dynamic or their ability to keep training at this level. 'If they run on the track and I tell them 66 seconds and they come around in 65 that is a yellow card. But if they run 64 then that is a red card for me, they will not lead again.' There are exceptions to this emphasis on control and patience – when we do 'speed' training on Wednesdays, for example – but Meseret is keen to emphasise that it is control on the other days that enables us to run fast on a Wednesday.

As we near the turning point my new training partner turns to me with a grin and says, 'On the way home we will suffer together.' I am still feeling quite good and I'm enjoying the company, so this comes as a reminder that most of the way back is uphill. He may have been a 61-minute half marathon runner, but even someone capable of pacing Haile struggles to do a 35-kilometre run after two months off. When we reach the 20-kilometre mark, Meseret stands with Tadesse next to a pile of water bottles. 'Ah, you have a celebrity pacemaker today,' he says, laughing. 'You have to make the most of it!' He runs alongside us for a hundred metres or so and tells us to make sure we push to maintain the pace on the hills. That is the challenge today. We have to keep the pace as even as possible for each kilometre, even if the kilometre is steeply uphill.

Maintaining a pace that is just about manageable but which you have to really think about and concentrate on – in other words the kind of controlled running Meseret was so keen on – is, according to the Hungarian psychologist Mihaly Csikszentmihalyi, the way to enter a state of 'flow'. The best moments, he writes, 'usually occur when a person's body or mind is stretched to its limits in a voluntary effort to accomplish something difficult or worthwhile.'

Such experiences may not be pleasant at the time they occur, a fact I could definitely attest to in relation to sections of running in Sendafa, but they can also be, according to Csikszentmihalyi, some of the best moments of your life.

In his book *Flow: The Psychology of Optimal Experience*, he explains this in terms of demonstrating control. 'Getting control of life is never easy,' he writes, 'and sometimes it can be definitely painful.' But, and here his turn of phrase couldn't be more appropriate in this instance, 'in the long run, optimal experiences add up to a sense of mastery – or perhaps better, a sense of participation in demonstrating the content of life – that comes as close to what is usually meant by happiness as anything else we can conceivably imagine.' In moments like this as a runner, when everything seems to click, you can seem like you are fully inhabiting the potential of your physical self – and this can feel pretty incredible.

By now the sun has burned through the clouds and the temperature is rising. I pour a little water on to my head and wash the salt – the athletes here call it *necc lab* or 'white sweat' – from my face. The *coroconch* surface, which felt forgiving and almost like it compelled momentum when I was feeling good, starts to feel like it is working against me, dragging me backwards with every footstep. When he can tell that I'm struggling, my new friend motions for me to run as closely behind him as possible, as if he can pull me up the hill on an invisible thread. When a small gap opens up between us it is like he can sense it, and he clicks his fingers and points to his heels again.

I try to do what my coach at home always told me to do in this situation: 'Just look at the back of the person in front of you and forget about everything apart from keeping them there.'

I decide that if I can do this until the top of the hill we're on, which is the biggest and steepest on the whole route, then I can probably survive until the end. I have accepted by this point that the rest of the run is going to hurt, but it does seem like my partner is going to keep his word that we will 'suffer together' all the way to the end.

We finally crest the five-kilometre long hill and he points out that we have a couple of downhill kilometres to recover before pushing on to the finish. 'And look,' he says, 'people to hunt.' I look up for the first time in ages – I've been making a thorough study of the sweat patch growing on his tracksuit top – and see a bus in the distance followed by a group of runners and then a series of stragglers. They must have turned around just before we did. I realise that I've never really caught anyone on a run here before and I feel a surge of adrenaline spread through my body. As we run at a steady pace down the hill I make up my mind to go for a long push to the finish when we hit the final hill. We have run more or less exactly four minutes for every kilometre since I was joined by my famous pacemaker and I hope that the control we have exercised is about to be rewarded.

He is clearly enjoying the idea that we might be able to catch the group in front and keeps turning around to grin at me and then wave his arm in a 'come on let's go' kind of way. I imagine that his excitement is on a similar level to when he realised Gebrselassie was about to break the world record in Berlin in 2007. When we do finally catch the back marker of the group in front, the runner we pass is clearly disgusted. '*Ayy, rucha*,' my training partner says, observing the pain on his face and shaking his head. 'Oof, running.' What a brutal sport, he seems to be thinking. Rather than just running past him, he turns to shout, '*Gaba!*

entreating him to 'enter' the pace that we are running and try to continue with us. Somehow, through a combination of pride and determination, he does, his footsteps syncing with mine.

This process continues up the hill until we are a group of seven. My new friend treats the other runners to a strange mixture of encouragement and insult. 'What the *hell*? The *farenj* has overtaken you,' is followed by, 'Only a few kilometres to go, everyone has a rough day sometimes.' I am totally knackered by this point, having never run over 30 kilometres in Ethiopia before. I don't want to falter at this stage, though, not now that we've managed to collect another five runners. My new training partner runs the final three kilometres with a big smile on his face, having recruited a whole group who required his considerable pacemaking abilities. The rest of us grit our teeth and propel ourselves on pure pride to the team buses parked at the roadside.

Hailye is clearly pretty relieved to see me make it to the end and gives me a high-five. 'We'll have to call Malcolm,' he announces. 'You finished 35 kilometres.' As the group's sub-agent Hailye is responsible for communicating to Malcolm who is in shape and ready to race at any particular point. A strong 35-kilometre run, he explains, always leads the athletes to demand that he call Malcolm and arrange for them to run a marathon 'outside'. 'Dubai or nothing, I want to run 2.03,' I joke back. My celebrity pacemaker just waves and continues up the road, and as I watch him recede I realise that it completely slipped my oxygen-starved brain to ask his name. I've covered the 35 kilometres in 2.20 and don't feel like I could have gone a great deal quicker. Tsedat and Birhanu, meanwhile, have somehow finished the run in less than 2.05, with Fasil only a minute or so behind. This is pretty amazing running on this terrain and they are clearly pretty excited about it.

Tadesse drags a huge plastic container of water out of the bus so that we can clean the dust from our legs and wash the salt from our faces. A few of the runners also change into newer shoes and tracksuits before we head back to Kotebe, clearly wanting to project a particular image of themselves as athletes. I really wasn't convinced that I'd be able to complete 35 kilometres, so I am in high spirits on the bus back. It is hard, in fact, to imagine that this is the same group of people who boarded the bus in the morning. The slow Orthodox Christian spiritual music that played to drowsing athletes when we boarded the bus is replaced with the triumphant rhythms of Teddy Afro's new album, *Ethiopia*:

> Even though the world calls her Backward today,
> She will be the frontrunner of the coming age
> Just let me repeat her name over and over
> Isn't Ethiopia my own name?

The bus ride back down to Kotebe is animated by hundreds of kilometres' worth of endorphins. On the starboard side, Tilahun and Selamyhun (neither of whom look older than 16) watch the highlights of the Manchester United match with Andualem (who looks 40 if he's a day). Andualem's disparaging comments are met with cries of '*Shimagolay!*', a term usually reserved for the elderly. At the front Hailye is trying to persuade a still sulking Zeleke to see the funny side of his having refused to let him in the bus after 30 kilometres. There's also an anecdote underway, as Hunegnaw recalls his win at the Jan Meda Cross Country and World Championships trials a couple of years previously.

'I was running so hard that Kenenisa, in the crowd, asked if I was trying to kill everyone!' (*Kenenisa* said that?) 'Even the Kenyans were scared when they heard about it!' (The news travelled *that* far.) 'People run 35 minutes for 12 kilometres in Jan Meda, not 32. And I led all the way!' (All *six* laps?!) The Jan Meda Cross Country is coming up in a couple of weeks and we are still in the process of negotiating whether I am permitted to run or not. And, given the legendary status of the race, I am still in the process of working out whether I want to. The Jan Meda Cross Country is tied only with the Kenyan equivalent for the title of toughest cross-country race in the world. 'At least when you get to the World Cross Country,' Hunegnaw laughs, 'there are only five other Ethiopians.' I don't have to prove that I will be competitive in the race, obviously, only that I stand a chance of completing the race without being lapped, which would be unheard of and against the rules. Finishing 35 kilometres in Sendafa was a test of endurance that Hailye thinks proves that I should run. Time will tell whether or not he is right.

5

FIELD OF DREAMS

The runners I train with all answer the question 'Is running work?' in the affirmative and, in fact, *sera* or work is the most common word for training. While they also agree that they enjoy much of the running they do, it is clear that without the twin motivations of competition and money they would stop. It becomes clear pretty quickly that my turning up at training every day without a race to prepare for is confusing for them, and sooner or later I will have to run a local race. Their attitude is similar to that of Norman Mailer, as related by William Finnegan in his surfing memoir *Barbarian Days*. Exercise 'without excitement, without competition or danger or purpose, didn't strengthen the body but simply wore it out.' The race on the horizon maintains the vitality of the runner, giving all the hours of work a purpose. It is also – like going to war – a good way to reveal your *idil*.

And so it is that I end up in a queue at the EAF offices in Gurd Shola with Hailye, clutching a letter of support from Scottish Athletics and kind of hoping that there will be some bureaucratic reason why I am not allowed to run in the 33rd Ethiopian National Cross Country Championships. On our way in we pass a group of junior athletes who have just collected their national team kit. They peruse the contents of enormous black Adidas bags emblazoned with the yellow, green and red of the Ethiopian flag, unwrapping bright red tracksuit bottoms and trying on their bright yellow tracksuit tops.

We make a more ragtag crew in the registration line. Most people are entered in the race through their clubs, so anyone in the queue to register as an individual is on the fringes of the sport. The young man in front of me looks no older than 18 and his shoes, crisscrossed with different coloured thread, look like they have undergone many repairs. I ask him what he thinks the race will be like and he answers in English: 'I think it will be very fast. More than any other race this one will be fast. It is only for the strong ones.' He sees the worry in my eyes. 'No matter, OK?' he says, placing his hand on my shoulder. 'First of all is full confidence, OK?'

I have looked up the results from previous years online and the list of winners is a who's who of top Ethiopian runners, although the curious thing is the conspicuous absence of the name 'Kenenisa Bekele', who never managed to win in Jan Meda in spite of winning a ridiculous 11 World Cross Country titles. The race in Jan Meda doubles as the World Championship trials and yet – in spite of many individual victories – only one man, Gebregziabher Gebremariam, has ever won the trial in Ethiopia and gone on to win the World Cross Country. 'Winning in Jan Meda takes so much from people,' Hailye says. 'It is very difficult to go on and win the World Cross Country too.'

The name that stands out on the list for me is that of Hunegnaw Mesfin. While most of the winning times are in the 34- to 35-minute range for 12 kilometres, that 32-minute winning run I'd heard him talk about on numerous occasions was right there on Wikipedia: 32.20. I can only assume the measurement of the course was approximate, given the altitude of 2500 metres, but it is still clear that his run in 2011 was extraordinary and it makes his frustration with his current form even more acute.

When we reach the front of the queue the official in charge of registration looks me up and down, frowns at my letter from Scottish Athletics and tells Hailye, 'Take him to see Dube.' Dube Jillo has been president of the federation for many years. We sit on plastic chairs in a large office with an open-plan layout, apart from the glass-walled cabin in which Dube sits. While many people work here, everything – from national team selections and release letters allowing athletes to go abroad, all the way down to me wanting to run as a guest in the Cross Country – has to be signed off by Dube.

A past winner of the Rome marathon, Hailye credits him with opening up more opportunities to run abroad. Before Dube, he tells me as we wait, it was only the small number of athletes who made the national team who would have the opportunity to run a few races abroad after an Olympics or World Championships. 'The reason he did that,' Hailye says, 'is because he was an athlete, and he knows the ups and downs, the difficulties, the hard work, what they deserve. If things go wrong, where does that athlete go? He's going to go back to being a farmer! That's difficult, so Dube made it possible for athletes to travel.'

We are called into the room. Dube is rather larger than in the days when he competed, and cuts an imposing figure in his suit and tie. Hailye explains the situation to him. 'Well, sure, he can run,' comes the verdict. 'But if he can't break 30 minutes for 10 kilometres he should run in the junior race.' I point out that at 28 I would feel a bit of a fraud in the under-20 category and we reach a compromise: I can run the senior race but I should drop out before the finish. I return to the queue and receive my first race number with Amharic text on it, which has to be taken back to Dube and signed for some reason.

Hailye explains to me that the classification of athletes into 'junior' and 'senior,' especially at clubs in rural parts of the country where birth certificates aren't always available, can be more about the ability of the athlete in question and their experience than about how many days remain until their 20th birthday. And in terms of ability I was still a junior at 28. 'You can finish the senior race, but if you are going to be lapped you must drop out,' Hailye says. 'So that you don't disturb the leaders.' I think back to running the Scottish National Cross Country the previous year. I finished seventh and negotiating lapped runners was an important part of how the leaders ran the last lap. Jan Meda would see the tables turned on me in as good a demonstration that it's all relative as you could hope to have.

The name 'Jan Meda' is a shortened form of *Janhoy Meda*, which means something like 'field of majesty' or 'field of the emperor', after it hosted a vast military parade and fireworks display to mark Haile Selassie's coronation. It is where Emperor Menelik displayed the canons captured from the Italians after the 1896 Battle of Adwa. Almost a century later, in the early 1990s, it hosted thousands of internally displaced Ethiopians during the civil war, and has played a pivotal role in modern Ethiopian history, staging religious festivals, coronations, military reviews and campaign inaugurals. The field is around two and a half kilometres long and perhaps 500 metres wide, walled in on all sides but open and expansive within the walls, with long grass during the rainy season and a parched yellow stubble for most of the rest of the year. The field hosts more horse racing than athletics events, as well as traditional Ethiopian sports like *gena,* a form of hockey, and *gugs,* a sort of rough-and-tumble horseback tag. There is a large stable in one corner of the field, but the horses are normally allowed to wander around, and will occasionally break into a spontaneous gallop and startle the runners.

Today, though, the horses are all safely ensconced in their stables. This is important business and the organisation is meticulous. I arrive with Fasil, who seems nervous, even though he's not running. He's not ready yet, he tells me, but will 'prepare well' for next year's race. Large Pepsi advertising flags have been erected on the road outside Jan Meda. Underneath a huge bottle are the words, 'Live For Now', which seems a singularly inappropriate maxim given the lifestyles of most of the runners I know, for whom 'Live For Next Year' would be more fitting. Daubed in foot-high letters on the wall as we walk into the field is the somewhat cryptic phrase, 'Muscles are the slaves of the brain. Muscles do not learn.' I hope I can think myself faster today.

As we try to find other athletes we know, one corner of the field is filling up with team buses. Large vehicles for the first division clubs like Mebrat Hayle and Bank, and smaller minibuses for clubs from further afield, whose athletes must qualify from regional races. We find Hailye, who is preoccupied with meeting people from the various clubs he has links with. As Moyo Sports sub-agent he is hoping to speak to some of the top finishers who don't already have contracts with managers, but there are other sub-agents here as well and competition to secure the best athletes can be tough. He tells me to make sure I let the officials know I am here, and to make sure I do what they tell me so that I'm allowed to run.

It turns out that I have to queue to have my number initialled by two different people, which takes a good 20 minutes of standing in the sun. Having done practically all of my training before 8 a.m., I realise it is going to be strange to run in direct sunlight and 25 degrees. Once my number is sorted, Fasil and Hailye join me for a jog around the field. 'Meseret is with the guys from Mebrat Hayle,' Hailye says, 'but he said to warn you it's going to be really fast. Like, you will be surprised by how fast it is. Even if you tell yourself you know it will be fast, you will be surprised.' He reminds me of the 10,000m race we had watched, where there were more drop-outs than finishers. 'You'll be the only one on the start line who doesn't think they have a chance,' he says, 'so they're all going to go for it and a lot of them will drop out. You have to let them go.'

Quite a few people are already in their spikes completing their warm-ups, and judging by the speed at which they are doing their pre-race strides letting them go shouldn't be too difficult. I put my own spikes on and, much sooner than I would have liked, we are called over for a last check of everyone's numbers. Even though I have no competitive ambitions in this race whatsoever, I am nervous as hell, the pent-up energy of the other runners on the start line contagious. The field is on a long gradual slope and we start on a 150m wide start line at the bottom of the field, with about a kilometre of straight, uphill running ahead of us. The ground is rock-hard and covered in tufts of dry yellow grass, and a hot sun blazes down on our heads. It could not be more different from the mud and sleet of Falkirk at the Scottish equivalent of this race a year ago.

The gun goes and Meseret is not wrong. The runners in front of me depart like a wave surging to break on a shoreline. I do a spectacularly good job of letting them go, first 10 metres and, by the time we get to the top of the field, at least 50 to the backmarker.

I look down at my watch, which says my pace is just over three minutes per kilometre. They must be absolutely flying at the front, uphill. I try to stay calm and settle into a rhythm, and I'm relieved to reach the top of the field and begin the gradual downhill back to the start. I hear the odd, '*Ayzoh, farenj*', as I pass spectators. The tone is sympathetic, if a little patronising. As in any race, I try to feel for the limits of effort, that circumference beyond which I know I'll be in trouble, so that I can stay the right side of the line. This is so much harder to do at altitude, though. Once you're in a little bit of trouble you can be in a lot of trouble very quickly, and it's harder to claw your way back to the right side of the line.

Meseret runs alongside me and shouts, 'Mike! Concentrate!' I have no idea if this means I should concentrate on running faster or slower, or just that I should concentrate. I negotiate a couple of wooden logs that have been laid across the course in case it wasn't hard enough to run at this altitude, and before I know it I've completed a lap and I'm at the foot of the uphill drag again. When I lift my head to look up the slope it looks like I'm not as far behind the second-last runner as I had been at the top of the hill. Perhaps it's the lack of oxygen or some kind of optical illusion, I think, as I focus on getting up the hill without working too hard. I put my head down and *concentrate* like Meseret told me. And when I lift my head again I find that, yes, he is coming back to me.

I feel a little surge of adrenaline and then immediately tell myself to calm down. The aim is to even out my effort in such a way as to run five laps before the leaders have run six. By the top of the hill I am close to catching him, though. He turns, snatches the quickest of glances at me and ducks under the tape to his left. Head down, he starts to walk back towards the start. Hailye had said this might happen. There's nothing that adds insult to injury more than assuming you're in last place and then realising you're about to be overtaken by a *farenj*. Hailye had explained the high percentage of drop-outs in domestic races as follows: 'If they know they will not finish in the prize money sometimes they will stop. They will save themselves for another day.'

I look to my left and scan the middle of the field, where I can see that already – with only a lap run – a fair few runners are walking back to the start or else lying prostrate on the floor. For them, as Hailye says, there is no shame in dropping out. They are making the obvious decision to accept that they are not yet ready to compete at this level. There is little point in soldiering on for the sake of it. Over the next couple of laps I maintain my steady pace and catch a few more penultimate runners, who all do the same thing as the first runner I caught, so that I remain in last place. While I had to think about controlling my pace on the first lap this is a less conscious effort as more time passes: I am simply incapable of deviating from a steady lope, feeling once again like my body has gone into a kind of self-preservatory auto-pilot.

It does feel good to catch the odd runner, though, and at the halfway stage I try to calculate how far away the leaders are. They are nearing the top of the hill when I return to the start/finish area, which as far as I can tell means they are still less than a kilometre ahead. If I can keep going like this I should be allowed to finish the race. My task is closer to that of an ultra runner trying to beat cut-off times than that of someone racing a cross-country. My mouth is dry and I can feel the skin on my shoulders starting to burn under the sweat. The bottoms of my feet are starting to get sore from running on such hard ground in spikes. These are not familiar cross-country running sensations for me.

As I reach the top of the hill I am closing in on another struggling backmarker. '*Ayzoh, farenj!*' is still the refrain from those standing on the sidelines, but it is delivered with a little more force now. 'Go *on, farenj!*' I still detect a little pity, but it does seem like there is also a respect garnered from not giving up. I realise how tired I am getting when it is time to negotiate the logs on the ground and I catch my toe on one and almost stumble. By the time I get back to the start/finish area I am struggling and there is no-one left within striking distance for motivation. Those who remain in the race are either running strongly or they have stopped. It will be a lonely last two laps.

As I head up the hill for the fifth time it becomes very tempting to stop – and I have every reason to do so. Everyone else who was having a bad day has pulled the plug already and I would only be doing what I was told to do. It would, actually, be the sensible thing to do. For some reason, I don't, though. Possibly I am not thinking clearly with the oxygen debt and the altitude. But I do berate myself for making the decision to run in the first place. The English professor, poet and runner Thomas Gardner describes this kind of mid-race wobble beautifully:

At some point in almost every race you get lost. You open your eyes and realise you're in trouble. Your heart rate rises, your confidence buckles and you're suddenly flailing around inside, with no landmark save for a familiar hatred of yourself and the ego that made you line up and race. You slow down and turn on yourself.

I think most runners can relate to this feeling. It is one that I, like Gardner, seem to have in 'almost' every race, the exceptions being the really good ones. You realise that your preparation wasn't as good as you thought. You're not ready to 'participate in such a world at such a pace,' as Gardner puts it. And yet the process of getting through what I would call a 'bad patch', and what Gardner is able to evoke far more eloquently, is hugely rewarding. Gardner again:

> The body does have limits, and your fingers will eventually fumble everything you love. But go on and think about what you could build there, "sentence by shunning sentence," your words most alive when they are most disappointed in themselves. Why else would you race? Why go back there, year after year?

This, it seems to me, is what racing, and running more generally, does for people. Because in every race there are far more losers than winners (and in Ethiopia everyone is racing to win). Because there seems to be something deeply human about always wanting a bit more, even if you run well. Because the other side of disappointment is hope and we thrive on imagining ourselves that little bit better next time. The number of conversations I've had with people who have just run a personal best and who still focus on the fact that they think they could have gone faster attests to this. We are not easily satisfied. And so, we keep going back, week after week, year after year.

Back in Jan Meda, Getaneh Molla (future Dubai marathon champion and 2.03.34 course record holder) is on the charge at the front of the race and is well on his way down the hill by the time I make it to the end of my fifth lap, but I am safely round without being lapped and I can relax a little. My race was to avoid getting lapped, so in a sense this is a victory lap for me. I am through my bad patch and determined to enjoy pushing myself through this last lap. If I was going to finish dead last in the 33rd Jan Meda International Cross Country I was going to do so with my head held high.

I run under the finish gantry to find Hailye, Fasil and Meseret. Fasil puts his arm around me as I put my hands on my knees to suck air. Already he's thinking forward – who would want to dwell on last place? 'If you stay here for the whole year and do your training properly, next year we will both come here and run really strongly,' he says. He is already sketching the training in his head, I can tell, imagining himself flashing round the field like Getaneh Molla. We are joined by a diminutive figure who Hailye has been chatting to since the junior race finished. Asefa Tefera took third place in the eight-kilometre race, having travelled here from the Debre Birhan University Club. In less than three years' time, as a Moyo Sports athlete, he will win the Osaka marathon in 2.07, but he doesn't know that yet. 'Today everything changed for me,' he says quietly. 'I am very happy.'

6

ZIGZAGGING TO THE TOP

On my return from Bekoji I move from Benoit's into the same compound as Hailye in Kotebe, about five kilometres from the city centre. We mark the occasion with a small party. Hailye buys a sheep from the local market, which stands in the corner of the compound, letting out the occasional nervous bleat, for most of the day. When the other runners arrive, the sheep is dispatched, butchered and frying in a huge wrought-iron pan on a wood fire within half an hour, the meat we will not eat that afternoon parcelled up in banana leaves for the neighbours. The floor of the compound is carpeted with chillies drying blood red in the sun, ready to be ground into the Ethiopian spice mix *berbere*, and we sit for hours discussing running and the races people are hoping to run this year. By now I speak a kind of specialised runners' Amharic: I can discuss the intricacies of an interval session and the pros and cons of running in different parts of the city, but I still struggle with everyday conversation about non-running matters.

We discuss my own attempts to improve as a runner and the emphasis is again on my learning by doing. As with any craft, running requires an apprenticeship in Ethiopia. If I am to run with Fasil and learn about the forest from him, I will need to run with him and his friend Tsedat Ayana, from whom he is, in turn, learning his trade. I am, then, to be apprentice to the apprentice. Tsedat is not a well-known athlete outside Ethiopia by any means at this point, but his reputation on the domestic scene is fearsome. He has recently won two of the races organised by the EAF for first division athletes and, given that all the top professionals in Ethiopia are contractually required to run at least two of these races a year, that means he is phenomenally good.

The distinction between national and international competition in Ethiopia is, in fact, more or less the opposite to the one we might make in Europe or the USA. 'When you go outside,' Fasil points out to me, 'there may only be six or seven athletes from Ethiopia and a few from Kenya, and the rest of the people there will be running for enjoyment only.' I'm not sure that this is how many serious club runners would think about it necessarily, but I let him finish. 'When you run a race in Ethiopia, though, you have to fight with hundreds of strong athletes and Tsedat knows how to win.'

Reputations are built not only on race performances in Ethiopia, but also on the times people run for particular training sessions around the city. There are two main roads that are used for what people refer to as 'asphalt' training, both of which are marked every kilometre with a white post by the roadside. One heads east out of Addis from Kotebe to Sendafa, an undulating road that rises more than it falls as you leave the city. Both professional groups and first division clubs, which are well provisioned, pay their athletes a decent salary and have their own buses, drive out to the road well before dawn to do a fast out-and-back run, 15 kilometres each way. The other road is through Sebeta, and is flat and fast at 'only' 2200 metres above sea level.

Ethiopian running is a tight-knit network, and if someone runs particularly well over 30 kilometres in Sendafa, word spreads quickly through WhatsApp and Facebook. Pretty much everyone does their asphalt training on Friday mornings – the only time they will run on the roads all week. With a big race coming up, texts will start coming in to Hailye and other runners in the group at about 9 a.m. on a Friday. Hailye will pull his phone out of his pocket and whistle. 'You know so-and-so?' he will say. 'Well, he's *ready*,' for Dubai or Frankfurt or Rotterdam or whichever race is on the horizon. Tsedat has been known to run 1.31 for 30 kilometres in Sendafa, and very few people can do that. He hasn't built the profile to get into a big race yet, but people know what he will be capable of once he does.

Tsedat is 20 years old and at exactly five feet (1.52m) tall he is small even by the standards of Ethiopian runners. He talks at a cadence to match the whir of his legs at the end of a race. As we walk up the cobbled road the next morning, our way lit only by the occasional street light, he explains to me why we have to meet at 5.30 a.m. for our runs in the forest above Kotebe when it doesn't get light until 6 a.m. With so many runners training so hard in and around Addis Ababa, he says, you have to be clever about where you do your running, when you do it and who you do it with. By starting to run in the pre-dawn chill, he explains, he and Fasil and others from our training group can avoid 'losing too much energy' through sweating. We will walk the 20 minutes to the forest just in time for first light. 'We'll run very slowly to begin with, and then when it starts to get lighter and warmer we will speed up,' he says. In order to run almost impossibly fast on the road on a Friday morning, you have to run improbably slowly for most of the week.

Getting up this early also leaves enough time to prepare breakfast and lunch and have a long sleep before it is time to run again in the afternoon. This is seen as vitally important for protecting a runner's 'condition', which is how most runners describe the delicate state of health and fitness – somewhere between depletion and vitality – required to run at the very highest level. Tsedat wants to get home in time to prepare eggs and avocado for breakfast and still get a couple of hours' sleep in before lunchtime, which means that even a day on which there is ostensibly nothing to do but run becomes quite tightly scheduled.

Our running in the forest is to be directly influenced by the environment around us. We are to wake up slowly with the forest. When we reach the edge of the trees, Tsedat crosses himself and starts to jog. Without this pre-run ritual I might have failed to notice the distinction between walking and running: we barely change pace for at least the first couple of kilometres, which is just as well given that we can barely see anything. Tsedat trained hard yesterday, so today he is keen to emphasise that this is intended to be an easy run, which he sees primarily as a way of massaging his aching muscles.

The part of the forest we are running in this morning is criss-crossed with hundreds of paths between the eucalyptus trees, paths created through thousands upon thousands of steps. And yet where I would be inclined to passively follow these paths, Tsedat consciously seems to avoid them, picking new routes through the trees in order to stay on less firmly packed ground. This explains the vast proliferation of tracks, which are created by the infinite ways of weaving through the trees. Viewed from above, the paths would resemble a huge latticework punctuated by eucalyptus trees.

I am reminded of something the anthropologist Tim Ingold wrote. He would point out that these are tracks on the ground, but also traces in the air, created by breathing as much as by the foot on the ground. They are paths of 'aspiration' in both senses of the word, a 'hope or ambition of achieving something' and 'the act of drawing breath'. Corridors of breath, the nature writer Barry Lopez would call them. Tsedat weaves his way through tight gaps between the trees, and dewy eucalyptus leaves scratch our faces and arms on the way past. The air at this time of the morning tastes like it is infused with menthol, and combined with the lack of oxygen it leaves a minty sting in my chest. We climb two or three hundred vertical metres over the course of half an hour, as the sun rises. And yet, such is Tsedat's skill at winding between the trees and gradually picking his way up the slope, it barely feels like we've been going uphill.

Ingold would call this kind of movement 'wayfaring' in contrast to more direct movement between two points – like Friday's asphalt training – which he would refer to as 'transport'. While he defines transport as a linear process concerned only with reaching a specific destination (or in our case covering the distance between two points as rapidly as possible), wayfaring involves a greater involvement with the landscape, emphasising the importance of the process of movement itself and the development of what he calls 'knowing-in-action'. Knowledge, he writes, grows along with the 'intensity and fluency of action'. Ethiopian runners seem to understand this pretty clearly, consciously building upon their knowledge of the forest alongside their knowledge of their bodies.

When I ask the Moyo Sports coach Meseret, who has a master's degree in sports science from Addis Ababa University, about the importance Ethiopian runners place on the forest he laughs and holds up his hands in a 'You tell me' kind of way. 'They think that if they run really high up into the forest they can pull energy from the trees up there,' he says, alluding to ideas about the fluid and transferable nature of energy that will become increasingly apparent throughout my time in Ethiopia. 'They are not thinking scientifically,' he adds. And yet, as the novelist Richard Powers notes in *The Overstory*, in a sense the runners are right. 'The secret of life,' Powers writes, is that 'plants eat light and air and water, and the stored energy goes on to make and do all things,' including fuel the best runners in the world.

After 50 minutes of running, Tsedat, Fasil and I are still barely more than three kilometres away from where we started, having zigzagged backwards and forwards, retracing our steps and running across the slope far more than up it. We frequently come to an almost complete halt as we duck through a gap between trees, before accelerating again. By constantly changing direction and avoiding firmly packed even ground, we avoid the repetitive strain on the muscles incurred by running in a straight line on the road. By the time we get back to the edge of the forest, miraculously, my legs do feel considerably better than when we started. When I ask Tsedat about the zigzag style of the run, he grins and says, 'This is Ethiopian doping! If you run like this you can do more without getting injured.'

I later ask Meseret about this as well, curious to know which coach came up with the idea of zigzag running. 'It is not an idea from a coach,' he tells me. 'It is unintentional, I think. No-one is planning to go zigzagging through the forest, but unintentionally they do a kind of training like that, and it gives them an advantage to be the best athletes in cross-country races.' The idea that this technique emerged *unintentionally*, and was developed intuitively by the athletes themselves, intrigues me, as does Meseret's deference to the runners' own expertise over his own. Clearly this style of running is integral to a specifically Ethiopian way of doing things and not something imposed by coaches or developed by sports scientists. It is a specific form of expertise that emerges from interaction with the environment of the forest and which is passed on from runner to runner.

While this way of running might seem to be a specific affordance – something offered by the environment to the individual – of the forests above the city, it is interesting to note that these forests have not always been there. According to historian James C. McCann, engravings, photographs and travellers' accounts from the 19th century indicate that a barren plain once stretched from Ankober in the north all the way to modern-day Addis Ababa. The blue-green forest that has become familiar to visitors to the city since the 1970s is in fact a 20th-century phenomenon, the first eucalyptus trees having been planted around St George's Cathedral during the reign of Menelik II. More recently, on 29 July, 2019, Ethiopia broke the record for planting the most trees in one day, a staggering 353,633,660 according to the government's minister for innovation and technology Getahun Mekuria. The large forests around Addis in which the runners train are the result of a similar tree-planting effort around a century ago.

Environmental campaigners Greta Thunberg and George Monbiot have recently called for more attention to be paid to 'natural climate solutions' such as tree planting, which have the potential to remove huge amounts of carbon dioxide from the atmosphere as plants grow. 'There is a magic machine that sucks carbon out of the air, costs very little, and builds itself,' Monbiot says in a video for the *Guardian*. 'It's called a tree.' Eucalyptus planting isn't considered to have been particularly successful from an ecological perspective. Eucalyptus lower the water table and therefore aren't particularly good for other trees, and they were planted primarily for their quick growth and utility as firewood. But the huge tree planting initiative at the turn of the 20th century has had a hugely beneficial and unexpected effect on Ethiopia's runners.

As we walk slowly back from the forest, Fasil recounts the dream he had last night. In it, a man in a suit gave handfuls of dollar bills to Mekuant, while another runner from our training group looked on empty-handed. 'That's tough,' Tsedat says, shaking his head. The runners are both in Wuhan for a marathon and both are hoping for a breakthrough. 'Fasil's dreams always come true,' Tsedat warns me and, sure enough, later in the afternoon the news filters through to Hailye that, while Mekuant finished third and won $10,000, the other runner from our group was unable to finish the race. That's the nature of running in Ethiopia. It offers the opportunity to make fantastic amounts of money to some, but as competition increases, so do the odds against doing so.

When I first got to Ethiopia I hoped to do some 'on-the-go' interviews while running, where I would ask people questions as we ran together. The idea was inspired by Ivo Gormley, the founder of GoodGym, who made a film called *The Runners* where he interviewed runners in Victoria Park in London from a plastic stool installed on a bicycle trailer. He found that people were able to open up almost immediately while running, even to a total stranger, and even when asked questions like 'Are you in love?' or 'What do you care about most?' He found that running stripped back inhibitions, allowing people to answer directly and honestly.

'Through their steps, their breaths, and their focus,' runners could respond unhesitatingly, he said. Given the single-file nature of running in Ethiopia, though, and the tendency to prefer communicating purely through finger clicks, this wasn't really an option for me.

Instead, I film some of our runs through the forest with a GoPro strapped to my chest. I want to ask about the route choices in detail, because they are so different to the way I would choose to run on my own in the same place. On the way back from one trip to the forest we stop at Fasil's new place to review the footage. He has moved out of our compound and is now paid 600 birr per month (around £17) to guard one of the partially built houses on the outskirts of Kotebe. There are quite a number of these, concrete skeletons with metal poles sticking up precariously between the floors. He explains that people often underestimate the cost of building and therefore run out of money halfway through. His job is to ensure that the bags of cement and other building materials aren't stolen before the money is found to continue building. He is often woken in the night by banging on the sheet metal around the yard and he has to climb up on to the second storey of the building with his torch to check for intruders. His immediate aim with his running is to be selected for a first division club and paid a salary like the other members of our group, so he can get some sleep. His task at the moment is the difficult one of trying to catch up while at a fairly serious disadvantage.

Fasil's room is made of corrugated iron and in the yard of the building. It contains a bed, a trunk and not much else besides a big brightly coloured poster of Jesus inscribed with Amharic text. We sit down on the edge of the bed and I ask him to talk me through a run we did earlier in the week. He humours me at first, clearly a little confused by my questions ('Yeah, so there we turned left, didn't we? To avoid all those sheep in front of us'). But as he talks, he develops a metaphor for running in the forest that we probably wouldn't have arrived at without the film.

'If you look there we are running very carefully and I am showing you where the stones are. You have to be careful to reach the places in your dreams.' For a while the footage is mainly of Fasil's back, distorted slightly by the fisheye lens, surrounded by the flashing green of eucalyptus leaves as we weave our way through tightly packed trees. 'You can't always find a comfortable place to run in the forest, though,' he goes on. We have emerged on to a steep slope littered with boulders. 'You might face big hills unexpectedly, especially if you are following someone else.' He pauses for a second to think about this as the GoPro shows him indicating to his left and right how I should dodge the boulders. 'Running is like that. You can't run and achieve what you want at once. There will be ups and downs before you are successful.'

We continue to watch in silence as Fasil disappears back into the trees for a while before emerging to cross a ploughed field, the deep furrows of which have to be carefully negotiated, before returning to the boulder-strewn slope. 'You see, the forest, then the ploughed field, then the stones, the field again, and back into the forest.' All of this involves running across, or up and down, a steep hillside. 'You see, there are many ups and downs in the space of one run. Running is like that. But if we keep going like this, our hard times will be over.' He repeats, gesturing towards the screen: 'If we just keep going like this, up and down.'

Fasil explicitly invokes the literal 'ups and downs' of training in the forest, the unexpected obstacles, tree routes and stones strewn across the path, as a metaphor for the running career. He clearly sees contingency and risk as not only inherent parts of training, but as a necessary barrier to pass through on the way to success; to be negotiated actively and with skill. The forest is a reflective space where runners think about their journey as athletes. For Fasil, running across the ploughed fields reminds him of the time in his life when he was responsible for driving an ox-drawn plough all year for his uncle in return for three barrels of wheat. The forest is also a place that enables runners to dream. It is the common denominator that links the greats like Haile Gebrselassie to those like Fasil who are just starting out. Not everyone can break records and run for hundreds of thousands of dollars in prize money, but everyone spends vast amounts of time in the forest.

While there may be thousands of runner-marked paths through the trees, each of the runs I go on with Fasil, Hailye or Tsedat is unique. We run with a general direction or a part of the forest we want to explore in mind and always knowing the amount of time we want to pass. Beyond that, it is up to whoever is leading – and to an extent the forest itself – to decide how we will actually cover the ground. Our running is always motivated by an attempt to create novelty or find new ways of passing through the trees. Above all, to keep things interesting.

When I was running in Edinburgh before I came out to Ethiopia I fell into some fairly boring routines, although I did find this satisfying in its own way. For long runs I would almost always run out-and-back on the Union Canal and the Water of Leith, and for shorter runs I would often just run endless laps of the Meadows, a flat park about a mile and a half around. Even after a few months in Ethiopia, on the occasions when I sleep in (and here this is defined as anything after 6 a.m.) I find that on arriving at the edge of the forest my natural tendency is to slip into the old habit of following the familiar and better-worn paths, following the same route as on my last run. I also gravitate towards the wider trails – ones Fasil, Hailye and Tsedat almost never use – so that I don't have to think as much about where I am running.

To try to recreate their style of forest running when I am on my own requires fighting against my own will towards the mundane. Staving off the boredom and monotony of running is a real concern for Ethiopians, and something our coach Meseret thinks about a lot. 'Running by itself is a kind of pain,' he tells me on one occasion, laughing. 'It is a kind of exhaustion. You know the feeling, how it is exhausting. You may drop it if you work alone. Now and then, now and then. Today, tomorrow, today, tomorrow. It is boring. If you take a footballer, every footballer runs for the sake of a ball. He looks at something in front of him. But with running there is nothing to look at. You can run if and only if you have a kind of vision inside.'

Part of the motivation for always seeking a new way through the forest, and for always running with others who might come up with unexpected and interesting routes, is to stave off this boredom. It means that it is important to try to run with a curiosity for your surroundings. Zigzagging up and down a new copse of trees, and following each row before doubling back on yourself, might add ten minutes to the run. Proceed in this way and before you know it, the 80 minutes you set out to 'pass' is almost over and it is time to turn for home. There is room for welcome surprise in this type of running, which is largely absent if you run the same tired route every day.

When I am back in Edinburgh on a short break about six months into my research I start running like this when I go to the Meadows. Criss-crossed with footpaths, rather than running laps

I follow the grass on each side of the paths, doubling back on myself at the end, to create a zigzagging lap that takes almost three times as long as a straightforward loop. Crucially, I find that if I run in this way I run for longer. My friend Mark, with whom I do a lot of running, jokes that there used to be just two ways of running in the Meadows, the Mulhare Way, named for Irish international track and cross-country runner Dan Mulhare, who has been known to run one-hundred miles of laps in a week, always in the same direction, and the Other Way. Now there are three ways. 'We'll call it the Crawley way, where you just run wherever you want,' Mark jokes.

The forest is also seen as a rejuvenating space where more intensive and pressurised forms of running are discouraged. In the afternoons in Ethiopia we sometimes run so slowly that the women hurrying to collect dry leaves from the forest floor to burn overtake us. This kind of running is seen purely as a form of therapy and an aid to recovery, and not as training in itself. GPS watches are pretty rare when I first arrive in Ethiopia, but it quickly becomes apparent that they are used in quite different ways to how they are marketed and used in other parts of the world. As we make our stiff-legged way up the hill to the forest one afternoon following a hard run in the morning, my friend Zeleke shows me the watch he won when finishing second in the Fuzhou marathon in China a couple of weeks previously. 'It says I burned 1600 calories yesterday,' he says, 'but to be honest I have no idea how I am going to replace them.'

He explains that he has started buying expensive imported food because it indicates calorie content on the packaging and is concerned to ensure that he doesn't 'lose anything' through training too hard. This is a concern that will be raised again and again by runners during my time in Ethiopia: that they will push too hard and 'burn themselves' by overtraining. Rather than using the watch to see how fast he can run, or to celebrate having burned calories as many people might, he uses the watch to see how *slowly* he can run in the forest. Three of us stand at the forest's edge for five minutes waiting for a signal (how many street corners and parks have I done this at over the last five years I wonder), and when we finally have one he starts the watch and we begin a familiar single-file procession through the trees.

We run in silence punctuated only by the swishing of three jackets and the tired scuffing of six feet until we hear a loud beep. Zeleke glances to his wrist and laughs. 'Seven minutes and 12 seconds!' he shouts. On subsequent days this becomes something of a game: we see how little running we can do in 40 minutes. But after using the watch for a while Zeleke starts travelling to other parts of the city to run – to the farmland in Sendafa, for example – where, he says, 'The kilometres come more easily' for the same amount of effort. The introduction of GPS watches actually starts to transform the way and the places in which he runs in this case.

On other days, though, the prescriptive use of the watch in forest training sessions is resisted by the athletes. On one of our excursions to Entoto, during rainy season, we sit watching the raindrops trickle down the windows and waiting for it to get light. Coach Meseret, wearing a thick sky-blue Adidas rain jacket, turns in his seat and explains that today's run will be a 'moderate' one. He takes the Garmin watch, which is used collectively by the team and given to a different runner for each session, out of his pocket and activates the GPS. 'I want you all to run for an hour and 20 minutes,' he says. 'The men should cover between 17 and

18 kilometres and the women between 14 and 15.' Teklemariam, who is employed to pace the female athletes, has his own watch. 'For the men, I will give the watch to Bogale today.' Bogale, who is sitting in front of me with his head bowed and his hood up, looks up and rubs his eyes before wiping the condensation off the window and peering out into the mist. He will have to lead the run through the forest this morning. 'I will check the kilometres at the end,' Meseret adds as we reluctantly step out of the bus into the rain.

As usual on a morning run like this, it is difficult to pinpoint the exact moment at which the run could be said to have started. We jog slowly into the trees in groups of two or three, most of us taking the opportunity for a last-minute pit stop before the run begins, some continuing their conversations in the meantime. Small groups of two or three then meander around the trees before resolving themselves into one long line, with Bogale at its head, and I assume that it is at this moment that Bogale starts the watch. We wind our way in gradual zigzags across the camber of the hillside, with Bogale making frequent hairpin turns and returning the way he has come. We are soon drenched by the cold rain percolating through the eucalyptus, but still running extremely slowly.

Bogale leads us down into a thickly forested hollow, which causes two hyenas to suddenly scatter up the bank to our left. The runners whoop with excitement – clearly this is not too unusual an occurrence – but a couple of them do stoop to pick up stones just in case. As my heart rate returns to normal I make a mental note to make sure I don't get dropped on this particular run, but luckily for me the pace remains leisurely as we continue to process through the forest. After 30 minutes or so of this careful meandering through the trees one of the other runners, realising that we have no chance of covering 17 kilometres at this rate, shouts to Bogale that he is going too slowly. 'Let's find an easier place where we can run quicker,' he says. Bogale ignores him. 'This is forest training,' he says. 'We have to go up and down.' We continue at Bogale's pace and I am able to enjoy the feeling of being an easy part of the group for once, comfortable in mid-pack, concentrating only on 'following the feet' of Tsedat in front of me.

Bogale continues to silently pick his way through the trees, shouting back only after an hour to let us know that we have 'killed' 60 minutes. When we reach the clearing where the bus is parked he finally begins to stretch his legs, and the line concertinas out and back across the field for the final 10 minutes. Our hour and 20 minutes up, he slows to a walk and heads over to Meseret to let him know that, 'There is a problem with the watch. We have no kilometres today.' My own watch shows that we have covered fewer than 15 kilometres.

Running at a pre-determined pace and succumbing to the pressure of the watch were seen as inappropriate on this occasion. Entoto is imbued with a particular power because of the number of churches within the forest – when I met Ryan Hall, holder of the American record in the half marathon, he told me Entoto was his favourite place in the world to run because 'with all the churches I feel like I can get close to God up there' – but equally, as Bogale reiterates, the forest is for 'going up and down', and for using the camber of the mountain intuitively to reduce the stress on joints and lessen the chances of injury.

I find the athletes' selective use of GPS watches interesting. Garmin's main advertising slogan is 'Beat Yesterday', which exemplifies the connection between capitalism and exponential speed, improvement and acceleration. For the Ethiopians, though, it is quite clear that you can't always 'beat yesterday' and that a vital component of speed is slowness. For many proponents of the quantified self movement of people who use tracking devices to try to make improvements in all areas of their lives, technologies like GPS watches remove some of the pressures of everyday decision-making. As the founder of the quantified self movement, Gary Wolfe put it in an interview with the *Washington Post*, 'Data is [sic] the most important thing you can trust. Certain people think a feeling of inner certainty is misleading.'

Most social scientists who have written about self-tracking devices have done so using the concept of 'technologies of the self' developed by the French philosopher Michel Foucault; that is, the way in which people perform 'Operations on their own bodies and souls, thoughts, conduct and ways of being, so as to transform themselves.' In Ethiopia, though, such devices are not merely concerned with 'selves' but with others. They are shared and used to monitor the pace of the group, not just the individual. And runners certainly do not trust the watches over their own 'feeling of inner certainty'. They draw upon them creatively and selectively, using them to slow down as often as they use them to speed up, and more often than not simply leaving them at home when they run in the forests.

The idea that the key to success in sport is in the exact measurement of physiological attributes and therefore the removal of any kind of wonder or surprise is also contested by the Ethiopian runners I know. Articles about the various two-hour marathon projects – first the haphazard Sub2 Project led by Yannis Pitsiladis, then the super-slick Breaking2 sponsored by Nike, and finally the successful Ineos 1:59 Challenge – circulate between runners on social media, but are met with a degree of scepticism. For my own part, I dislike the way these projects framed expertise as primarily the domain of white sports scientists and apparel designers. In the coverage of the Breaking2 attempt, for instance, much of the attention is placed on the 'input of science and technology' rather than on the knowledge and skill of the runners themselves.

One break in the footage of the Breaking2 event, for example, features an interview with Dr Phil Skiba, described as an 'MD performance engineer'. 'My goal,' he says, 'is to tell [the runners] something they don't know. "What do I *really* have under the hood?" That's the question.' Dr Brett Kirby, the lead physiologist of the Nike Sports Research lab, says in another clip that, 'We took them to the laboratory and said, "Let's put you through the full tests and see what you're really made of."' The idea that someone in a laboratory would know more about what a runner is 'really made of' than they would themselves, after years spent running, learning from other runners and dreaming of success, makes little sense to the runners I know.

Nike's scientists continually invoke the metaphor of the human motor (speaking of 'engines' and 'gas mileage') in their commentary on the Breaking2 project and yet their testing, and the accompanying imagery, like the photographs of Kenyan marathon world record holder and Olympic champion Eliud Kipchoge with a mask on to measure oxygen consumption, are misleading. The testing all took place *after* the decision to aim for a two-hour marathon. It is irrelevant to the event itself, which was always going to consist of Kipchoge, Lelisa Desisa of Ethiopia and Zersenay Tadese of Eritrea running at two-hour marathon pace for as long as they possibly could. Lelisa had wins in Boston and Dubai to his name at this point, and Zersenay was a five-time world half marathon champion and world record holder. In spite of this vast experience, what the emphasis placed on testing does is to reinforce the idea that the expertise lies with the scientists. As one of the commentators put it during the coverage, as the camera pans up from Kipchoge to a cyclist behind him holding a stopwatch, 'You can see in that shot over the shoulder of Kipchoge, the scientists on the bike, communicating, looking at stopwatches – the science is really the key to this possibility.' I think the quest for the two-hour marathon has generally been good for running. I was in a pub the night that Kipchoge ran 1.59.40 and a surprising number of people seemed to be talking about it. His sentiment that, 'We need to make everyone into social runners,' is one I am absolutely in favour of. It is the framing of expertise in a way that detracts from the runners themselves that I have a problem with.

As one young runner put it to me when praising Haile Gebrselassie's appointment as head of the EAF towards the end of my time in Ethiopia, 'Science does not work for Ethiopians. A doctor does not know time, a doctor does not run. If mind and legs are not one, it is impossible to run.' In fact, this kind of statement was not far off the philosophy of Eliud Kipchoge. 'Running is thinking,' he is fond of saying. Rather than focus on the embodied expertise of the athletes involved, though, all of these projects have tended to focus on the expertise of those funding them. The three runners involved in the Breaking2 project are presented as bringing the raw materials of belief and 'spirit' to the project, and a naive physicality upon which Nike's scientists could work. Lelisa Desisa, the Ethiopian runner, is described as a 'happy guy' by one commentator, who adds, 'I think he'll bring that spirit to this possibility.' Zersenay Tadese of Eritrea is quoted as saying, 'If you make the effort then God can do his part'.

Throughout the video, the runners' own watches, as well as their own embodied sense of time and rhythm, are portrayed as obsolete because of the more prominent timing technology provided by Nike. In fact, when Zersenay starts his watch at the beginning of the attempt – a habitual gesture of many runners when they start a race – it is met with laughter from the commentary team. 'I found it interesting that Zersenay started his watch at the start,' one commentator says. 'He didn't trust the very sophisticated timing we have here.' Nike, it is implied, possess sophisticated knowledge about time that he cannot be expected to match. And yet, as Alex Hutchinson, one of the few journalists invited to cover the project, comments, many of the scientific interventions were acknowledged to be unreliable. They had found that it was 'difficult to predict' how Kipchoge would run, 'because his visit to the lab for testing had been his first time on a treadmill.' He had 'looked extremely uncomfortable', according to Hutchinson.

The sports scientists involved had also expressed surprise, Hutchinson notes, at the sheer volume of running Lelisa was doing according to the GPS data they were receiving in Oregon from the watch they had asked him to wear during his training. When I mentioned this to Hailye he frowned and said, 'Yes but he probably wasn't always the one wearing the watch,' as if this were self-evident. He would almost certainly have lent it to other runners at some points and would probably have done some of his own running without a watch. Zeleke, Tsedat and others were intrigued by the focus on the two-hour marathon, but wary about the effects it might have on their own careers. As the fastest marathon time receded further from the realms of what seemed possible, so did the times people were expected to run in order to secure sponsorship from a brand or a time bonus at a race. The focus purely upon time was also understood to put more pressure on runners physically, and to bring with it more chance of burnout and to increase the likelihood that people would be tempted to dope.

Learning to zigzag through the forest, and use the variety of surfaces and inclines in particular ways, is seen as just as important to building expertise as a runner as learning to run to the watch. Running with intuition and creativity, and knowing when to focus on slowness rather than speed, are important skills and are the foundations upon which everything else is built. By running in a way that lessens the stress on joints and minimises repetitive movement, people are able to do more, as Tsedat is keen to emphasise. And this, in turn, allows people to do crazy things sometimes.

7

CRAZY IS GOOD

'We're going to have to do a lot of running at Arat Shi,' Birhanu warns me. Birhanu Addisie was the first of several runners in the Moyo Sports team to come from a small club sponsored by the Amhara Water Works Construction Enterprise in Gondar in the mountainous north of Ethiopia. He grew up a stone's throw from Ras Dashen, at 4550 metres above sea level Ethiopia's highest mountain, and had used some of his prize money to set his family up with a trekking business to lead tourists up the mountain. Abere and Selamyhun came from the same club and signed their contracts with Moyo Sports on his recommendation. Having heard him talking about marathon training I've said I want to accompany Birhanu on some of his training runs leading up to Rome marathon.

'And we'd better take Fasil with us,' he adds after a few moments thought.

'Why Fasil?' I ask.

'Because Fasil,' he says, 'is crazy.'

'And crazy is good?' I query.

'Crazy is good,' he replies, grinning.

How do you go from being five kilograms overweight and not having run a step for three weeks to running a 2.09 marathon after

113

just five weeks of training? Birhanu dropped out of his two previous races and, in spite of showing flashes of brilliance in training, he seemed to have lost some of the fire required to succeed at this level. At the Shanghai marathon six months before he had gone through 5 kilometres in an astonishing and suicidal 13.32 and not lasted very much longer. When I ask him about it he tells me he had a problem with his leg because of 'water vapour' rising from the road. His next race is in Nigeria. In the build-up to the race I ask him and his friend Abere how they are feeling. Abere says, 'It's going to be hard, but I've made a decision never to drop out of another race, even if I faint at the finish.' Birhanu says, 'I don't know, Mike, I've heard it's going to be hot.' I send his manager Malcolm a text saying I am worried that Birhanu is lacking confidence. Abere finishes eighth, wins $4000 and appears in a photograph on Twitter prostrate on a mattress on the tarmac, volunteers pouring cold water over his head. He has to be put on a drip, but he's done what he said he would. Birhanu drops out a little after 15 kilometres, again because of a problem with his leg. This time it is more than just 'water vapour'; he's been kicked by one of the Nigerian runners on the start line, he tells me. 'In a race you can only concentrate on one thing,' he says later. 'You can't think about running, about protecting yourself and about the heat at the same time.'

Hailye and I meet up with him in Hirut Café on his return from Nigeria and he orders a pizza. Hailye raises his eyebrows at this, but says nothing; Birhanu is dispirited enough. His tendency to overfuel on Italian food has reached the extent to which he's earned the sobriquet Birhanu Pizza from the other runners. A few weeks previously, in the same café, I'd seen him eat a huge bowl of spaghetti before ordering a takeaway pizza. He grinned sheepishly

at me on his way out of the café and said, 'In case I get hungry in the night, you know?' We chat about what happened in Nigeria and he says he didn't feel right before the race. He talks about the importance of a single-minded focus and of not having a 'divided mind'. He has decided to blot everything but the Rome marathon from his mind in the following weeks.

As we walk home up the hill, Hailye says that he thinks it will help that it is the beginning of the fast for Lent. Lasting for the 55 days leading up until Easter on the Ethiopian calendar, this means that Birhanu will cut out all meat and dairy. A simple diet consisting primarily of vegetables and grains is one all Orthodox Christians, many of whom are vegan, regularly return to on Wednesdays and Fridays year-round, as well as during specific fasting periods. Hailye thinks that the timing of the Lent fast this year will help Birhanu. There will be no more pizza for one thing. I agree, but think the transformation will be psychological as well as dietary: the fast represents a clear rupture, a chance to purify body and mind and start again. The next time I meet up with Birhanu I ask him whether five weeks is really long enough to prepare for a marathon. 'That is *long*,' he says, fixing me with a meaningful look, 'if you train like I do.' Won't the Lent fast make training even harder? I ask. 'Hard is good, Mike,' he says simply. 'This is marathon.'

I suggest that the first week of training will have to be relatively gentle, so that he can ease back into full training. 'We will run two to three hours every day that there is no group training,' he says. 'Sundays included.' Sunday is traditionally a rest day for Ethiopian athletes. 'Sunday will be three hours,' he says. 'Three hours is nice.' He tells me that he has agreed to meet Fasil the next day to run for two and a half hours at Arat Shi. Literally, Arat Shi means four thousand, an estimate of the altitude. Actually it's not quite that high, but as usual it's the *belief* in the altitude that counts. *Belg*, the short highland rainy season that normally lasts two weeks, has outrun its course this year and seems likely to continue until the main rainy season starts. Parts of the forest have turned into a clay-like, cloying mud, red-brown in colour and impossible to shift once it has attached itself to the soles of your trainers. This is the other reason to go to Arat Shi. This makes it even harder. Hard is good.

* * *

When we meet Fasil just before 6 a.m. the next day it is still dark. I expect him to be pretty exhausted having run 39 kilometres in the morning and another nine in the evening the day before, but he has a big smile on his face as usual and is clearly impatient to get going. 'Fasil is 100 per cent emotional,' Birhanu tells me. That, apparently, makes him the best person to lead a two-and-a-half-hour run on the side of a mountain. 'Aren't you tired this morning?' I ask him. 'I am never tired!' he replies, beaming. This has become something of a catchphrase. A four-word phrase in English, this is rendered in one word in Amharic: *aldekemegnem*. I guess we're ready to run then.

Arat Shi is a 20-minute uphill walk from the compound and my stomach is already rumbling by the time we get there. We walk a few cobbled streets between corrugated iron buildings, past the odd large newly built house. Birhanu and Fasil both know exactly who owns these houses. Some are owned by Ethiopian Airlines pilots. They drive Mercedes and reportedly make as much money from duty-free imports as they do from flying planes. The majority, though, are owned by runners. 'Impressive place,' I comment. 'Hagos Gebrhiwet,' Fasil responds, referring to the famous Ethiopian 5000m runner, who won medals in the last two World Championships and is one of the few people to have beaten Mo Farah in a sprint finish. 'That place is more or less a palace,' I say, pointing up at a three-storey house with a huge balcony and three prominent security cameras. 'Gete Wami,' Fasil says, grinning. I remember watching Gete, a former 10,000m world champion and Berlin marathon winner, race against Paula Radcliffe. There are reminders of just how high the running stakes are at every corner.

As we walk up the hill the corrugated iron buildings give way to wooden fencing and the little 'souks' get progressively more compact. These are sort of hole-in-the-wall convenience stalls. As you walk further up the hill towards the forest they get smaller, their bananas more expensive. They are 15 birr in town, 16 halfway up the slope and 17 at the forest's edge, testament to the difficulty of hauling them up here. We pass three churches on the way to the forest, and Fasil and Birhanu stop for a minute or so at each, crossing themselves, dipping their heads and whispering. I linger awkwardly, the only one to pass by the church without acknowledging it. It rained unseasonably hard yesterday afternoon and by the time we reach the forest our shoes already have an extra sole of clay-like mud. Fasil stops to carefully scrape it off before we start running, which seems to me a futile gesture as we are about to be running through it for two and a half hours.

As usual we set off slowly, winding our way through the tightly packed trees. I have got used to this style of running now, and I'm no longer surprised when Fasil suddenly decides to loop right round a tree and go back on himself, or make a 90-degree turn by ducking under a low hanging branch. We work our way in gradual zigzags, like a ship tacking into the wind, up a long slope, before dropping down into a gully. This route is even more difficult than usual, and Fasil seems to be picking out the thickest patches of mud and the loosest scree slopes. We end up in a gully from which the only way out is to climb between bushes with inch-long thorns, one of which manages to embed itself in the top of my head. After we have been walking carefully for a couple of minutes, pulling ourselves up the slope with the exposed roots of the trees, and after I have extracted the thorn from my head, I venture: 'Can't we just run on the easy paths up there?' He grins and shrugs as if to say, 'Where would the fun be in that?!'

After a few more minutes I start to get kind of annoyed, first with Fasil and then with myself; I know I'm only in a bad mood because I'm exhausted. 'I'm going to go back up and find somewhere easier to run on my own,' I say. 'No, no,' he tells me. 'There are way too many hyenas around here.' Ah. I continue to follow him through the valley, the scraggly trees with their cartoonishly long thorns looking more and more like Scar's den in *The Lion King* every second. I've been warned about certain parts of the forest and heard rumours that anywhere from one to eight runners have been 'taken' by hyenas while running alone in the forest in the past few years. Fasil told me he accidentally ran alone into the middle of a clearing and found himself surrounded last year. He said he backed away slowly, telling them, 'I'm just here to work, please leave me be.' It worked for him, but it's not an experience I particularly want to replicate. I have no choice but to labour on through the mud.

I turn round to see how Birhanu is faring; he is floating along, a serene look on his face. He is wearing two tracksuits to make things a bit harder, but there isn't a single bead of sweat on his

Club runners compete in an ultra-competitive local road race in Sebeta.

Teklemariam stands by the team bus waiting to hand out water bottles to his teammates.

Coach Sentayehu addresses his athletes after a training session in the forest in Bekoji.

The group fly past during a *coroconch* run in Sendafa.

Malcolm and Hailye in Sebeta.

Fasil runs early-morning hill repetitions at the edge of the Yeka forest.

Abebe Bikila leads the 1960 Olympic marathon in Rome, running along a torch-lit avenue.

Wami Biratu and Abebe Bikila train together on the track in Addis Ababa Stadium.

Jemal Yimer competes in the World Athletics Championships in London 2017, where he finished 5th in the 10,000m in 26.56.

Kenenisa Bekele celebrates his second 10,000m Olympic Gold medal with his teammates, Sileshi Sihine and Haile Gebrselassie.

Birhanu readies himself for the start of training in Akaki to the south of Addis Ababa.

The author on his way to a 2.20 marathon in Frankfurt in 2018.

Jemal Yimer runs 300m repeats on the track in Addis Ababa Stadium, one of only two Tartan tracks in Ethiopia.

The author runs one of the criss-crossing paths created by runners in Yeka forest.

The author and his partner, Roslyn Malcolm, after a run at Entoto.

Runners from Moyo Sports train on the asphalt in Sebeta, running a session of fast 2km repetitions.

Zeleke rests on the team bus after training.

Hailye shares a joke with the driver after training in Sendafa.

A coach times a training session on the grass track in Gondar, at 3,100m above sea level.

Coach Messeret, wearing the scarf of the Ethiopian Electric Corporation running club, observing training from the team bus.

Tadesse waits to hand out water bottles at the turning point of a run in Sendafa.

Tsedat celebrates after his breakthrough win at the 2019 Seville marathon in 2.06.36.

forehead. We now have a good inch of leaden mud on the bottom of each shoe to haul across the ground. He smiles at me encouragingly. This is clearly exactly what he had in mind when he enlisted Fasil as leader. Birhanu is a far more experienced athlete, having won the Amhara region 10,000m championships and competed abroad on numerous occasions. It might therefore be expected that he would lead our training runs. It is what he calls Fasil's 'freshness' that appeals to him, though: he runs with less of an ingrained sense of what training ought to be like and therefore in a way that keeps things interesting. We drag ourselves up another steep slope, our sharp exhalations of breath turning to mist in the overcast morning air.

Eventually we emerge in a clearing and we can run a bit more freely, following the usual pattern of runs here. Fasil especially likes to start running in the densely packed forest on the edge of the mountain, where every step you run you have to think about carefully placing your feet, and dodging in and out of tree roots and low-hanging branches, then to seek out more expansive ground when we have warmed up. As we gradually speed up, Fasil leans into the tighter turns round trees and then accelerates on smoother ground, before easing off again when we enter clumps of trees or negotiate stony descents. By starting in the forest on the roughest terrain we ensure that we don't go too fast early on. In the clearing he opens up his stride and we start to really move. The run turns into an environment-dictated *fartlek*; we run fast on the easy ground before slowing again in the forest or as we cross roughly ploughed fields.

As I start to tire the views get more spectacular, but I am less and less able to take them in. When I do manage to look up, I can just make out the city, shrouded this morning in a faint cloud cover, far away across the plateau. My attention zeroes in on following Fasil's feet and *just keeping going*. I am faintly aware of the fields and trees flashing by in my peripheral vision. Eucalyptus, eucalyptus, tree root, clearing, branch, eucalyptus. But my attention is now mostly focused *inward*, not outward. On the sensation of each footfall. On the cry of my lungs and the ache of my legs. 'Absolute unmixed attention is prayer,' the philosopher Simone Weil wrote. Running has always been the closest I've got to religious experience. The last hour passes unimaginably slowly.

Finally we stop several kilometres away from where we started; exactly two and a half hours have passed, so training is finished. Fasil has been glancing at his watch for the past few minutes, but I am careful to point out that our time is up. If he goes over the allocated time by more than a few seconds he is liable to decide to add an extra 10 minutes, so that we finish on a nice round number, and I'm in no mood for that today. He starts to cough violently. I am not the only one who struggled up that last hill when we were so tired from yesterday. He thumps his chest. '*Akayelegn*,' he says; it burns.

Almost immediately he and Birhanu launch into a series of quick-feet drills and strides, the mud finally flying off their shoes. 'Is that really a good idea after such a long run?' I ask Birhanu in English. He doesn't understand and just says, 'Come on,' motioning that I should join him in the exercises. My legs are wrecked. I sit on a big rock and wait for them. Fasil is a raw talent, having only started running a year ago. He takes off down a faint path at full pelt, striking the ground heavily with his forefoot and using his arms to power himself forwards. His stride is a bit ragged round the edges, but you would never know he was this new to running. Birhanu is serenely efficient with a high pick-up to his stride; the soles of his shoes flash behind him as he 'follows Fasil's feet'. As they run four flat-out strides in perfect synchrony a shepherd boy steps out on to the path. He has to tut the sheep out of the way as they fly past and shouts encouragement to the runners as they run away from him.

My watch tells me we have run 31 kilometres at 4.45 per kilometre. That seems very slow given how exhausted I feel, but as Birhanu points out, 'That was up and down.' This is an understatement. We can't have spent much more than 10 minutes on flat ground and the outsides of my shins are throbbing from the effort of staying upright on the steep camber. Birhanu bounces from foot to foot like a boxer, as if the momentum of the run compels him to keep moving. He looks ecstatic. 'Tomorrow, three hours!' he beams. 'This air is *nice!*'

This is something you hear a lot. Runners describe the air in different parts of the forest as 'nice' or 'special' or 'powerful'. Our coach Meseret sees in this a misguided attempt to understand the science of altitude. 'They think there is *more* oxygen the higher you go,' he tells me, 'and that you can get energy from the air itself.' He shakes his head when he talks about this. 'They don't understand that the energy comes from food,' he says. 'They think they get energy from the air and the trees, and that they don't have to eat. They think they are plants!'

Actually, though, I think they understand it just as well as he does. By training up here you get more oxygen *in your blood,* because the low levels of oxygen stimulate the natural production of erythropoietin (EPO), which then stimulates the production of red blood cells and increases your body's blood-oxygen carrying capacity. In turn, this gives you more energy when you return to 'low' ground at 2500 metres. There is something about being up here, above the hustle and bustle of city life, as well; it feels like you are transcending the ordinary, tapping into some kind of elevated magic. There is no-one up here. It is just us and the hyenas. It makes it feel like we're doing something daring. Something special.

We have finished our run a 40-minute walk away from the house and I was hungry before we even started training. Fasil keeps giving me concerned pats on the shoulder. '*Dekamah zare?*' he asks me every couple of minutes. 'Are you tired today?' 'Yes,' I tell him in English, 'and I could have done without you choosing the most difficult, dangerous route possible, and without having to trek for hours to get home!' He smiles wryly and just says, '*Ayzoh, ayzoh,*' (keep going) and my irritation gradually lessens as we walk down the hill. I feel like a petulant child on a long car journey. I trudge slowly. Fasil looks absolutely fresh, and walks with a spring in his step and a swing to his arm. As we walk down the hill he takes my hand affectionately. Ethiopian men often hold hands, something that initially surprised me but which I've got used to now. '*Ayzoh,*' he says again. That run was hard, but it's over now and we can rest. Poor Fasil, it's not his fault he's stronger than me. I'm glad he couldn't understand my little tantrum.

We stop for *tella* – lightly fermented beer – on the way home. I sit on a tree stump sipping tentatively at mine, picking out the odd piece of straw and caught between wanting to slake my thirst and not wanting to deal with an upset stomach. Fasil drinks two litres and seems like he could do the whole run again.

* * *

Dave Brailsford, general manager and chief guru of Team Ineos, formerly Team Sky, the cycling team that took Bradley Wiggins,

Chris Froome, Geraint Thomas and Egan Bernal to Tour de France glory, made the idea of 'marginal gains' famous. The idea is that if you do enough tiny little things better in terms of nutrition, recovery and injury prevention they will add up to an appreciable improvement. Team Sky slept on special mattresses regardless of where they raced, carried in a team bus that was effectively a hotel and spa on wheels. A nutrition expert delivered personalised meals to their houses. They did everything they possibly could to minimise exertion outside of training and to accelerate recovery. The idea extends to running. The American record holder for the mile, Alan Webb, used to count his non-running steps every day, trying to minimise the amount of time spent on his feet while he wasn't training. Runners also talk about the '20-minute window' after training, which sports scientists say is the crucial time to eat something containing carbohydrates and protein if you want to recover quickly.

So what do the Ethiopians make of this? After training one week in Sebata we got stuck in traffic and it took us over two hours to get back into town. On the way, coach Meseret suggested we stopped off at the stadium in town – known simply as 'Stadium' because it is the only one – for the Addis Ababa 10,000m races. We made it just in time for the first race at 10 a.m., and sat in the sun to watch an 'A' and a 'B' race, by which time it was 11.30 a.m. None of us had eaten since the night before and we had all got up at 4.30 a.m. It was over three hours since we'd stopped running. I turned to Meseret and said, 'When are we going to get some breakfast? I'm starving.' He laughed and slapped me on the knee. 'Don't worry, Mike!' he said. 'You will become strong.'

On 'non-programme' days we walk for at least 25 minutes to and from training, so there's no way anyone is hitting the

'20-minute window' so many runners obsess over after *any* run. The recovery drinks and protein shakes most Western athletes swear by are notably absent here too, although their use does seem to be increasing, especially among the wealthier athletes. When I ask most runners about them, I am told that Abebe Bikila ran on *injera* and *beso*, and he did just fine. *Injera* is the pancake-like bread and *beso* is the simplest of fuels – roasted and powdered barley, shaken up with several tablespoons of sugar or honey. We rarely go a day without drinking at least a couple of litres of the stuff. 'This is Ethiopian power bar,' Teklemariam tells me.

And the walking? I ask Hailye whether it wouldn't be better to run straight from the door; we could get training over with quicker. 'And besides,' I say, 'doesn't all this walking tire people out?' He shakes his head. 'Most of them grew up on farms miles away from the nearest road. They are used to walking for many hours. This is easy for them.' All the walking, he tells me, is just extra training. 'What is wrong with being tired?' he says. 'This is running.'

And what of sleep? Paula Radcliffe used to nap religiously for two hours every afternoon. Galen Rupp, the greatest American distance runner of all time, reportedly sleeps a total of 14 hours every 24. One of the assumptions people make about East African runners is that, 'All they do is eat, sleep and run.' The runners I train with, though, rarely sleep more than seven hours at night. Many of them share a bed with another runner and sleep on a thin mattress on a concrete floor. No customised mattresses for them. In the afternoons they often 'take rest', but usually two or three of them will be in the room and the radio will be on. More often than not, two runners will be chatting while a third lies shrouded in a towel, as though laid out for embalming. They can't get a huge amount of sleep like that. In the compound we live in, the dog barks throughout the night and chanting from the church around the corner starts as early as 4 a.m. Most nights I am woken several times by something going on outside. We do, however, grab our sleep when we can, especially when power cuts leave the compound in the dark at 6 p.m. '*Mebrat tafa, Hailye tafa,*' Fasil jokes. 'When the lights go out, so does Hailye.'

Fasil, Birhanu and I return to the compound just in time, banging on the gate as the heavens open. There is no drizzle in Ethiopia. When it rains, it really rains; huge droplets pelting off the floor and quickly turning to rivulets in the streets. We retreat into Hailye's room and he gestures towards the rain before saying, 'I thought it might do that. I'll make *kikil*.' It is the last day before the Easter fast starts, so we will make the most of it by eating one of the meals most clearly associated with 'condition'. *Kikil* is a spicy soup made by boiling meat and marrow-rich bones, and Hailye is not messing about, retrieving a bag containing two kilos of meat that he bought this morning and preparing an enormous pot.

He opens the door to the room slightly, making the noise from the pounding rain even louder, and lights the charcoal in the bottom of a cook stove in the corner of the room. The room soon fills with smoke and becomes stiflingly hot, which Hailye assures me is a good way to avoid the colds that tend to come with the rainy season. As the soup starts to boil too the mixture of steam and smoke means I can barely see Fasil and Birhanu on the other side of the room. We sit patiently listening to the rain, knowing that we have little else to do for the rest of the day except eat and rest.

I ask Fasil about the route he chose for our run this morning. Had he deliberately tried to make it difficult? Hailye translates my question. The answer is simple: 'Yes.' 'Why?' Hailye asks him. '*Akayelegn.*' Because it burns. Another simple response. 'You have to go up and down and run on the difficult ground,' Fasil goes on, reiterating what he told me before. 'You have to run across the stones and up the slopes and through the mud. Then you will have endurance and strength. It gives you everything.'

Fasil laughs and launches into a rapid-fire speech in Amharic that I struggle to follow. 'What is he saying?' I ask Hailye. 'It is just a kind of proverb,' Hailye replies. 'He says that there was once a priest who knew many things: he could read in three languages and he had written many books on religious issues. He was a very important man. His wife thought that she was very clever, too; she was married to the priest, after all. But then one day he went away for a few days to a monastery and she washed all of his bibles in the river.' 'I see…' I reply. I don't see. 'What does that mean exactly?' I ask. 'I don't know!' Hailye laughs. I think, though, that what Fasil was trying to say was something along the lines of: 'You have spent eight months with us now, asking us questions and writing things down. But you still don't understand a thing.'

I still have a way to go, it seems, and I am reminded of how grateful I am for being able to talk through my experiences in Ethiopia with my partner Roslyn every evening, albeit over a temperamental WhatsApp connection. She is spending long days in the stables in Somerset, immersed in the routines of mucking out, caring for the horses and riding, as well as in trying to understand why it is that spending time with horses might help children with autism to speak. She is as tired as I am at the end of the day, but it makes the process of doing ethnography far less lonely when we are able to unpack the day's events together.

I get in touch with Zane Robertson, the New Zealander who, along with his brother Jake, has spent the best part of a decade in East Africa, and he has the following to say about the forest:

> Personally I think the Ethiopians are making the best of a bad situation. Some of the places they run are absolutely crazy and not runnable for the normal runner. I adapted to this because I was forced to when there was no other option on an easy day. I think the forest training makes the mind busy, the legs and feet strong and the agility increased. It's an amazing benefit but also a huge risk for injuries. Adapt and overcome is what the Ethiopians are great at.

I contact Zane online in the end, because every time I see him training in Ethiopia it is with an intensity that I don't want to disturb, usually wearing a pair of on-ear Beats headphones. He is embodying the Ethiopian runner's way of life far more fully than I could, and is rewarded with some astonishing performances, including a 59.47 half marathon. His interpretation of forest training makes sense to me, though, the environment forcing an increase in agility and building strength even while it makes the risk of injury higher. In a sense it raises the stakes: train in the forest and you will get stronger *if* you can survive it. He goes on:

> Ethiopian runners are very strong mentally. They are willing to 'do or die'. Some of them aren't the most gifted runners form-wise. The key to their success is playing the card they were dealt like it was the card they wanted.

He signs off his correspondence with four emojis that seem to sum up both his approach and that of many of the Ethiopians I know: prayer hands; 100 per cent sign; smiley face; flexed bicep. Zane reminds me of the sports philosopher Bernard Suits' definition of sports as the 'voluntary acceptance of unnecessary obstacles'. Accepting more obstacles, Zane suggests, brings improvement for those who are able to overcome them.

Hailye, Fasil and I spend the day listening to the rain intermingling with the tinny music from Hailye's phone and eating endless bowls of *kikil.* 'Add more!' Fasil keeps saying. 'This is "condition" for the next two months.' The meat is delicious and falls off the bones, which we then split to get to the marrow. The theory is that this will rejuvenate our own bones and joints, allowing us to withstand the running we are doing. The room by now is like a furnace and sweat drips off my forehead. I do as I'm told and eat five or six bowls of soup before dozing off on the sofa next to Birhanu, who has been lulled to sleep by the rhythmic drumming of the rain, with a Kenyan Airlines blanket acquired on the way back from a marathon he ran in Lagos draped over his head.

Before I know it Hailye is shaking my shoulder and I wake to see Fasil tying his running shoes on a chair on the other side of the room. This can't be good. 'What's happening?' I manage. 'Rain's stopped,' Hailye says. 'Afternoon training.' 'But we did two and a half hours this morning,' I protest, getting uncertainly to my feet and feeling how leaden my legs are. 'Yes, but we had *kikil,* so we should run,' is his response. I don't understand the logic of this, but I decide to accept it and go to retrieve my mud-caked shoes beside the door. 'It has been raining for hours so it will just be very slow,' he says. 'For recovery.' The small vegetable patch in the middle of the compound is absolutely sodden, with rain still dripping from the banana leaves. There are huge brown puddles all along the cobbled street that leads, to my relief, towards the closest patch of forest.

Hailye didn't run in the morning, because he was accompanying his girlfriend Kumeshi to a visa appointment, and he seems worryingly spritely. 'I'll lead,' he says. 'I've been running in this bit of forest for years, so I'll be able to avoid the mud.' Given that I am slipping around just walking on the mud that has spread out on to the roadside, I take this with a pinch of salt. Once we start running Hailye does manage to avoid the worst of the mud, though, and manages somehow to scuff the layer that does build up on the bottom of his shoes mid-stride. I try this and almost trip myself up; I am utterly exhausted from our excursion in the morning.

We make our way up the slope as usual, avoiding the red-brown paths and sticking to the tufts of grass along their edges, and for the most part staying upright. It starts raining again and we are soon soaked through, but we still make our way up the slope, jumping across the little rivers that have formed in the downpour. The *kikil* sloshes ominously in my stomach, but it is clear that Hailye is thoroughly enjoying himself, leaping across the puddles like a steeplechaser, and his enthusiasm is infectious. We reach the top of the hill after about 50 minutes and he takes off back down the hill in a long diagonal through the trees, covering me in mud from his flicking heels in the process.

We finish the run by sprinting in a foot-wide channel that is by now half-full of rainwater, like we're on some kind of log flume, the water splashing out to either side. Hailye slows to a jog and turns round to see if we are still with him, a big smile on his face. 'That was an unusual kind of "easy" run,' I say when I catch my breath. 'I was enjoying myself too much,' he says. I turn to Birhanu and Fasil, who look like they could quite happily have splashed about in the forest for another hour. 'If you can make it fun, it's so much easier,' Hailye adds. I couldn't agree more. As we wander back to the compound in the rain, I feel elated. I've never done three and a half hours of running in a day before.

* * *

Birhanu calls me a couple of weeks later to invite me round for juice. Before he started training for the race he went to Mercato, the biggest market in Africa, and bought himself a Chinese juicer. He has decided that all of this going to cafés and playing pool has to stop. The Amharic word for this is doing *zur*, which literally means 'laps'. When you're training this hard, *zur* are for the track, but it also means any activity that compromises your ability to rest between training sessions. If you go to the shop you are doing *zur*, or if you pop by to see a friend or have to go to the EAF to get a release letter for a race. Off the track, *zur* are very bad and are to be avoided at all costs. So Birhanu has resolved to spend no more time 'warming up a café seat,' he tells me. It's three-hour runs and plenty of avocado juice for him.

I ask him to outline his training for Rome in a bit more detail. 'First,' he tells me, 'is the forest.' This is where the foundations are laid. The higher he runs, he tells me, the slower the pace he can train at, but still get incredibly fit aerobically. 'If you train at Entoto, you can go up to 3500 metres above sea level,' he says. 'Up there, you can go as slow as six minutes per kilometre, but when you come down you will fly.' After the forest, he says, is *coroconch*, the rough road. This is the next stage in getting the legs ready to race a marathon. The rough road offers a firmer surface, on which you can run a little faster, but it's still an uneven, challenging one. The *coroconch* road is *never* flat and you still have to think carefully about where you are putting your feet. It is still very hard work.

A couple of weeks into his new training regime we go to Sendafa and I'm still far from convinced that Birhanu's five-week plan is feasible. The transformation, though, is sudden and dramatic. Birhanu gets on to the bus for training swathed in his Kenyan Airlines blanket. His eyes shine brightly and his cheekbones are prominent again. He must have lost three kilos. He leans conspiratorially over to me and says, in English, 'I think I am winning in Rome.'

On the two-and-a-half-hour rough-road run I bail at an hour and 45 minutes and clamber into the bus in time to watch him run away from everyone over the final 45 minutes, his arms swinging violently across his chest, but no sign that this apparent squandering of energy is doing him any harm. He runs 40 kilometres with 1400 metres of ascent at between 2550 and 2800 metres above sea level in two and a half hours. As he climbs back in the bus I say, 'You know, Birhanu, I think you might be right.'

The final stage is asphalt training. Even the most seasoned Ethiopian marathon runners train on the road once a week maximum and always on a Friday. Nobody runs on asphalt during their formative years, or until they are about 18. Birhanu didn't set foot on the roads until he'd been running in Gondar for four years. It is seen as too unforgiving a surface. It drains your energy. A simple three-stage process, then. Until you realise that in five weeks Birhanu has covered close to 1500 kilometres. 'You could have run halfway to Rome!' I tell him. 'Impractical,' he replies, straight-faced. Birhanu's build-up for the marathon is a mini version of the trajectory of a young athlete. First he spends ten days in the forest to get strong, then he runs on the *coroconch* road, and finally he hones his speed on the asphalt. It is a process, again, of gradual adaptation. First you get used to the surface and then you get used to the speed.

Once he has done the big *coroconch* run, Birhanu knows that he is ready for the two big sessions on asphalt: 30 kilometres flat out and 5 x 4 kilometres at race pace or faster. In his case this last session is the real indicator. He runs his four-kilometre reps at 3.00 per kilometre pace at 2200 metres above sea level – 2.06 marathon pace – and runs the single recovery kilometre in 4.00. He knows there are very few people in Ethiopia, and therefore the world, who can do that. He thinks he is ready for anything in Rome, even the dreaded cobblestones.

A few days later I meet him in the same café in which he had sheepishly ordered a pizza five weeks ago. He will get a taxi from here to the airport en route to Rome. He sips from a two-litre bottle of mango juice, his demeanour completely transformed through the five weeks of hard work. 'Hey, Birhanu,' I ask him in parting as I wish him luck, 'you know about Abebe Bikila's run in Rome, right?' 'Of course I know,' he tells me, reaching down to remove his shoes and holding them aloft. 'If I am winning by a long way, I will run the last few hundred metres like this.'

8

TO WIN IN ROME WOULD BE LIKE WINNING 1,000 TIMES

Abebe Bikila is running past the Axum obelisk, the patter of his bare feet, which has accompanied him for an hour and 45 minutes, now lost in the noise from the crowds lining the road. Darkness is falling and the *sampietrini*, the bevelled stones of black basalt on which he runs, have cooled noticeably. 'In Africa, this is the hour when the animals drink,' says the BBC commentator, vacuously, and this is not Africa, but Rome. Abebe is running at a pace of five minutes 10 seconds per mile, in red shorts and a simple cotton vest given to him at the training ground of Emperor Haile Selassie's Imperial guard in Debre Zeit, south of Addis Ababa. He wears no watch, however, and has no way of knowing how fast he is travelling or how far behind him the other runners are. His gaze is impassive and steady. Onni Niskanen, the Swedish army major who Haile Selassie put in charge of his training, has told him to make his bid for victory here, at the Axum monument.

It is Saturday, 10 September, 1960. Earlier in the evening, as he warmed up in a swirling mass of bodies in the cloisters of a church, he had made the decision to remove his shoes. Not to prove anything to anyone, or to show that Africans needed nothing in order to win, but because he felt he would run better barefoot.

He wrote the numbers of the competitors he thought he needed to be wary of on the back of his hand. Sixty-nine for Popov from the Soviet Union. Twenty-six for Rhadi the Moroccan, a fellow soldier. He thought about what Haile Selassie had said to him before he left: 'To win in Rome would be like winning a thousand times over.'

The Axum monument, where Abebe makes his bid for victory, is a 24- metre tall obelisk that was built during the fourth century by subjects of the Kingdom of Axum, an ancient Ethiopian civilisation. In 1937 after Mussolini's invasion and occupation of Ethiopia, it was taken from the city of Axum in the Tigray region as war booty by the Italian Fascists, cut into five pieces and transported to Rome. When the monument was finally flown back to Ethiopia in 2005 the runway at Axum had to be extended specially to allow it to land. At the time it was the biggest and heaviest piece of airfreight ever transported. Its symbolism on this occasion is no less huge. When the Ethiopians fought off the first Italian invasion in 1896 they did so barefoot and without guns, against a boot-wearing, heavily armed Italian force. Here, once more, is a barefoot Ethiopian defeating better-equipped opposition and doing so at a moment of incredible historical significance. No fewer than nine African countries gain their independence during the Olympic Games themselves, between August and September 1960. The Rome Olympics are also the first to be widely televised, so a large global audience is able to witness the first gold medal be won by a sub-Saharan African.

'But who is that quiet Ethiopian?' the BBC asks in its commentary. 'When he entered for the marathon he gave a time better than [the legendary Czech runner] Emil Zátopek's, but nobody believed that his stop-watch could be right.' In two hours

15 minutes and 16 seconds of running Abebe Bikila changes distance running for ever. He runs the last few hundred metres through a torch-lit guard of honour made up of Italian soldiers. 'From this moment on,' a crisp Queen's-English-speaking voice tells us, 'the name of Abebe Bikila will rank alongside those of Nurmi and Zátopek.'

Abebe crosses the line and keeps running through the Arch of Constantine. A little unsure of what to do, he half-continues to follow orders by performing the warm-down exercises Niskanen taught him, shaking his arms out to loosen them from the crooked carriage they have held for the past two hours, and he half-dances, a spontaneous reaction to a victory only he and Niskanen saw coming. He then lies on his back and bicycles his legs in the air to loosen them. Fifty-six years later when I ask people in the forests around Addis where they learned their esoteric warm-down exercises, they still refer to this moment. 'It's what Abebe did,' they tell me, simply. There is a rhythm to the Ethiopian warm-down far more joyful than the conventional jog and it started here.

* * *

Birhanu Addisie runs in matching Adizero singlet and shorts made from a 100 per cent lightweight polyester mesh, which, according to the manufacturer, features a 'bold graphic designed to make you stand out as you speed past' on the front. To his left and right run four fellow Ethiopian runners and five Kenyans. Three of them wear the exact same Adidas kit, a black and green stylised spiderweb pattern. Five wear Nike kit almost entirely identical to the Adidas kit; for some reason the two companies compete not only to sponsor the best athletes, but to produce the most similar kit. It is

Sunday, 10 April, 2016, and 9.45a.m. Birhanu responds to a beep and glances at the Garmin watch on his wrist to see that he is running at a pace of four minutes and 50 seconds per mile, a pace he knows he can run at for a very long time, but not a pace he is certain he can hold all the way to the finish. The other runners' watches chime almost simultaneously and they make their own private calculations. Birhanu's five foot eight (1.78m) frame takes up a surprising amount of space on the road. His friends in Addis joke that it is best to give him the space of two men because 'he runs like a boxer' and a mistimed elbow in the ribs can leave it difficult to catch your breath at this speed.

With the Axum monument safely back in Ethiopia, Birhanu has to make do with a marker to tell him that he has reached 35 kilometres. He is almost two kilometres beyond where Abebe would have been at this point and is finally starting to feel the effects of the searing pace he has set. He was the only one to follow the pacemaker to 30 kilometres, so when he dropped out he was left in no-man's land with the chasing pack a scant 15 seconds back. Far from running purely on feel as Abebe did, he runs staring at a giant red-lettered clock mounted on the back of a car. A couple of kilometres later the group catches up and Amos Kipruto counter-attacks. The others try to react, but only Birhanu is able to dart in behind him. 'I was just doing what I've always done,' he tells me afterwards, 'trying to follow his feet.' Watching the footage back his eyes don't waver from Kipruto's heels.

Given his awareness of Rome's history, this is a race that Birhanu desperately wants to win. We might think of Haile Gebrselassie or Kenenisa Bekele as the stars of Ethiopian running, but many of the runners in Addis have slightly longer memories. 'The real heroes,' Birhanu says, 'are Abebe and Wami.' They were *real* heroes. They were genuine soldiers. They ran before there was any money in the sport; when love of country was the sole motivation; and they ran barefoot.

Wami Biratu, Birhanu tells me, is the grandfather of Ethiopian distance running. He was the one Abebe Bikila looked up to and he was the one who was originally selected for the Rome Olympics after beating Bikila by over a mile in the trial race, only to succumb to illness before the games. I had to tell Birhanu, ashamedly, that I'd never heard of him. 'Well you don't need to talk to me about it,' he said. 'Go and see him yourself.' 'So he's *alive?*' I replied. 'How old is he?' A quick calculation put him at least in his late eighties. Abebe Bikila died young, at 41, in 1973. 'Alive?' Birhanu replies, incredulous. 'He's still *running*, Mike. He's 92.' I had to meet him.

* * *

The following Sunday I meet Jegenna, Wami's son, outside Juicy Bar in Arat Kilo, the same part of Addis where I take my Amharic lessons. *Jegenna* means hero. 'Like father like son,' I say. He is a slight man, smartly dressed in a suit. He opens his briefcase and hands me photocopies of an article about Wami from *Runners' World* magazine, which is a nice thought, except that the article is in Finnish. We fold ourselves into a minibus taxi and head towards the Italian Embassy, next to which Wami happens to live. 'If you ever want to come and visit without me,' Jegenna said, 'just come up here and ask the first person you see. Everyone knows Wami.'

We reach a detached concrete house and duck through the corrugated iron gate. Wami is pacing on the balcony and turns at the sound of our arrival to peer at us. He has lost most of his sight and hearing. He is a big man, over six feet tall and powerfully built. His son says his voice was imposing enough before he lost his hearing. Now it is borderline deafening. 'So who is this you've bought to see me?' he roars. I try hard to remember the correct formal pronouns in Amharic and to explain who I am. 'What?!' Wami shouts. 'This man is as quiet as a mouse!' We go inside and sit down, and Jegenna explains that the best way to do this will be to direct my questions to him so that he can relay them. He perches on the arm of the sofa and shouts my first question into Wami's ear at the top of his voice, twice.

I have got used to conducting interviews with runners who seem to consider speaking an unnecessary waste of aerobic power. They answer my questions in the softest of voices as concisely as possible. With Wami it is a little different. He settles himself in his chair, braces his hands on his knees and takes a deep breath. 'My name,' he shouts, 'is Shelakabash Wami Biratu!' *Shelakabash* is a military term meaning 'boss of a thousand'. 'I never eat without *chechebsa*, milk and honey!' *Chechebsa* is a rich, buttery pancake. 'I always say, the dog and the poor man will never feel ashamed!' His answer to my first question is over 40 minutes long and only comes to an end when his son shouts several times in his ear, 'That's enough for now, Dad!' Wami ran the Great Ethiopian Run this year following the vague shadow of his son through myopic vision on 91-year-old legs. Wami Biratu does not know how to stop. His story is best told in his own words:

I was born in Sululta, up past Entoto. I was a runner before I was an athlete. I would go out as a boy and find animals to race against. There were many animals. There were antelope, porcupine, partridges, rabbits. From morning to night I caught

138

them without becoming tired. Soon I could even run 40 hectares with the horses. One day my mother came back from Addis with coffee wrapped in newspaper. On the newspaper there was this skinny soldier. It said he was a fine runner and I thought, 'What, this little guy?' I decided that I would beat him. I could feel it in my body. All of my thoughts became decided on this.

After two or three years I finally went to Addis to visit my brother. I heard that the army were hiring in the Old Airport area of the city, so I marched right up there and told them I wanted to join. I undertook the official training and I was assigned to the Second Amhara Division. In the first November, a friendship race was organised with current and former members of the army. I ran and I won. From that day onwards my dreams were realised. Every morning I started training in the cold before 6 a.m. and 7 a.m. I was usually finished. Sometimes I used to run to my mother's farm, drink milk and then run home, which was over 50 kilometres. I have run for 64 years and I have never once given up or dropped out of a race.

At this time there was no Athletics Federation and there was no marathon running in Ethiopia. There were only occasional races between army divisions in the presence of His Majesty, Haile Selassie. I would win the 5000m, the 10,000m and the road race, which was 15 kilometres, 32 kilometres or, on one occasion, 50 kilometres. Before the competition we would dig the track ourselves. At that time we would win 7 birr (25 pence) per race, but sometimes His Majesty gave us 200 birr. In 1952 Abebe Bikila came from his army division to race, but he became tired and returned to his division empty-handed. I said, 'This boy can be effective in the future,' and finally they allowed Abebe to come and train with me. He became my responsibility.

We were both selected for the Olympics and moved to Debre Zeit in order to train. Major Niskanen came from Sweden to train us and he promised His Majesty that we would win three races in the 5000m, 10,000m and the marathon. I asked him how he knew and he said he had been timing me, and that my times were better than the Europeans. He said other nations did not have the same potential as Ethiopians. Then, six days before we were supposed to travel, I faced a terrible fever and swelling all over my body. Abebe participated in the marathon and he became the motor for Ethiopian running.

They asked him at the Olympics: 'How many times were you a champion before?' and he told them, 'The champion was sick and they left him at home. I was never a champion before today.' After the Olympics we went together to Osaka marathon in Japan. I was still recovering, but I led for many kilometres before finally Abebe won. I finished second. In that race Abebe ran in shoes, but I still ran barefoot. After the race I sat down and my feet were bleeding. I peeled the soles off my feet and threw them away. My blood became part of the soil.

The Japanese gave us many things. I received a radio and a camera. No-one had these things in Ethiopia at that time. I said to Abebe, 'You can keep yours as you won, but I will give mine to the government.' Later Abebe gave me his radio and it was the only one in the Piazza area of Addis at the time. It used to be very quiet around there. I played the radio every day for the army division between midday and 1 p.m. After Abebe died I set up a marathon in his honour. I also founded the Addis Ababa Sports Council, and the Jan Meda International Cross Country, and I established race walking in Ethiopia for the first time. I will always run in Jan Meda. That is a special place for me. Every year I go back and I run a lap and I greet the people. Only death can separate me from that field.

By the time Wami stops talking night has fallen and a power cut has left us in the dark. A single candle flickers in the corner as Wami's voice fades. He has been talking for over two hours. As he stands to show me some photos, his son tries to pass him a walking stick. He waves it away imperiously. Using the candle, he shows me a photo of him leading that race in Japan. Sure enough, he runs powerfully, barefoot, 50 or so metres ahead of a pack of athletes led by Bikila, who wears white running shoes. Wami is built like a boxer, his shoulder muscles straining with the effort. It almost looks like his larger-than-life figure has been superimposed on the photo.

I thank him and as we say our goodbyes I ask him if he has any advice for the current generation. He tells me it is so different now he is not sure what to say. Midway through our interview a young man in a tracksuit had come into the house to visit. They clasped hands for a moment before the young runner kissed both of Wami's knees in veneration and left, leaving me his phone number 'to give to a manager.' When Wami was running competitively, he tells me, Addis was very different. Bole, now the wealthiest area of Addis, with high-rise buildings and neon lights, was still farmland and he could run right through it. Addis was 'empty' and unpaved.

Now, he says, it is crawling with cars and athletes have to travel outside the city to train.

'I remember when the cars first arrived,' he says. He was running from his house to the army base and a general asked him if he wanted a lift. The road was rutted and crowded with cattle and horses. 'I told him, "No!"' he recalls, before adding mischievously, 'I was in a hurry, you see. My car was my two legs and my eyes.' He says the main advice he would give to the current generation is not to take advantage of such modern comforts. 'They should still run from here to Entoto,' he says. 'Running up that hill it feels like you're carrying a child on your back. It makes you strong.' He also cautions against complicating things. 'Tell them to drink water,' he says. 'Water gives you power. If you mix it with other things you lose energy.'

* * *

At 35 kilometres Birhanu takes a few sips from the seventh bottle of Go Electrolite energy drink he has prepared for the race, before throwing the bottle to the side of the road. Amos Kipruto is the world record holder for 30 kilometres, a record he broke while pacing the Dubai marathon. He is now running his first major marathon in his own right and he is not messing about. Selamyhun, Birhanu and I watch the footage back in Birhanu's room in Kotebe a week after the race, as the two of them run stride for stride along café-lined streets. 'It's a nice place, isn't it?' I comment. 'It's not a nice place,' Birhanu replies. 'Cobblestones.' For the best part of the last two hours this has been a constant refrain. Every time the runners enter a cobbled section he says, 'See, cobblestones,' with a shake of the head. 'Disgusting cobblestones.'

As we watch the video, every time the footage shifts to an aerial view Birhanu and Selamyhun count the athletes remaining in the lead group. At the beginning Selamyhun asked how deep the prize money was and Birhanu told him there was only money for the first five. They quickly count the remaining runners and subtract the two pacemakers. After five kilometres, reached in 15.00, 11 are left. 'Two pacemakers... so four have to go.' After 10, reached in 30.05, 'Nine left. Two to go...' After 25 kilometres there were six runners left; one was a pacemaker. 'OK, the money is here,' Selamyhun says and seems to relax. 'What were you thinking about at this stage, Birhanu?' I ask. '*Mashenef,*' he replies. Simply, to win. 'How?' I ask, hoping for a bit more of an insight into his tactics. 'By finishing first,' he says, with the tone of someone explaining a simple concept to a child. Fair enough.

'Up to 35 kilometres I was sure I was going to win,' he tells me. 'My energy was full.' Kipruto hits the front, though, and runs the next three kilometres in 8.40, on the cobblestones and through a number of tight turns. At the moment that Kipruto takes the lead, Birhanu leans in closer to the screen and says, 'Look closely. *There.* The race started.' Most viewers would have missed this crucial moment. All Kipruto does is increase the pace by a few seconds per kilometre. Birhanu hangs on for dear life for four kilometres, but is dropped at 39 kilometres, leaving him safe in second place. 'I made a mistake,' he tells me. 'I shouldn't have tried to go with the pacemakers earlier on. I was the only one who went with them. *Big* mistake. Crazy man.' The 'crazy man' impulse is one he's determined to overcome in subsequent races. It is what got him through the training that got him to the start line, but marathons rarely reward impulsive decisions.

'The last two kilometres took eight minutes,' he says, wincing. Selamyhun can beat that. 'They took me 8.46 in Korea,' he says. One rash decision in the previous 40 kilometres can easily cause an implosion like this. Sometimes it happens even if you've been careful. Going through 41 kilometres, Birhanu was all alone, and couldn't see anyone behind him, but he very nearly got caught by three runners right on the line. Watching the race back is excruciating. As he wobbles through the final metres, arms aloft to acknowledge his second-place finish, a mad sprint threatens to engulf him from behind. Not until he crosses the line, and they crash into him, does he realise how close he'd been to a humiliating and costly finish.

'I had no idea,' he says. 'There was no-one there. I checked. How did they come? Just imagine...' He says he doesn't think he could have done much about it if they did catch him. 'I was dancing by that point,' is how he puts it. I know the feeling, like your limbs suddenly have a mind of their own. He won $5000 for second place. If he'd lost another couple of seconds he'd have been down in fifth place and won only $1000. You can do a lot with $5000 in Ethiopia. He has already built a house in Gondar and set his family up in business, but runners have a limited amount of time in which to establish themselves financially.

The legacy of Abebe Bikila's victory cannot be overstated, but much has changed in the landscape of Ethiopian athletics since he was running. As my friend Benoit Gaudin puts it in a paper he wrote with his Addis Ababa University colleague Bezabih Wolde, organised sport was more or less a '*terra incognita*' until 1960, with no physical education programmes in schools and no manuals available in Amharic. The first sports clubs were formed during the imperial period, when Emperor Haile Selassie began to change the structure of the army and the Imperial Guard, opening up the ranks of non-commissioned officers and officers beyond the nobility, and thereby making the army 'a way out of the harsh peasant condition' and a good way to secure paid work, the possibility of promotion, and other advantages like literacy and free medical care.

Onni Niskanen was assigned the role of coaching Ethiopia's top military runners in the late 1950s, because he was in Ethiopia to develop physical education in the Ethiopian public-school system. It just so happened that he arrived at a time when Scandinavia was at the cutting edge of distance running expertise and he was also a close friend of Gösta Olander, one of the designers of the *fartlek* training used by the world's best middle-distance runners at the time. Benoit is therefore keen to emphasise in his paper that, 'Contrary to the myth of the natural Ethiopian runner,' Bikila had undertaken 'rigorous, planned and diversified training.' The emphasis that is often still placed in commentary on East African runners running barefoot, or to meet their transport needs of getting to and from school, underplays the strong institutional support on offer in both Ethiopia and Kenya.

The extent to which athletics has been driven by the state – and motivated by patriotism and national pride – can be seen clearly in the fact that up until the year 2000 all of Ethiopia's Olympic medallist came from the army clubs. The structure of institutions and competitions that characterise Ethiopian athletics is, if anything, more developed than in many European countries. The athletics clubs competing in the first division in Ethiopia – in track and road races and in cross-country – all pay their athletes a salary large enough to live on without having to do other forms of work. These clubs usually have direct links to the state, with Defence

(Mekelakeya), the army club, featuring prominently alongside the Federal Police, Ethiopian Electric Corporation (Mebrat Hayle), Commercial Bank of Ethiopia (Bank) and the Federal Prisons clubs.

Alongside these clubs, headquartered in Addis, is a huge network of smaller clubs, working primarily with junior athletes, which provide food, accommodation and kit as well as coaching. These can be sponsored by regional branches of the police or army, by local companies or even by the regions themselves. Gaining access to a club in the first place usually requires competing in some sort of trial race, as does moving from a local club to one of the bigger Addis Ababa clubs. My friend Aseffa, who started out at a club in Asella, tells me about lining up for a 3000m race with 80 other runners and being told that the club had space for the first three. 'If you are fourth, come back next year,' he recalls being told. He went through a similar process when moving from that club to Mebrat Hayle.

The domestic race calendar in Ethiopia is furiously competitive, and the organisations which sponsor the first division clubs seek the prestige that comes with winning races like the Jan Meda or the Great Ethiopian Run. This competition schedule, though, exists in parallel with international races that allow athletes to win huge amounts of money, access to which is available through the (mainly European and American) managers who negotiate with race organisers, and arrange visas and travel to races in exchange for that 15 per cent of an athlete's earnings. In many ways, the international side of the sport is subsidised by the clubs in Ethiopia: without them, athletes would not have the time or resources to reach the level which allows them to be competitive on the international stage. Because race winnings are unpredictable and uneven (and can dry up for extensive periods of time in the case of injury), most athletes rely on the salaries from their clubs.

Our coach Meseret works with the Moyo Sports group on Monday, Wednesday and Friday, and with Mebrat Hayle on Tuesday, Thursday and Saturday. He explains to me that for both runners and coaches, 'It is difficult to live in the management system if you don't have some sort of money to be self-sufficient,' provided by running for a local club. For the vast majority of runners, though, the motivation to compete comes from the opportunity to win tens of thousands of dollars at races abroad. This means that for someone like Meseret the challenge is to negotiate and 'keep the balance between these two systems in order to sustain the lives of the athletes.' It is a battle for him to ensure that he has strong athletes available for domestic competitions and that they are not running in races abroad that would interfere with this.

In fact, the EAF still retains control over who can and cannot run abroad, issuing 'release letters' which athletes must have in order to obtain visas to compete abroad. They will not issue these if they feel racing would interfere with an athlete's domestic schedule or with their national team duties. In many ways, as Meseret puts it, 'The clubs do the development work, but they do not bear the fruits.' The structures that have been in place since Bikila first put Ethiopian distance running on the map in 1960 have played a hugely important role in the success of Ethiopian runners. Imagine, for example, if the Royal Bank of Scotland, Scottish Power, and 15 or so other companies each employed 20 full-time distance runners. Scottish long-distance running is, in fact, pretty strong at the moment, but the likes of Callum Hawkins (Scottish record holder in the marathon), Jake Wightman (Scottish

1000m record holder) and Andrew Butchart (Scottish 3000m and 5000m record holder and 6th placed finisher in the Rio Olympics 5,000m) might have even more company on the world stage with this kind of support.

While Wami is keen to note the extent to which the sport of running has changed in Ethiopia, the advice he gives to resist what he sees as modern comforts is still heeded by many. While Hailye, Fasil and others have access to a training bus to travel out of the city to places they describe as more 'comfortable', they sometimes embrace discomfort in ways that surprise me. They also still run through the middle of the city sometimes, in spite of the traffic, but they do so when pretty much everyone else is sleeping.

9

WHY IT MAKES SENSE TO RUN UP AND DOWN A HILL AT 3 A.M.

It is 3 a.m. and I have just woken from a fitful four-hour sleep. I am already wearing running shorts, and I quickly pull on a T-shirt and tracksuit and step outside. It is pitch black and my breath turns to mist in the cold air as our dog barks at me. Fasil is washing his face at the outdoor tap. He has a night off his job guarding the half-constructed building and shared Hailye's bed last night. He beams, clearly surprised that I have kept my word about joining them for this particular session. '*Ante farenj aydellum*,' he says. '*Jegenna neh*': you're no foreigner, you're a hero. Hailye just pats me sleepily on the shoulder on our way out of the gate. We jog slowly to Kidane Mehret church and 400 metres down the asphalt hill in silence before Hailye turns, crosses himself, and leads our first run up the hill. The only light comes from the occasional bare bulb hanging outside a kiosk and by the seventh or eighth run I have learned that, like a watched pot, the hilltop comes faster if you watch your feet rather than the summit.

This training session is one Hailye and Fasil refer to as *rejjim dagut*: long hills. There are two distinct kinds of hill training here and they require different kinds of hill. Short hills require a steep incline of around 80 to 120 metres and these must be run flat out with a slow jog or walk back down the hill. Long hills can be very long – sometimes 500 or 600 metres long – but are run at a steady, sustained pace on a slightly gentler gradient. 'How many times are we going up and down the hill?' I ask Hailye. 'Maybe 12,' he says, before changing his mind. 'We will just keep going for an hour,' he says. 'If it is short hills, there is no limit, you just push and push until you can't go anymore.'

The searing pain in my lungs increases very gradually as we near the top of the hill, but, just as I think I won't be able to keep up, Hailye swings round in the road and heads back down the hill, maintaining a steady pace on the downhill. I am just about shaking the light-headedness that had built by the top of the hill when Hailye again swings across the road and heads back up the hill. It is 3.30 a.m., but already there are women, cotton *shammas* clutched tightly around them to ward off the cold, sitting outside the church at the top of the hill. 'What are they doing out here at this time?' I ask Hailye between breaths. 'They probably walked overnight to get here,' he replies, as though this were the most normal thing in the world.

The women sit huddled together, and watch us impassively as we continue to run up and down the hill and I slowly run myself into a daze. Somehow Hailye manages to modulate the pace so that I can just, barely, gritting my teeth, keep up until the top of the hill, when he turns to head back down. Later he tells me that he was listening carefully to my breathing, wanting to ensure that I was working hard, but not going over my limit. I have deliberately stopped looking at my watch, but finally, after an hour, Hailye stops. '*Beka*,' he says. Enough. As we jog home he tells me, 'Now you should have a cold shower outside and then you should sleep. That's going to be the most wonderful sleep.' The cold shower seems to be an important part of making the most of this middle-of-the-night ritual, so I strip down to my shorts and pour several buckets of freezing cold water over my head. The first one is a shock and I start shivering violently, but in the end I kind of enjoy the tingling, wide-awake feeling of my skin. The wide-awake feeling doesn't last long when I climb into bed and I fall into a deep sleep.

I wake, feeling sore and slightly jet-lagged, to Fasil knocking on my door to announce that they have made a 'special breakfast' to compensate for our overnight excursion: fried meat with scrambled eggs and chillies, served with a dozen bread rolls. Even moving my legs slightly under the covers brings a heavy stinging feeling, but one that is in a way satisfying, like worrying a loose tooth with your tongue. This training session marks the start of the time – six months or so after I arrived in Ethiopia – when Fasil first tells me I am becoming *habesha,* a term denoting unified, proud Ethiopia. I feel that I have been through a rite of passage, and that my relationship with Hailye and Fasil changes after this. Fasil jokes that when I go back to the UK I will be able to run races and say, '*Ciao farenj,*' at the beginning – literally 'bye-bye foreigners' – and win easily. '*Ciao farenj*' quickly becomes something of a catchphrase every time we do a good training session. It occurs to me that these midnight runs have probably been happening for months while I slept, blissfully unaware of the hard work that was going on in the hills around me. This kind of insight into Ethiopian running is one that I could only have arrived at by being here for a long time and involving myself as much as possible in the lives of the runners around me. So what is specifically Ethiopian about running up and down a hill at 3 a.m.?

Hailye decides that he needs to run up and down the hill in the night because he is dissatisfied with his 'condition'. He has gained a bit of weight recently and his job as sub-agent means that he doesn't have quite the same drive to train as he once had. He is *too comfortable*, basically, and he sees this as having spoiled his running. He tells me that he was running better when he lived on a mere 200 birr a month (around £7). Back then, he had no access to the team bus that takes us out of Addis Ababa three mornings a week to access the environments deemed by our coach to be the most beneficial for training. He didn't have the money for public transport to these places, so he had to wake up in the night – when there were fewer cars and people on the streets – and train in the city. There is a morality here that is tied to a memory of poverty, of doing justice to a past self. When Hailye emphasises the importance of the cold shower that follows this kind of training, and the quality of the sleep we would have after this session, he ties work and rest into a moral system that rewards particular kinds of work and sacrifice, and which makes the same hill repetitions worth more at 3 a.m. than at 3 p.m.

On another occasion, when he is suffering from typhoid, Hailye still insists on running in the forest. He puts on two tracksuits in spite of the temperature being in the 20s, to 'encourage sweat' and we walk slowly up the hill. 'Are you sure this is a good idea?' I ask him. 'It is always better to run than to sleep,' he says. '[Cristiano] Ronaldo will not play if he has a cold. [Gareth] Bale will not play. They will rest. *Farenj* will all rest, but *habesha* will work.' Several times he comes to a stop, crouching and holding his forehead and complaining of dizziness. In spite of repeated entreaties to go home, he keeps running, saying, 'I have to struggle, I have to face it.' Running through an illness – usually with a clove of garlic up each nostril – is often portrayed as making you stronger, an attitude very much at odds with the conventional medical viewpoint. Demonstrating a willingness to suffer and to continue without complaint is part of building 'condition'.

Again, this is a long way from the logic of marginal gains and making enough tiny changes – 'one per centers' - to the way that you run and rest to add up to a significant improvement. Ethiopian runners do, of course, place emphasis on rest. I was frequently told not to 'do laps', which is how people refer to walking around between training sessions, and to ensure that I slept after morning training. On the way back from our midnight hill reps, I unzip my jacket, hot from the running in spite of the pre-dawn chill, and Hailye's response is to zip my jacket back up for me. 'Careful, careful, it's cold,' he says. When I question the logic of this in light of his just having told me we should take a cold, outdoor shower when we return home, he merely shrugs. While Ethiopian runners clearly do place an emphasis on focusing on little things that will improve performance (zipping up a jacket to avoid a chill, avoiding 'warming up café seats' and walking around on errands), there is also a strong focus in Ethiopia on *maximal* gains, like the middle-of-the-night hill repetitions, and cultivating a sense of power and 'dangerousness'.

A common adjective to describe a strong runner in Ethiopia is *adagenna*: dangerous. Cultivating a sense of 'dangerousness' is therefore an important part of being in 'condition'. Often this 'danger' is connected to training environments, especially to high-altitude, 'cold' places. Before I go to either place, I am told that Bekoji and Debre Tabor – both over 3000 metres above sea level – are 'very dangerous' for their altitude. Often runs in particularly challenging places, or middle-of-the-night excursions, are planned and discussed days in advance. In this way, by the time we set out we feel like dawn raiders or like we are engaged in something risky and adventurous.

Cultivating 'dangerousness' in your running is not always a case of artificially creating a particular feeling. Sometimes the danger is quite real. Hailye has talked about the asphalt long run he used to do before he joined a club or could afford to travel outside of the city to train, a 35-kilometre run that took him on a tour of the city. When I ask if he would recreate the run for me one night he seems amused that I have asked. After all, we have the bus now and can go wherever we want. I can tell he is keen to see if I am serious, but it is also clear that he is a bit apprehensive. 'Sure, we can go,' he says. 'But you'd better leave your watch here and you should wear your cheapest shoes.'

He explains that there are two main things to be worried about at night. The *lebboc* – thieves – who know that a runner's asphalt shoes can be sold for quite a lot of money on the secondhand shoe market. He often refers to these people as *jibboc*, or hyenas, preying as they do on the vulnerable in the night. And then of course there are the literal hyenas. 'The route we will take will follow the main transport routes,' he says. 'It is best that there are cars and the lights from cars around.' The one time he had real problems with hyenas, he told me, was when he went for an asphalt run with Fasil at 2 a.m. and their run coincided with a power cut. 'We were heading towards the city centre,' he says. 'You know the place just beyond Kotebe, where there is sometimes a big sheep market?' I know where you mean, I tell him. On a patch of semi-cleared forest there is often a big gathering of farmers keeping groups of sheep in check with leather switches, where the ground is strewn with sheepskins and cast-off bits of meat.

'Well, we got there,' Hailye goes on, 'and there's usually some light from the bars and streetlights down there, but all of a sudden,' he snaps his fingers for emphasis, 'the light went out and it was pitch black. There were no cars around so we had to stop completely and wait for our eyes to adjust. I couldn't even see the ground in front of me properly, but when we stopped I could hear something sort of scampering around and when my eyes started working I could see that there were about six or seven hyenas on each side of the road. Fasil grabbed my arm and said, "Which way shall we run?" and I said to him, "We do not run. We wait until a car comes with its lights on." So we waited. I could hear my heart beating in my chest and I could hear the hyenas breathing, they were so close.' I was starting to go off the idea of the run slightly at this stage.

'Finally,' Hailye continues, 'I heard a car coming up behind us and we could see the light from its headlights start to spread out around us. When the car was about to go past, I said to Fasil, "Now we run with the car," and we did the fastest interval I have ever done. We kept up with the car for hundreds of metres.' He thinks this is the funniest thing in the world now. 'Don't worry Mike, no power cuts this time,' he says. We decide to do our run on the Thursday night before the Dubai marathon, because, Hailye reasons, 'Lots of people will be doing their long run in the night so that they can watch Dubai.' I've been known to get up at 6 or 7 a.m. on a Sunday in the UK in order to get a run in before watching the London or Berlin marathons, but Dubai starts at 6 a.m. – 5 a.m. Ethiopian time. We were planning on getting up early enough to have 35 kilometres done and dusted by 5 a.m.

Our route is quite a simple one, following the main arteries of the city, which during the day are plied by mini-bus taxis. We will first leave Kotebe and run past the place where Hailye and Fasil had their run-in with the hyenas on the way to Megenagna, a huge roundabout and transport hub. From there we will head to Mexico, another huge roundabout named in honour of one of only five countries who refused to recognise Italy's annexation of Ethiopia in 1935 (there is a corresponding Plaza de la Ethiopia in Mexico City). We will then head towards Bole, the most prosperous area of downtown, and back towards Megenagna again, before returning to Kotebe. Hailye and some others have managed to persuade a carpenter, who uses his workshop to screen Premier League matches on DSTV at weekends, to set it up for us to watch Dubai at 5 a.m. It is going to be a surreal night.

By this point I have developed an evening routine designed to minimise the amount of time needed between waking up and leaving the compound, but which isn't that great for falling asleep quickly. I use my stovetop moka pot (an Italian one I buy in a department store – by far the most expensive purchase I make in Ethiopia and the most necessary) to make six shots of espresso, which I top up with a little bit of hot water. I then pour this into a thermos flask for the morning and lie down about 9.30 p.m., in a room infused with the smell of freshly brewed Ethiopian coffee, to hope for sleep.

Five hours later, the familiar knock on my corrugated iron door and the usual discussion about me drinking coffee on an empty stomach. Hailye only seems to drink coffee last thing at night before going to sleep and doesn't understand why I want to drink it at this hour. I'm not sure I can get going without it. We leave the compound at 2.30 a.m. and head out along the cobblestones to the start of the asphalt road, using the light from the bare bulbs hanging outside kiosks. When we reach the asphalt and start jogging down the hill, Hailye clicks his fingers and motions for me to move to the right to avoid not the usual tree root or stray rock, but a swaying figure gamely trying to make his way home after a heavy night in town.

On the way out of Kotebe there are still a few bars open, with neon lights and large advertising hoardings for beers – the red and yellow of St George competing with Walia's looming blue ibex logo and Habesha's afro-wearing, sideward-glancing woman. A few shouts follow us from the bar – not because we are running necessarily, because that isn't all that unusual at this time here, but because there aren't many *farenjs* who run at this time, and possibly because I'm wearing the Ethiopia tracksuit jacket I have acquired, its yellow and green the closest thing I have to fluorescent clothing. The noise from the bars quickly dies down, though, and as it does my heart rate rises on the approach to the spot of Hailye's encounter with the hyenas. To my relief the electricity is still working tonight, but you can still only see a few feet into the trees at the side of the road and I can't help feeling impatient to get moving a bit faster.

I feel a far more heightened awareness of my surroundings at this time of night, alert to any noise or sudden movement. There is not much traffic, though, and we slip into a nice rhythm, my footsteps following Hailye's on the road. As usual I feel like I make more of an impression on the road than he does. I try to run as lightly as I can so that my footsteps don't drown his out. Every hundred or so metres there are corrugated iron constructions, some of them raised off the ground on wooden platforms, which house the guards who patrol the streets or watch over the kiosks and market stalls at night. Occasionally we see one of the guards themselves, holding a torch or a *dulla,* a thick wooden stick.

In the bus station below Megenagna roundabout there are small groups congregated around fires and others huddled in blankets. We pass Haile Gebrselassie's Marathon Motors building, from which he sells imported Hyundai cars, and Alem Fitness centre, owned by his wife. We have to keep our attention on the road, though, because with no pavement and little street lighting we rely on the attentiveness of drivers and our own wits to keep ourselves safe. Lights blink away in the high-rise buildings around the roundabout as we head downhill towards Kebena, where I lived with Benoit, and then along the long straight road to Arat Kilo. After a while, even on this most unusual of runs, I start to zone out from my surroundings and watch instead Hailye's heels flicking away in front of me. We have run a little over 15 kilometres by the time we reach Mexico and I have to snap out of my reverie to negotiate a footbridge over the roundabout.

We head back towards the stadium and Meskel Square, the huge parade ground from the socialist era and the focal point of both the religious festival from which it gets its name and for recent anti-government protests. A bank of stone steps a few hundred metres long faces the stadium on one side of the square and already, at 4 a.m., we can make out dark figures running up and down. From there we head south-east into the outskirts of an area referred to as Chechnya – so named because its neon lights remind people of the footage of tracer missiles from the conflict. This is Addis Ababa's red-light district and it shows no signs of slowing down at this time. From there we head north and up a long gradual hill, before Hailye speaks for the first time in about an hour. 'We've done a bit of a detour,' he says. 'But I thought you'd like the name of this street.'

After almost 30 kilometres, we return to Megenagna by running the two-kilometre long Kenenisa Avenue. I am relieved to see the roundabout, my legs feeling pretty tired from such a long run on the roads. All of the longer runs we have done recently have been on Sendafa's rough road or in the forest, both of which are more forgiving surfaces. I realise how hard it must be for those who don't have access to transportation to get them to more favourable places to train. They are desperately trying to catch up and get to a higher level while unable to access the environmental resources that they are told are so important. When we are within striking distance of Kotebe, Hailye announces that we will 'add some intervals' and slows to a jog before motioning for me to come alongside him. After 20 seconds or so of jogging he claps his hands and begins a now familiar series of post-run intervals. Each one is slightly faster and slightly longer than the last, until we are loose and have shaken some of the long-run lethargy from our legs. We finish the run by jogging very slowly and swinging our arms to loosen them.

We have seen seven or eight other groups of runners – usually in twos or threes – in the course of our run, so I am curious to see how many people will show up at the carpentry workshop at five. Hailye is not worried that the runners won't show up. He's concerned that the carpenter will sleep in. By the time we get back to Kotebe just before 5 a.m. the day is just beginning for a lot of people. Workers stand by the roadside waiting for lifts and the queue for minibus taxis already stretches along the road. Athletes in Nike and Adidas tracksuits stand waiting for the buses that will take them to asphalt training in Sendafa or Sebeta. It is strange to feel smug about having already finished training so early in the morning.

To Hailye's relief the carpenter has opened the workshop and is busy preparing a projector screen, and rearranging worktables and planks of wood into a rudimentary, albeit splintery, seating arrangement. A few runners are here already, the sweat drying on their tracksuits after their own long runs. Ten minutes later, to my amazement, the room is more or less full and, lit with just a small lamp and the light from the projector, has the feeling of a tense (and sweaty) cinema. There is a nervous energy in the room in spite of the long, depleting runs that we have just completed. We can be fairly certain that someone who the runners have known for years, perhaps someone from a training camp at home, or a more recent training partner in the forest, or else just a neighbour, will win enough money in the next two hours to achieve lifetime financial security for themselves and their extended families. We can also be fairly certain that the vast majority of total prize money across the men's and women's races – some $816,000 before any time bonuses are added on – will be coming back to not just Ethiopia but to Kotebe itself.

We can also be fairly certain that the race won't be won by the favourite, by one of the fastest runners in the field on paper or by a previous winner. In the race's history only one man, Haile Gebrselassie, has managed to win it twice. Two years previously 18-year-old Tsegaye Mekonnen won the race in his first ever marathon. Not only that, but Mekonnen's best half marathon time going into the race was 1.02.53. When he crossed the line in Dubai in 2.04.32 he had therefore run back-to-back half marathon personal bests. Last year's race was won by Lemi Berhanu, who ran a PB by over five minutes in only his second-ever race outside Ethiopia. Dubai epitomises the winner-takes-all, one-race-to-change-everything nature of marathon running. It can catapult someone who grew up on a highland farm and left school at 13 to unimaginable wealth in just over two hours.

Dubai resonates with Ethiopian runners for this reason. Very few Kenyans run in Dubai, because the race doesn't pay large appearance fees like most of the other big marathons. Given that most of the top Kenyan runners only run two marathons a year, they see the race as too big a risk, as to run poorly in Dubai is to earn nothing. And yet it was the race that more or less all the Ethiopians I met wanted to run, even if their best marathon times were minutes (and in some cases 10 or 15 minutes) away from the time it would take to win. There was precedent, in Dubai for these kinds of transcendent performances. It was known as the place 'where the time comes' of its own accord.

The runners in the room are not surprised, then, when the race sets off at breakneck speed. We watch without much comment for the first hour as a huge group runs down the wide, pan-flat Dubai motorway, lit, as we had been an hour previously, only by the odd streetlight. There are only four turns in the entire marathon in Dubai, which the runners seem to approve of. 'Curve *t'iru aydellum*,' I am told – 'corners are no good.' A total of 16 men go through the halfway mark in an incredibly quick 61.39 and maintain that pace to break the 30-kilometre world record. Perhaps the most astonishing thing is that in spite of myself and Hailye providing relatively efficient translation services, no-one seems particularly astonished by how fast they are running. In fact, the main emotion seems to be disgust whenever someone inevitably falls off the group. 'Pfft, Tilahun can't keep up,' someone says as Tilahun Regassa – who will still go on to run 2.08.11 – lets a few metres open up between himself and the others.

In the end the race becomes slightly more tactical and thoughts of a world record become less important than who is going to take away the $200,000. It starts to look like Lemi Berhanu might become the first since Haile to take back-to-back wins as he opens up a gap on Tesfaye Abera in second. I look up the start list and point out that on paper Abera has only the 17th fastest PB in the field. 'Yeah,' Hailye says, 'but he's right there, isn't he? And Tesfaye has *finishing*. He used to be a 400m runner!' The English word 'finishing' is often used in discussions of the end of races, either as a place ('finishing *lay*' – at the end) or, in Hailye's usage, as an ability. Tesfaye is six foot four (1.93m), which is enormous for an elite marathon runner, and given the foreshortening effect of the camera this makes it pretty difficult to tell how big the gap is.

A couple of Lemi's friends are screaming at him as he strains for the line. '*Na! Na!*' they shout – come, come – willing him towards them from their vantage point on the camera motorbike headed for the finish line. Both sides of the road in Dubai are lined with Ethiopian migrant workers in what look like carefully choreographed outfits – in the top levels of the stand people wear white robes and red, yellow and green scarves, while in the lower levels they wear Ethiopian national team football shirts and wave huge flags. Hearing the sudden roar of this crowd Tesfaye remembers his sprinting days and takes off over the final 200 metres to win convincingly, holding his head in shock as he crosses the line. Just as Lemi did the year before, he has produced a personal best by over five minutes. His life will never be the same again. Behind him, though, such is the depth of the race that three men who run faster than his previous best time fail to win even a cent of prize money. 'That's marathon,' Hailye says when I point this out later.

We make our weary way back up the hill as people make their way to work, and it strikes me that the people I am living with do not share the neat division of night and day into time for resting and time for exertion. Running is essentially an option at all hours of the day and night, as is sleeping. The important thing is not the time that is spent on things, but the energy exerted. And if you don't feel like sleeping at a particular time, that is fine too. One night I am woken up at 3 a.m. by Hailye clattering around in the garden and, assuming it is time to get up, start pulling on running clothes to head out too. When I finally check my watch I open the door and ask him what is going on. 'I couldn't sleep,' he tells me. 'I was lying there wondering what time Tsedat would cover the 35 kilometres tomorrow, and then I remembered I'd forgotten to water the garden, so that's what I'm doing.' By this point I am wide awake so I help him with the watering before going back to bed for another hour.

Given that a big part of Hailye's job as sub-agent is to mediate between Edinburgh-based manager Malcolm and the athletes, and another big part of his job is to make sure that runners get to the airport on time, he sometimes gets caught out between local *habesha* and *farenji* time. He often has his watch set by the Ethiopian system, counting the hours from six in the morning (1 a.m. for 7 a.m., 2 a.m. for 8 a.m. etc.) and his phone on 'normal' time. One night he went to bed especially early, tired from two runs and trips to embassies to check on athletes' visa applications. When he woke up his watch said 5.30, so he quickly got dressed and started heading down the hill to training, assuming that this was *habesha* time and it was therefore 5.30 a.m.

It was only when he got down to the main road and started to wonder why there were still so many people in the bars that he realised his error. 'I called Fasil and said, "Is there some sort of festival on?" and he was like, "Go to bed, Hailye,"' he tells me, laughing. Anxieties about missing sleep before a big session or a race don't seem to exist. I remember asking Tsedat how training had gone after one particularly impressive long run. 'It was pretty great,' was his response, 'especially after I'd been up helping my brother sell a truck all night.' Why his brother was selling a truck at night I thought it best not to ask.

The night running that we do, more even than the particular places or environments we run in, brings home to me the importance of cultivating a particular feeling, or sense of importance and adventure, in your running. It isn't just a case of following a training schedule to the letter, of managing to fit in all the running you need to do and not worrying about when or where it is done. The hill reps run at 3 a.m. have a very specific value. I for one can now stand on a start line and think, 'Well, I bet nobody else has done that.'

10

WHERE DOES ENERGY COME FROM?

That there are forces at play that I don't always completely understand becomes quite clear to me over the course of my time in Ethiopia. When the wind whips up a dust cloud in the *coroconch* as we are standing around after training, for example, Fasil will cross himself repeatedly. When I look to Hailye for explanation he says, 'He thinks it could be a devil and he has just done a hard run so he doesn't want them to take his energy.' I first notice this kind of thing in the forest, where we occasionally come across small piles of torn white paper on the paths. The runners cross themselves and give these strange little paper cairns a wide berth, muttering about witchcraft, and I avoid them too. It is only months later that I learn from my friend Ed Stevens, who set up Run Africa with his wife Rekik to support young athletes and give foreigners the chance to train alongside them, that these paper trails were actually set by the Hash House Harriers (the 'drinking club with the running problem'), a non-competitive running club with branches all around the world.

While sports scientists and, I imagine, the majority of runners in the West tend to think of the athletic potential of an individual as self-contained, and as bounded within one body, energy in Ethiopia is seen as trans-bodily. It can flow between people, it can be shared and it can even, on occasion, be stolen. A runner's 'condition' then is constructed and maintained through their relationships with others, through the sharing of food and through sharing the pace in training. This expansive view of the capacity to harness energy means that people can be wary of each other. Because they believe they have more to draw upon than the resources of their own bodies, though, it also explains their beliefs in the possibility of dramatic and unlikely improvement.

The anthropologist Stephen Gudeman describes something similar when he discusses the world view of peasants in Latin America. 'The current of strength,' he writes, 'comes from the earth and other elements that include wind, rain and sun,' and ultimately from God. 'Humans do not create these sources of strength, nor do they create strength itself. Instead, they secure, transform and remake it. They are conveyors but not creators of strength. Their work "helps compose" strength, that is, they put it together in ways that can be used by themselves and others.' In a similar way, Ethiopian runners seem particularly aware that they are drawing strength from the environment around them, as well as from those with whom they live and train. They are not only what they contain, their own particular desires, personalities, muscle and mitochondria, but also the forces that come to inhabit them at any particular time and the energy they are able to mobilise from others.

Coach Meseret will often begin training sessions by reiterating the importance of working together and sharing the responsibility of running in a controlled way. This morning, as we sit on the bus in Sendafa before warming up, is no different. 'Many Ethiopian athletes will come to the medium level,' he is telling us. 'But only a few can reach the edge. If you ask why, it is not because you are unable to run. Rather, it is a lack of self-management.' This lack of self-management is never purely thought of in terms of the individual, though, as he goes on to explain. 'A person who pushes beyond the pace I give you, especially in the build-up to a race, is killing himself and he is killing others.' To run in a way that is controlled, then, is to demonstrate a commitment to the group and a willingness to help others.

I hear something similar about the importance of those around you from Jeroen Deen, the Dutch massage therapist to many of the top runners in Ethiopia and Kenya. I often meet Jeroen to watch Diamond League races in the Ararat Hotel, where he talks almost without drawing breath for three hours, his stories about the various runners he has treated punctuated at roughly 30-second intervals by his reading out the splits from the Diamond League website on his iPad. He tells me that the majority of the running injuries he sees are back and hip injuries sustained by overtraining. On one particular evening we are joined by one of his massage therapy students, Haju, who is also a runner, and Jeroen addresses the following to both of us. 'I call it the Boulevard of Broken Dreams. You can think of it as Meskel Square, that huge square in the centre of town, full of the runners who didn't make it; who trained for three to ten years and never really made it. Some of them went to a couple of races, made a few dollars here and there, had some fun, but they didn't make it.' At this point he grabs Haju by the arm. 'And that's why I'm not like a lot of physios who only want to treat the top athletes. Because I can advise people like Haju and say, "Hey, my friend, how long have you trained for now? Every time you get injured you know where that comes from? Because you trained too hard, you trained harder than you can train. Your body tells a story, eh?"'

You trained harder than you can train. This is the very distinct possibility that many of the runners I know face. Their desire to work hard is unparalleled, the potential rewards for doing so stratospheric. The consequence of this is that much of the role of the coach, and of the support team around athletes, is one of holding them back. Jeroen has trained many other massage therapists like Haju, all of them runners who were struggling but who wanted to continue to work within the sport, and he is keen to emphasise that the therapist's role is broader than just the treatment of specific injuries and niggles.

Jeroen is also keen to express his surprise that people interested in marathon running performance never come to him, because he (or 'one of my Hajus' as he puts it) has worked with three previous world record holders. And he is also keen to emphasise that while many people look for one basic cause of success, his is a more holistic approach. 'The most important thing is that you help the athletes to make a circle of people around them,' he says. 'You are in the middle, you have the manager, then there is the family, there is your church, there is your charity, there is everything that is in your life. All of those circles have to work for the individual to succeed.'

In many ways, though, this list of influences on athletic performance is only part of the story. The balance of pacemaking responsibilities, and the choice of people with whom to train, is vitally important for a number of reasons. Back on the bus in Sendafa, Meseret continues his team talk. He explains that he wants to 'give' the first five kilometres to Teklemariam and Fasil, because Teklemariam is just coming back from injury so can't be relied upon later in the run. Then Andualem and Tilahun will take over for five kilometres, followed by Hunegnaw and Aseffa, before Tsedat and Atalay, two of the more experienced athletes, have their turn. In the final five kilometres of the 25-kilometre run the athletes are 'free' to run as fast as they like. Meseret wants to ensure that even those returning from injury are given the 'responsibility' to do some pacemaking and that everyone feels like this 'duty', which is taken very seriously, is divided equitably among all the runners.

It is cold in Sendafa when we emerge from the bus just after 6 a.m. A hazy bluish fog sits over the fields of chickpeas that line the asphalt road and smoke rises from the round *tukuls* in the distance, where farmers are just waking for another day's work in the fields. We have to try to run fast today, which means that our warm-up will be a long and gradual one. We begin with a short wander and an appraisal of the Valencia marathon champion Leul Gebrselassie's new Toyota, before starting with the slowest of stiff-legged first kilometres. We will run mostly uphill for the first 20 kilometres before turning around and I can already tell it's going to be a tough day for me. '*Ayeru kabad naw zare,*' Tsedat says. The air is heavy today. Running at 2700 metres above sea level is never easy, but it does feel like particular days are worse than others. Today I feel short of breath as soon as we start jogging, which is never a good sign.

The asphalt road in Sendafa consists of rolling hills that go through a number of small towns. There is no pavement, but it is possible to run on the road's gravelly edge, which becomes necessary whenever one of the huge Isuzu lorries comes careering past or when we have to negotiate our way around one of the larger herds of donkeys. Our forest, mountain and *coroconch* runs have been spectacular and almost perfect training environments, whereas asphalt training can actually be quite perilous here. Ethiopia has some of the most dangerous roads in the world. I have yet to come across a vehicle with a functioning seat belt and wearing one is widely considered as displaying a lack of respect for God. The idea that life and death on the roads is in the hands of a higher being is often evident in the driving styles of the truck and minibus drivers, and I am often left in shock by their more audacious acts of overtaking.

There are also fewer regulations on exhaust emissions, meaning that running on the asphalt often means having to suck in thick diesel fumes along with the thin air. It is not my favourite kind of running here, which is also perhaps to do with the objectivity of the roads: I become more acutely aware of how much slower I am running than I would have been at sea level. Our warm-up this morning follows the usual pattern. We jog very slowly for the first 10 minutes at perhaps seven minutes per kilometre pace. Then we gradually speed up to around four minutes per kilometre by the 20-minute mark, before winding the pace up to closer to three minutes 20 pace over the final 10 minutes. As usual, we slow to a jog just as I am about to get dropped, before immediately launching into a series of 'intervals' consisting of around 200 metres of hard running followed by 30 seconds of jogging.

This is followed by about 10 minutes of synchronised loosening exercises. These are performed in lines of three or four athletes, and involve a lot of arm swinging and in-time stamping on the ground. They are focused as much on ensuring that the shoulders and torso are relaxed as they are on warming up the leg muscles. I have to be careful with some of the more explosive exercises, which leave my hamstrings extremely sore. The idea is to be as relaxed as possible before we start running and also as in tune with each other as we can be to make the train of athletes as smooth as possible. By the time we have completed these exercises and changed into racing flats, our warm-up has taken the best part of an hour. The first five kilometres are to be run in 16.00, then the second in 15.45 and the third in 15.30 to bring the athletes to 15 kilometres in 47.15. Finally, Tsedat and Atalay will lead from 15 to 20 kilometres in 15.15 before they let rip for the final five kilometres. I have no chance of keeping up on a run like this and Meseret tells me to set off halfway between the women's group and the men's group, and run in the no man's land between them.

This is not ideal for my purposes in terms of research and writing, so I decide to try to hang on for as long as I possibly can before jumping on the bus at 10 kilometres and watching the rest of the run unfold from there. As we line up by a white post that tells us we are 25 kilometres from Addis, Meseret addresses the group. 'I need you to co-operate today. Let me tell you one thing: if you never lead you won't be a winner. But if you never follow you won't be a winner either.' I have about a minute to try to get my head around this idea – that getting the balance right between leading and following is the key to success – before I am in too much oxygen debt to really think about anything apart from not being left behind within the first kilometre.

The pace doesn't feel that fast, but almost immediately I can tell that this is going to be one of those runs where it feels like I'm running through a different, more resistant, substance than air. If I can get to five kilometres with the group, I decide, I'll be happy. We form one long single-file line, like cyclists in a team time trial, with Teklemariam and Fasil alternating at the front and me at the back. Our footsteps fall into step straightaway, so it feels like our legs whir along underneath us like pistons in one long train.

I imagine we are each joined by an imaginary thread to the runner in front and behind us, and I'm conscious that as the runner at the very back, who is unable to contribute to sharing the pace, I am perceived as a drag on their ability to run fast.

I focus on just trying to keep up with Hunegnaw in front of me, while keeping half an eye on the road ahead. We dodge a big horse-drawn cart on the left and then a series of *bajaj* auto rickshaws coming down the hard shoulder on the wrong side of the road, and I'm conscious that this is harder work than it would be on a clear road. We are heading vaguely uphill, and pass through a small town with roadside bars and cafes from which people shout encouragement or else simply the standard descriptive '*farenj!*' I manage to hang on to the group for the first five kilometres. Teklemariam and Fasil do an excellent job of getting us there in bang on 16 minutes, and then Andualum and Tilahun overtake them and accelerate and immediately a gap opens up in front of me.

My only thought now is to limit my losses to avoid slowing Meseret and Hailye down in the bus, and I put my head down and run as hard as I can. This road seems to undulate when you're in the bus, the long uphill drags relieved by short downhills. Today, though, it just feels like varying degrees of incline and reminds me of my out-and-back runs along the coast at Portobello in Edinburgh. Often I would run out past Musselburgh, thinking, 'This running into the wind is tough, but at least when I turn round I'll have the wind behind me,' only to turn around and find that, somehow, I seemed to still be running into the wind. Sendafa was like this but for hills.

With great relief I make it to the 10-kilometre mark and, by virtue of not wanting to hold training up too much, find I have run my best time for 10 kilometres since being here, just outside 32 minutes. I collapse on to the bus's leather seats for a few minutes, the sweat pooling around me, before pulling myself together to watch the rest of the run – which would turn out to be rather eventful – from the bus.

I join Meseret at the front of the bus. He holds a notebook scrawled with hundreds of splits from past training sessions rolled up in one hand and two stopwatches – one for the men and one for the women – in the other. A large wooden cross swings like a pendulum inside the windscreen, clonking me on the head every now and then, and we race to catch up with the runners at the 15-kilometre mark. After a couple of kilometres, though, the driver Birhanu spots one of the female runners, Mulu, at the side of the road. She is waving her arms to get our attention and as Birhanu slows down she points to a small knot of onlookers who are crowded around something on the grass verge by the road.

'*Minden naw?*' Meseret shouts to Mulu. 'What's going on?' She explains in Afan Oromo rather than Amharic, which leaves me none the wiser, but Meseret nods and, grabbing a Bible and a bottle of water that are stashed in the glove compartment, jumps out of the bus and shoves through the crowd. One of the other female runners, Birhan, is writhing on the ground and speaking in tongues, as far as I can tell. Meseret crouches over her with the Bible and pours water from the bottle over her head, pinning her down to stop her from moving around. I have a limited view of what is going on from behind the crowd, but gradually she starts speaking in more recognisable Amharic. 'Help me,' she shouts and keeps repeating, '*Mebrak, mebrak, mebrak!*' Lightning, lightning, lightning!

Before long she falls silent and Meseret roughly hauls her up into his arms and carries her to the bus, where he lets her fall across two seats, seemingly still semi-conscious. 'Let's go,' he tells Birhanu. Mulu, meanwhile, has started running again in a vain attempt to catch the others. Meseret seems unconcerned, and returns to his post at the front of the bus and his stopwatches. 'What happened there?' I ask, tentatively. 'She thinks someone has cursed her,' he explains. I've talked to Hailye about this before, but this is the first time I've seen witchcraft manifest itself so dramatically. There is a widespread belief that it is possible for runners to steal each other's energy through a form of witchcraft called *metat*, usually by taking an item of their clothing like a sweaty sock to a *debtera*, or witchdoctor, who uses this to take energy and bestow it upon someone else. 'In this way,' Hailye had explained to me, it was possible for a runner to take 'six, seven or eight athletes' power and then run with the strength of a hyena' before rewarding the *debtera* by killing an ox or a sheep for them if they won a race.

Previously when I had talked to Meseret about this, he had explained *metat* in terms of psychological weakness. 'As a runner you're not always going to be fully fit,' he said. 'Sometimes your fitness will go, sometimes come, sometimes condition comes and condition goes. So when their condition is gone they think, "Oh, it is *metat*," and they leave.' Often runners who had fears about this would travel hundreds of miles to monasteries to drink holy water and subsist on a very limited diet (often just a couple of handfuls of chickpeas a day) for a period of time determined by the local priest, and they would return to training exhausted. Speaking as a coach educated to Master's level, he was keen to explain *metat* in terms of 'poor education' and 'psychological weakness'.

Birhan is clearly afflicted by something that looks very real, though. Regardless of whether you 'believe' in this kind of thing or you think it symbolises the high levels of competition and distrust in the sport, it is impossible to deny that the belief in spirits does something in the world. Meseret's response is actually one that a priest might have made. He keeps a bottle of holy water and a Bible in the bus for this express purpose, and is also able to explain what has happened in terms the runners are more familiar with. 'The spirits don't like hard work,' he says, and this is why runners are especially vulnerable to them. The holy water is intended to allow Birhan to continue to train and, in fact, once she comes around she demands to be let off the bus to continue running. The idea that spirits dislike hard work lends a clear moral dimension to the idea of hard work and it is often those who appear to achieve without working hard, or who made a sudden and drastic improvement, who are found to be suspicious. This resonates with the work of other anthropologists, who have identified 'taking without sweat', or amassing mysterious wealth seemingly without toil, as suspicious behaviour in many places around the world.

In his book *Witchcraft, Intimacy and Trust*, Peter Geschiere writes that, 'In modern contexts as well, everyday life is still haunted by the tensions between, on the one hand, the fear of an intimacy that can give the ones who are close a dangerous hold over you and, on the other, the need to establish at least some form of trust with one's intimates in order to collaborate.' This describes the tension for runners quite neatly – they know that they must collaborate in order to succeed, but they also know that they must eventually compete as individuals, so they need to gain an advantage over others if they can. This is, in a sense, a version of the problem identified by Jean-Jacques Rousseau in his story about a stag hunt. When you're hunting for a big prize – in Rousseau's instance, a stag – you need all the hunters to collaborate in order to be successful. If a hare crosses the path of one of the hunters, he has a choice. Does he go after the hare on his own, ruining the chance of a successful stag hunt for his own benefit? Or does he ignore the hare and stick with the group?

Building trust between the runners in the team requires sharing resources equally, whether that means pacemaking responsibilities, food or hospitality. This is often spoken about in strongly moralistic ways by the runners I know. Back on the bus, we pick up Hunegnaw and another runner, Gojjam, at the 15-kilometre point, where they are sitting on a pile of concrete slabs by the roadside. Gojjam gets in and sits down before coughing violently. 'I did your turn at the front today,' he tells Hunegnaw. 'And my soul almost came out.' He coughs some more before adding, 'Leading is hard, it's like bearing someone else's burden.' This act of sacrificing your own energy for your teammates is not without reward, as Gojjam predicts that this gift will be returned at some point. Working hard on behalf of someone else also has a larger significance, as Meseret is keen to point out: 'If you are morally good there is no hesitation and no doubt between friends. If I need to lead, I will lead. If my friend is leading, I will take over from him. He is not asking me to help him, but because I am morally good I know that if I do that I will get a reward from God. There is no argument, there is no blaming others. If people are morally good they know what is right and what is wrong; they have already differentiated.'

In Meseret's view, there is a strong symbolic value to working hard together that is not to be disturbed, something that is about to come to a head in a big way today. Once Tadesse has collected the water bottles scattered along the roadside, we head off to catch up with the runners between 15 and 20 kilometres. When we do, we find Tsedat at the back of the group, rather than the front, and Atalay, with whom he was supposed to be leading, alone at the front. When Meseret shouts out of the window to ask Tsedat if there is a problem, Tsedat ignores him, keeping his eyes on the runner in front of him. They continue like this until we approach the turning point at 20 kilometres, from which they will run the final five kilometres downhill to the finish. As we approach the turn, Tsedat moves up around the outside of the group until he is on Atalay's shoulder and then, after swinging round to make a 180-degree turn in the road, he hits the front and accelerates, hard.

Within seconds he has a gap on the rest of the group and it is clear that he wants to make a bit of a statement with this last five kilometres. 'Interesting,' Hailye says, turning to me. 'Something has pissed him off.' Tsedat is the picture of compact efficiency. There is almost no energy wasted in upwards movement and his head seems to stay the same distance off the ground as he propels himself forwards, his legs whirring away at a cadence I try – and fail – to calculate with my watch. He runs the kilometre between 20 and 21 kilometres in 2.53, at almost 2800 metres above sea level, the gap to the others growing bigger with every stride. What was a carefully marshalled group is now in complete disarray.

We pull up alongside him at the 18-kilometre mark and Hailye shouts, '*Berta!*' – 'Be strong!' – out of the window. Tsedat turns to us and a big smile spreads across his face before he has a quick check of his watch, and continues pounding out his punishing tempo. We accelerate to avoid holding up the traffic behind us and park by the road marker that shows us we are 40 kilometres from Addis. As Tsedat approaches, the others are barely in view and Hailye shakes his head. 'He does this occasionally,' he says to me. Tsedat stops his watch – he has covered the last 5 kilometres in 14.23 – and continues to jog slowly down the road without a glance behind him. He knows the damage that last 5 kilometres will have done.

When he returns, though, the runners form the second focal point of the day for local farmers, as a crowd gathers round to watch Atalay and Tsedat dispute what went wrong on the run. Meseret barrels over and orders us all on to the bus to discuss what happened 'peacefully', much to the disappointment of the farmers who were clearly enjoying seeing the usual serenity of the runners broken. Back on the bus, the windows starting to steam up, Meseret asks Hunegnaw to explain what happened.

'Well, it seemed like Atalay was going a little bit too fast,' he starts, 'so Tsedat refused to help him with the pace. Atalay got annoyed with him, so Tsedat went to the back of the group. But he was clearly capable of leading, you saw what he did at the end there...'

'Atalay was running at 2.58 per kilometre pace up the hill,' Tsedat interrupts. 'Which is crazy. I turned round and I could tell that only Hunegnaw could cope with that, so I told him to slow down and he didn't. That's why I decided to finish alone.'

'Yeah, what a hero,' Atalay says, sarcastically.

'I am a hero for myself,' is Tsedat's retort. 'You were going at the pace that felt right for you, not the pace we were told to run.'

'Well you came first anyway, what a hero,' Atalay repeats.

'Yes, I am a hero for myself. Next time I will lead the whole session alone and you'll see who Tsedat really is.'

In my more than a year in Ethiopia this was the only time I witnessed a major argument about people 'disturbing the pace' or allowing individualistic desire to overrule the desire to build the team. But it was clear that there was a constant concern to ensure that the hyper-competitive nature of elite marathon running did not encourage selfish behaviour to take hold. In Meseret's view, selfish behaviour is exacerbated by the competitive nature of modern life in Ethiopia. 'The problem is,' he tells the runners, 'that nowadays most people are becoming selfish, so they don't want to lose energy for you. They just want to be benefited upon your shoulders.' This is true, he says, in many aspects of life in Ethiopia, where it is becoming increasingly difficult to find stable employment and where even those with university degrees are finding it very difficult to find work.

The atmosphere on the bus on the way back to Kotebe is understandably muted. Tsedat sits on his own at the front, still fuming after what has happened on the run and how the others have reacted. I sit with Hailye and ask him what he thinks about Meseret's diagnosis of the problem. 'He has a point,' Hailye says, 'but I think that athletics itself also changes their behaviour. They were farmers before, they helped each other with farming, harvesting, collecting grains and making a house, and stuff like that, but athletics itself is a competition. You train for competition, you compete. Life itself is a competition for them when they come to athletics. By hook or by crook they want to achieve something better than their friends.'

The large sums of prize money on offer, and their highly unequal distribution, means that running exacerbates a winner-takes-all, survival-of-the-fittest mentality. If you read what anthropologists have had to say about Amhara Orthodox Christians, though, it would seem that this idea predates running in Ethiopia by quite some time. I was lucky to have two experts on the subject – Diego Malara and Tom Boylston – in Edinburgh while I was doing my PhD. As Tom puts it in his book *The Stranger at the Feast,* 'Ethiopian Orthodox Christians understand people to be basically individualistic and perhaps fundamentally selfish, but they do not consider this to be a good thing. Rather, individualistic urges must be tempered at all times by social and moral constraints.' The main way that people do this, according to Tom, is through eating and drinking together, which 'counteracts the centrifugal motion of individual people pursuing their own ends.'

Meseret joins us, having taken his usual stroll up the bus to check on individual athletes. He sits down and grins. For him, managing the egos of the athletes and encouraging them to work together is one of the challenges of his job that he enjoys most. The competitive energy has to be harnessed in order to get the most out of the runners. 'The misuse of the pacing system is created if one of them is not interested in the other, so my job as a coach is to create trust first and then to develop confidence based on the trust they have in each other,' he tells us. 'And today we'll do that with bananas.' Before I can ask him what he means he is standing at the front of the bus announcing that to make up for their 'mistake' Tsedat and Atalay will shortly be disembarking to buy 10 kilos of bananas to be shared on the way home – eating together, as Tom suggests, will heal the rift in the team. After a feeble protest, the runners do get off the bus with Fasil, who helps them to haul bags and bags of bananas on to the bus. These are distributed carefully to ensure that everyone gets their fair share and soon the mood is much better, the music is turned back on and there are banana skins flying all over the place.

Birhanu, the driver, has also picked up on the tension and has his own ideas about how to resolve it. On the way back to Kotebe he abruptly pulls the bus over at a roadside bar, announcing that he is going to buy a round of drinks for everyone. Hailye raises his eyebrows at me and shrugs. Clearly this is an unusual occurrence. We file into a big room, the floor strewn with leaves and the chairs still on the tables from the night before, and Birhanu hustles off to find someone to bring us some drinks. To my surprise at 9 a.m., a couple of the runners order Habesha beer, so I do too. They look as curious as I feel about Birhanu's motivations for stopping the bus and when we're all sitting down he stands up to speak.

'Let me just say a few words,' he begins. 'What I would like to say is that it would be nice if we gather like this sometimes. I have a lot of experience with get-togethers. Sorrow with people is beautiful, as is happiness with people, and eating and drinking together is important. Your happiness is my happiness, so we should come together to show our love and to strengthen our unity. Cheers!' He raises his bottle of Ambo flavoured water and everyone applauds. Hailye then stands up and says, 'Often we don't all get a chance to speak to each other openly. I think it would be nice if everyone said something about what the team means to them and what they aim to do in the future.' As an anthropologist I can't believe my luck and scramble to find my notebook. 'You first, Teklemariam. I think you went bald from knowledge, not from carrying loads on your head.'

Teklemariam laughs nervously and stands up. 'Thank you, Birhanu,' he begins. 'Truly, we love and respect you. You have done your job with love. You are like a father figure to us, even if you are still able to sprint and hand out the water. Hailye is like a brother, not just a representative. This group should be a place where we learn from each other and share things, where we help and understand each other. It would be great if we could all contribute a small amount of money every week, and then a couple of times a year we can visit monasteries and historical places together. Let us keep this in mind and let God allow us to do it.' He sits down and someone shouts, 'Tsedat!' He begins to rise then sits back down. 'I think the same,' he says, suddenly bashful. The speeches continue, with the runners emphasising the importance of the group and of working together.

Then Mekasha, who is new to the group, is encouraged to say something. 'I spent a lot of time in a monastery when I was growing up,' he begins. 'The nuns let me live there if I worked in the garden and I could focus on my running. Gathering like this is a form of going to church. I moved to Addis three years ago to join a professional group, but I wasn't strong enough to withstand the training at that time and I decided to go back home. Now I have left everything again to come to Addis, because sometimes you need to lose something in order to get something. Even if I can't get two things, I can get one through my running; I am healthy even if I do not have money. Even if I have no money I have a goal. I have hope of gaining something tomorrow. As our elders say, "A pregnant cow does not crave milk." I remember reading a book in the monastery. It said that the human mind is like a farm. It will grow whatever you cultivate, so you have to distinguish between the wheat and the chaff, and focus on the good.'

He pauses briefly to think and shuffles his feet, which are clad in an old pair of pink Asics trainers. 'It's like it says in the gospel: "Fill up your stomach with food, but fill your mind with words." That is why it is important for us to come together sometimes and encourage each other. Some people say that athletes only think with their legs. Let us show them that we are thinking with our minds, we are breathing with our lungs as we lead ourselves by our own minds.' There is murmured assent and the nodding of heads, but this proves to be difficult to follow. Mekasha has drawn attention to the realities of the sport; that you might not be strong enough, and have to return home; that you may have only your health to show for years of toil. But that the group is there as a potential source of support and inspiration, that should not be underestimated.

Most of the time Meseret feels that his job is primarily about creating a sense of togetherness and unity that will allow the runners to progress together without overdoing things. The idea is that they will run together, and therefore know that everyone else is doing the same thing and not trying to gain an advantage unfairly, and this is why it is so important to him that people don't miss any of the group training sessions. When at one point we have to cancel two sessions because of protests in the outskirts of Addis Ababa, the runners come back in various states of exhaustion and end up strung out along the road rather than in the usual group formation. Meseret explains that this is because some of them saw this time without group training as an opportunity to push the intensity of their training up in order to improve before returning to the group. Operating as a team is explicitly intended to protect the energy levels, livelihoods and dreams of all the individuals within it.

Underlying all of the emphasis on teamwork and improving together, though, is the reality that sooner or later everyone has to compete as an individual. The first race abroad is vitally important for any young athlete. With the sheer number of runners seeking an opportunity to run abroad, performing poorly in your first race overseas can make it your last, or else mean a long process of proving again that you are ready to run at that level. I wonder what it must be like to board a plane for the first time in such circumstances and how it must feel to run at sea level when you have never in your life been below 2000 metres in altitude. When Selamyhun goes to the Istanbul half marathon with Bogale, who, as he puts it, has never been 'outside' before, I decide to go with them.

11

THE GAME IS WORTH THE CANDLE

The elite athlete hotel at a major road race is like a boarding school for narcoleptics. The days are timetabled for you, and you are told what to do and where to be by race staff. Meals are eaten communally and it is very rare for anyone to leave the confines of the hotel except to jog. And if you are not being told what to do or jogging, it is very likely that you will be asleep. I share a room at the Istanbul half marathon with Ben Somikwo, a young Ugandan runner at only his second overseas race. When I arrive and let myself into our room, all the lights are on and Nigerian gospel music plays loudly from a phone. Ben, however, is fast asleep. I sit down on my bed and he wakes up. 'Oh, hello,' he says, rubbing his eyes. 'When will it be 7.30?' I tell him it will be 7.30 in about half an hour and he nods, turns over and promptly goes back to sleep. I assume 7.30 is dinnertime.

Before the gun goes off for the race on Sunday morning, there is the anti-race. The competition to see who can conserve the most energy; who can avoid the stairs the most; who can spend the most hours sleeping and the least time worrying. I get the feeling Ben is going to be an absolute champion at this.

I think back to my first encounter with the Ethiopian legend Haile Gebrselassie, in a conference room of the Millenium Hotel in Glasgow's George Square. The hotel had been taken over for the Great Scottish Run and I sat nervously with the other Scottish runners, feeling more than a little out of place in the company of some of East Africa's best athletes. We shared the kind of pre-race chatter you will hear before any race, anywhere. We ensured that everyone knew that we'd had a cold, a niggle, an interrupted build-up to the race of some kind. Some stretched, others fiddled with safety pins. A Spanish runner used a long elastic band to try to get some flexibility into his early morning hamstrings.

And then Haile walked in, a big smile on his face, his chest puffed out in a combination of pride and simple barrel-chested lung capacity. The room fell silent. The Emperor had arrived. I remember vividly the contrast between his smile and the tension on the faces around him. Carefully, Haile placed his bag against a wall and a chair just the right distance from it that he could lie with the bag as a pillow and his feet up on the chair. He interlaced his fingers on his chest and had the 20-minute snooze of a man slightly fatigued from a morning of gardening.

On the way to the start line he obliged, first, all those who wanted to take his photo on the way. He wished other runners good luck, hoisted a child into the air for a father's iPhone. Like a politician, his smile never wavered. Unlike a politician, his smile seemed genuine, infectious. There was nowhere, apparently, he would rather be. This is the kind of calm I now try to channel before a race, reminding myself that I'm there because I want to be, because I enjoy this. As any runner will know, though, this is easier said than done when you start to feel the nerves building. Staying in a hotel with all of your competitors for two days before a race it is more or less impossible to avoid.

I knock on the door of Selamyhun and Bogale's hotel room, and Selamyhun opens it with a tub of beige powder in his hand. 'Ah, Mike,' he says. 'You're just in time for *beso*!' *Beso* time happens about three times a day in the lead-up to the race. They have each bought two kilos of the so-called Ethiopian power bar – the roasted, powdered barley that's made into a drink – with them, in their hand luggage along with their racing shoes. Bogale, who has been sleeping, jumps out of bed and says, '*Ej wada lay!*' – 'hands in the air!' – his favourite phrase at the moment, picked up during obligatory army drills with the Ethiopian Defence Club. This show of bravura masks an anxiety Bogale never shows in Ethiopia, though. For the most part he has become quiet and withdrawn, not his usual ebullient self. He repeats '*Ej wada lay!*' every few minutes, like a mantra. 'Even when my sister called I said, "*Ej wada lay!*" to her,' he tells me. 'It was to reassure her that everything is fine.' I think it is more a case of him trying to reassure himself and hope he can gain some confidence by the time the race starts.

These bursts of energy also belie their tiredness, they tell me at dinner. Since their race earlier in the week in Bursa, several hundred kilometres away in north-western Turkey, they have been doing *zur* – laps – but in the off-the-track sense of activity that is detrimental, because it prevents you from resting effectively. They flew to Istanbul the week before and then on to Bursa for a 15-kilometre race in which they finished second and third in just over 44 minutes. Large portions of the race were on what Selamyhun calls 'ceramic' – hard tiles that beat up their legs. They then took a nine-hour bus trip to Denizli, where they stayed with Moyo Sports' sub-agent in Turkey, Khalid Azza. From there they took another nine-hour bus ride back to Istanbul, arriving last night. Because they are 'fresh' athletes who are yet to build up an international profile, the idea is for them to gain experience in Turkey by running two kinds of race, a relatively small one (in Bursa), and then a big and highly competitive race in Istanbul.

Khalid is more than just a sub-agent. He plays the roles of host, training partner and impromptu motivational speaker. He is also, seemingly, indefatigable. He comes from Morocco and was once a serious runner himself, but is now settled in Turkey and fluent in Turkish. He ran the race with them in Bursa and had to be at work on the Monday morning following the bus journey. He trained with them morning and evening either side of a full-time job in international trade. He arrives tonight having jumped on a flight from Denizli to Istanbul, straight after work, and bounces into the restaurant.

As we sit waiting to eat we eye up the competition. Watching the Kenyan athletes pad around the hotel it's hard to believe they can move at any speed at all. Leonard Patrick Komon wears hotel slippers, a pair of basketball shorts and, incongruously, a big black leather jacket. He walks tentatively, like he's checking with each step that the ground can support his weight. 'You see that guy?' Khalid asks Selamyhun. 'He's run 26 minutes for 10 kilometres on the road.' This was in Utrecht in 2010, when he ran a world record, and scarcely believable, 26.44. Selamyhun's name means 'Let there be peace' and he is normally very easy going. Suddenly he looks vulnerable, younger than his 19 years. 'On the *road?*' he says. 'That's impossible.'

I wish Khalid hadn't said anything. Our coach in Addis Ababa talks a lot about what he sees as the 'psychological weakness' of Ethiopian athletes and the challenge of nurturing their confidence alongside their fitness. In Ethiopia, that English term 'condition', used by athletes to describe what shape they are in, has come to mean far more than just an approximation of fitness. If athletes seem complacent before a race they are described as 'over-condition', implying that 'condition' is as much a psychological state as it is a physical one.

Meseret, with his masters in sports science, decries the fact that many athletes believe that energy can be drawn from the trees or from the sun, or that the results of a race will ultimately be determined by God. And yet these beliefs feed a runner's confidence and are highly influential. In travelling to higher and higher places to train, athletes are hunting elusive 'condition', which is why everyone always exaggerates the altitudes involved. As both a psychological and a physical state, 'condition' is a fickle and mysterious entity which 'comes and goes' with little warning. It therefore needs constant and unwavering attention, and a few misplaced words can have a disastrous effect.

The downside of the faith Selamyhun has in the power of altitude is that the alchemy of his belief is reversible. He believes the power is a transient one, prone to evaporate at any time. This is only the second time he has been to sea level and I suspect that this adaptation is a learning curve just as steep as the one travelling the other way. I always find it takes me a while to trust the extra oxygen in the air and my legs' run-away desire to go faster. This feeling must be far more pronounced in someone who has spent his entire life above 2500 metres.

I've seen Selamyhun run 44 minutes for 15 kilometres in Sendafa, at 2700 metres, with an uphill opening 10 kilometres. It is therefore staggering to me that he couldn't run faster the week before in Turkey. I would run 46 something for 15 kilometres at sea level (based on a 10-mile best of 49.37), but if I could break 52 in Sendafa I'd be over the moon. It's that much harder. I tell him to trust his feeling on Sunday, but I can see his confidence is on the wane. 'I can feel my condition ebbing away. We've been away from Ethiopia too long,' Selamyhun says. 'It's only been six days,' I remind him. '*Chigger yellum*.' No problem.

I suspect he's suffering mainly from having had an excessive amount of time to sit thinking about the race. In his book about the Ali-Foreman World Heavyweight Championship fight in Kinshasa, titled simply *The Fight*, Norman Mailer writes of 'the quiet boredom of men who are obliging themselves not to feel tension too early.' This ability to suspend nervousness is a difficult one to cultivate and if you're unable to do so the physical toll can't be underestimated. I join Selamyhun and Bogale for post-dinner *beso* – 'There is no problem with *beso*, Mike, only condition' – and as I leave Selamyhun says, 'Don't worry, Mike, men may die of sickness, but not just because they are scared.' I hope he's able to maintain this attitude until Sunday morning.

A training run has been organised for the following morning at 6.30 a.m. A shuttle will pick us up from the hotel, which is in a busy part of town, and take us somewhere more conducive to jogging. Everyone heads to bed at 9 p.m. I am wide awake, so I sneak out for a beer when no-one is watching. It really does feel like boarding school. Twenty-eight-year-old men shouldn't feel this guilty about having a beer on a Friday night. When I get back to the room I find it impossible to sleep. The fact that Ben is sleeping like a baby, with the light on and the television tuned to a gratuitously violent Korean drama, and isn't disturbed by my entrance but continues to snore gently, is infuriating. The ability to sleep in a stuffy, unfamiliar hotel room in a bed next to someone you only just met is a real gift for a distance runner. I finally fall asleep around 2 a.m., having turned my alarm clock off, reasoning that my body probably needs sleep more badly than it needs to jog.

* * *

There's an infernal racket at the door. Selamyhun is banging furiously on it and shouting, 'Mike, training!' I look across and Ben hasn't moved since the night before. He is blissfully unaware of the banging. Sleepily I make my way across to the door. Selamyhun is bright-eyed and incredulous. 'Mike, *minden naw?*' he says, '*Libes, libes!*' – 'What the hell? Clothes, clothes!' Before I can say I'm not actually feeling 100 per cent up for going jogging just now, thank you very much, he is thrusting my tracksuit top into my hands and has succeeded in shaking Ben awake, saying, 'Training, training!' Ben, who presumably had heard nothing about the training run the night before, accepts this with a nod as relatively normal behaviour, sits up on the side of his bed, stretches and says, 'Thank you, Jesus!' He says this quite a lot. He is very grateful.

Before I know it we've been bustled into the lift and chaperoned on to the bus, where everyone else is waiting patiently to go to training. For the second time in a few hours I feel like a naughty schoolboy. We are driven to a patch of waste ground made up of stubbly grass and dirt, about 400 metres by 50. The Turkish athletes are off the bus first and, gingerly, we all start to run together. The Turkish guys keep glancing back, clearly wondering why some of the fastest runners in the world look like they're just trying out jogging for the first time and aren't too sure about it at all. Our first kilometre takes six and a half minutes.

191

Gradually, though, and predictably, the pace is wound up, first to four minutes per kilometre and then to well under that. This is not quite what I'm in the mood for at 7 a.m. after four hours of sleep. I look across at Leonard Patrick Komon, who floats serenely across the ground with his mouth closed. I feel like I'm running through a different medium to the others. I also feel like I'm coming down with something, the beginnings of a cold lodged in my throat, and my legs feeling sluggish and heavy. Eventually the pace rises enough that people start to drop off and slip into their own pre-race rituals of drills and stretching. Bogale leans nonchalantly against a tree as I jog past. 'Aren't you full?' he asks me in Amharic. 'We haven't had breakfast yet,' I reply. 'No, aren't you full of running?' he says. 'It's enough, race tomorrow.'

By mid-afternoon I'm definitely sick. I go down to the lobby and find most of the Kenyans and the Eritrean Zersenay Tadese, one-time world record holder for the half marathon, sipping tea. I sit with Tadese who introduces himself to me as he spoons sugar into his tea. By the fifth absent-minded teaspoonful I think perhaps I'm distracting him and point to his cup, which is in danger of overflowing. He adds one more spoonful before carefully stirring. The small cup is at least half sugar. I ask him how he's feeling before the race and he shrugs. I ask him what time he expects to run and he grins sheepishly and says, 'At this point, we don't know.'

I've seen the footage of his 58.23 half marathon. He is on his own for most of the race, hammering out a relentless and unbelievable tempo. There is no wasted energy; he somehow seems to run – in defiance of physical laws – with no upward movement at all. It is mesmerising to watch. 'How did you feel that day in Lisbon?' I ask him. I want to know how it felt to run a sub 28-minute 10 kilometres and then *do it again*. How was it possible to pour out that much speed and energy in less than an hour? 'My body felt good that day,' he says. 'There were no limits.' I ask him if he's felt like that before or since. 'Once or twice,' he says.

It is a rare state of body and mind that allows an athlete to run under three minutes per kilometre for an hour. To run even faster is rarer still and to have a transcendent day like that one in Lisbon happens once or twice in a career, if at all. I had spoken to Ryan Hall, the American record holder in the half marathon, about these moments when he was in Addis earlier in the year. He said that when he ran his 59.43 American record for the half marathon, running every step of the race alone in Houston in 2007, he had a 'once in a career day' where he thought 'anything was possible.' In hindsight, he said he wished he had trusted the feeling and gone even harder.

When we spoke in Ethiopia Ryan was in the process of accepting that his career was coming to an end, having struggled with inexplicably low energy levels and poor performances for a couple of years. He told me he had spent the best part of the last 10 years fighting his body in the hope of having one more day like that. Countless thousands of training hours were encompassed by that one hour of transcendent running. 'Those 60 minutes made all those years of work worth it,' he told me. He felt like he was doing what he was made to do.

But is it possible to describe that feeling in words? Of course not. Even David Foster Wallace, who describes sporting genius better than anyone else I've read, put it like this: 'The real secret behind top athletes' genius may be as esoteric and obvious and dull and profound as silence itself.' If it is a mystery to the athletes themselves, then we mere mortals can hardly expect to articulate it. When I asked Ryan what he thought was the most frustrating thing about running, he said it was that it was 'impossible to isolate one variable' to explain why he wasn't running well. He would spend whole runs trying to think of little things he could change or improve upon. How could he get slightly more sleep? Tweak an already exhaustively considered diet? Change a meticulously planned training schedule *again*? The problem, he realised, was that sometimes you just mysteriously feel incredible and there is no way of pinpointing why. And perhaps it is this mystery that attracts people to running. For the Ethiopian runners I know it is definitely more art than science. For each day of feeling mysteriously good, though, there are usually others spent feeling inexplicably awful, and being able to process that is an important part of being a runner.

On race morning Ben's alarm goes off at 5.20 a.m. He rolls over and says, 'Yes! I will get up,' before promptly falling back to sleep until my own alarm at 6 a.m. We sit facing each other on the side of our beds and he looks at me and says, 'We are about…' I rub my eyes. 'We are about?' I ask. 'Yes! We are about… to go!' he exclaims. I now definitely have a full-blown cold and I'm glad that he seems to have enough enthusiasm for both of us. After breakfast we are bundled back into the bus and taken to the start on the coast. Hailye had texted me the night before to say good luck, and I'd replied saying I had a cold and was feeling pretty awful. I read his response on the bus to the start. 'Don't worry, Mike,' it said, '*Gunfan condition naw*' – 'a cold is an indicator of condition.'

There is definitely a fine line between being in top shape as a distance runner and being ill. You have to get as close to that edge as possible without going over it. I'd never heard of a cold being seen as a sign that you must be fit, but in a way (I try to convince myself) it makes sense. As I warm up with Selamyhun and Bogale

I tell myself that I will be fine once the adrenaline starts flowing. 'What's your plan for the race?' I ask Selamyhun. I wonder whether he might consider setting off a little slower than the leaders, given that two world record holders are targeting a sub 60-minute race. 'What do you mean?' comes the response. 'I will go with the leaders for as long as I can.'

The course is a long out-and-back along the coast, and I go through two miles in about 10 minutes and feel awful. I can still just about see the lead group with Bogale and Selamyhun gamely hanging on at the back, and I will them to keep it up. I am slowing down already and have accepted by five kilometres that it is not going to be my day. Approaching the turning point I see Zersenay Tadese hammering along at the front of the group, with Selamyhun still holding on for dear life at the back. Bogale is already a hundred or so metres behind and looks to have accepted, as I have, that his race is run. By the time I get to the turn I'm feeling truly awful and slow to a walk in the hope that I can jump in one of the race cars for the women's race. When no cars appear, I realise that the best way to get back to the start is actually going to be to run and start to jog tentatively again.

First, the lead women whir past, their steps light and their breathing quiet. Then the serious Turkish club runners, and older athletes with eccentric breathing patterns and running styles honed over many years competing at races like this. They pass me without looking, focused on the road ahead and their own races. After 10 or 15 minutes of jogging the number of people passing me starts to increase rapidly and suddenly I am in a throng of brightly coloured t-shirts. It occurs to me that this is the only time I've ever run in the middle of the field like this. People are actually talking to each other. They ask if I'm OK. There are smiles. Someone has a selfie stick and another group stop for a photo with some friends at the side of the road. I realise I am thoroughly enjoying running in such a huge mass of people, the sense of collective endeavour infectious. My mood is completely transformed.

I don't catch up with Selamyhun and Bogale until we got back to the hotel. Selamyhun had slowed dramatically over the last eight kilometres and ran a shade over 64 minutes. Bogale ran over 66 minutes, slower than my own half marathon best. I'd seen him run so much faster than that in Sendafa, over huge hills and with 30 per cent less oxygen to breathe. It seems pretty clear that the pressure of racing has been too much for them and I expect them to be disappointed. By the time I get back to the hotel, though, they seem to have already processed the fact that they didn't run well on this occasion and they are already looking to the future.

'Today it was not my day,' Selamyhun tells me. 'But, you know, maybe it wasn't my time to run well. Maybe if I had won all that money I would have bought a car and died in a car crash. God will know when I am ready to win big money.' This way of thinking is connected to the beliefs in *idil* I have already described. The way to best cultivate your *idil* or 'chance' is to live virtuously and train hard, above all with patience. By leaving the final word to God, there is an acceptance that in spite of what you do in training and how hard you work it may just not be your time. This sense that everything will work out in the end as long as you approach your running with the right disposition, and approach training and racing without expectation, makes it easier, in turn, to cope psychologically with success and failure.

Khalid has also had a slightly disappointing run and tells me that he has struggled to motivate himself to train hard since arriving in Turkey from Morocco. 'When I get my Turkish citizenship,

196

I will start to train hard again,' he says. 'Then maybe I can make a national team. It will be worth it then.' It occurs to me that a large part of what keeps us running are the stories we tell ourselves about ourselves, and that crucially these stories are oriented towards the future. The French sociologist Pierre Bourdieu would understand this in terms of *illusio*, the process by which people make their activities and actions meaningful to themselves. Connected to the latin word *ludus*, meaning game, the term *illusio* suggests a playful act of meaning-making in which imagined futures play a big role. Crucially, for anthropologist Robert Desjarlais, *illusio* is 'forward-looking, as it is tied to a person's ideas of future endeavours and commitments.' I think there are few places where this is more true than with distance running.

In deciding to become athletes, the Ethiopian runners I know have made a conscious choice to try to 'change their lives' through running, which has meant restructuring their lives according to a definable set of future goals. They have had to convince themselves, as Bourdieu puts it, that *'Le jeu en vaut la chandelle'* – the game is worth the candle that is burned to play it. While the sacrifices may be greater for most Ethiopian athletes, these are choices all runners make to a greater or lesser extent. We must all come up with ways to convince ourselves that the game is worth the candle. The way in which running encourages us to think forward and focus on the future makes processing a bad race easier. After a couple of hours all four of us are plotting a next race.

'I think I want to run a marathon before I give up,' Khalid says. 'I want to – how do you say it? Meet the wall.' I had found out about a week before the race in Istanbul that the Manchester marathon course where I ran 2.19.39 in 2015 was a couple of hundred metres short. I had, therefore, gone from thinking of myself as a sub-2.20 marathon runner to suddenly not even *being* a marathon runner. Like Khalid, I knew that I didn't want to give up on serious running until I'd run 2.20 for real. And Selamyhun was already plotting his return. 'I won't take any rest,' he said. 'I'll go to my club and train hard and come back stronger.' Within a couple of hours we had all gone from feeling despondent to having a newfound sense of purpose. Through setting goals and thinking to the future we were each playing conjuring tricks with ourselves to keep ourselves going.

12

TAKING THE AIR

Selamyhun pitches the idea to me over the phone a few days after our return from Istanbul. He is back at his club, the Amhara Water Works Construction Enterprise (AWWCE) athletics club, near Gondar, and his voice, 600 kilometres away from where I sit in the compound in Addis, keeps breaking up. 'You know altitude training?' he is saying. 'Of course,' I reply. 'I came to Ethiopia to train, didn't I?' I can almost hear him shaking his head. 'No, no, Mike. This is altitude training for people who live in Addis.' The club is 3100 metres above sea level in a remote area of the highlands. It sounds exhausting. I book a week-long trip, keen to get a sense for where Selamyhun started his career.

On the final leg of my journey, all I know is that I have to get a bus heading west. Abere and Birhanu are both spending some time at the club too, recovering from marathons. Abere tells me he will call once I'm en route and I should give my phone to the driver so he can tell him where to drop me off. Given the unpredictability of the phone network this is not the most watertight of plans. Sure enough though, an hour into the journey he phones and asks to speak to the driver, who tells me not to worry. The bus has been climbing steadily since we left

Debre Tabor, the nearest town, and the temperature is getting noticeably colder.

We gradually come to a halt in the shadow of a forested mountain, and the driver turns to me and tells me that I have arrived. The only buildings look like a series of barrack dormitories in a stubble field surrounded by barbed wire. The other passengers look at me expectantly. Was this really where the *farenj* was trying to go? I'm thinking the same thing and slightly unsure about whether to get out of the bus until, finally, Selamyhun scampers out of the nearest building, closely followed by a large number of curious athletes in matching blue tracksuits. He pulls me out of the bus, slings my bag over his shoulder and announces that it is time for a tour.

We are accompanied by coach Desaleyn, who has a dramatically receding hairline but who at 35 is young for a coach and wears his blue tracksuit top tucked into matching bottoms, and Gebre, the athlete representative in the camp and seemingly also the head of PR for AWWCE. 'Our enterprise is responsible for 74 projects, building roads and getting water,' he tells me, before offering me a bottle of Guna mountain water, named for the nearby mountain and produced by the company. They often refer to the club simply as 'Guna', a sign of the importance of the mountain. First they show me the dining room. A meal plan taped to the wall has pasta for breakfast on two days and suggests a diet heavy in carbohydrates and vegetables.

The club is one of many that were set up with the support of the EAF, with the idea being that they would be funded in part by the state and enterprises like the water company, and in part by the towns themselves. The implementation of the new clubs has been varied, with some of them chronically underfunded and lacking in resources, as documented in the award-winning 2012 documentary *Town of Runners,* which follows two runners from Bekoji who have very different experiences at the clubs they are sent to. This particular club is well equipped, and the runners receive a salary and three meals a day in the canteen. This kind of support, which is offered to hundreds of runners across the different clubs in the region, makes local competition fierce – and thus the odds against performing well enough to progress to Addis high.

Desaleyn fiercely wants the athletes he works with to succeed, but he is aware that a career in athletics will not be possible for all of them. Many runners therefore alternate between attending school in the mornings and training in the afternoons, and vice versa, keeping both options open, but extending the amount of time they are at school for. A few of the athletes in their mid-twenties are therefore still attending school, the salary they are paid by the club enabling them to do so. They show me the room where we will be staying, three single beds and two portraits on the wall, one of the Virgin Mary and one of Meles Zenawi, the late Prime Minister of Ethiopia. The rooms are all shared and Desaleyn believes strongly that avoiding spending time alone is vital to avoid athletes losing hope. 'If they stay on their own there is the problem of thinking too much,' he says.

This is especially important for those athletes who are unable to run for a period of time due to injury or illness, and Desaleyn is keen to point out the links he sees between physical activity and mental health. 'When they are running it is OK,' he tells me, 'because even if they are feeling worried about the future in the afternoon, they will go for a run and it will relax them and they will come back feeling happy.' This is definitely something I can relate to, having experienced running as a comforting way of bookending the day for years. 'You know what it's like,' he goes on. 'It's a kind of addiction.' Next is the gym room, with home-made weights with wooden bars and cement ends, made by dipping the pole into cans of wet cement. 'They're not perfect,' Desaleyn says. 'You have to swap sides after 10 reps to make sure you don't get out of balance,' he adds, demonstrating. 'Anyway, the weights aren't that important. What we really want to show you is our track.'

He sets off up a faint path in the grass outside the building. On the hike up the hill a farmer joins us, casually sowing seeds to each side of the path using the same motion the athletes use in one of their warm-down exercises. Worryingly, I note the difficulty of making conversation at this altitude even when just walking. I ask the farmer what he thinks about the runners, whether he minds them running all over his fields. He likes to watch them run, he says, adding, 'I try to help in any way I can.' Behind us, one of the athletes who has tagged along is laughing. 'Potatoes,' he says. 'That's how he helps.' The coach says the local farmers weren't always so supportive. When they first started the camp many of the farmers had never heard of the exploits of Abebe Bikila or Haile Gebrselassie. 'They used to shout, 'Stop, stop! Even a horse can't run like that! Your heart will explode!' he says, 'They thought we were crazy.'

Finally we reach the top of the hill, where a clearly defined grass track has been etched into the grass with millions of lung-sapping steps. At first they marked it out with stones, Desaleyn tells me, but the inside lane is now permanently marked into the ground. 'From here,' he says, gesturing, 'you can see in all four directions.' The ground slopes downwards from all sides of the track, which sits on its own plateau. He then points away down one slope and adds, 'Down there you can see the cloud level.' The track is 3100 metres above sea level, he reminds me. 'Sports scientists say it is too high,' he says. 'They say it is inadvisable.' He looks thoughtful. 'And what do you think?' I venture. 'It is advisable,' he says simply. 'When you go to other places, that's simple to win.'

Kimir Dingay, the settlement where the track is located, literally means 'Pile of stones'. Apart from the camp, it is an apt description. There is not much here, which is, I suppose, the point of a training camp. 'This is virgin land,' coach Desaleyn tells me. 'The air is special'. It is a place where it is possible to 'bring change' for the young runners. I recall that Sentayehu, who has discovered so many world-beating Ethiopian runners, predicted that the next crop would come not from Bekoji but from another high-altitude place, where there were fewer preconceptions about the sport. Desaleyn, whose name means Excited, is extremely proud of the altitude and keeps asking me to check it with an altitude app on my phone, before comparing it to the other camps he knows about. These have similarly enigmatic names and I feel a bit like I've wandered into *Lord of the Rings*. 'They say that Feras Bet (The Place of the Horses) is high,' he says, 'but it's not as high as Kimir Dingay.' Another athlete chips in with, 'They say the highest is Nefas Mawucha (The Place Where the Wind Comes),' which elicits vigorous head-shaking from Coach Desaleyn.

Desaleyn explains that Kimir Dingay got its name during the Era of Lords, the period of Ethiopian history from the mid-18th to mid-19th centuries when the country was ruled by regional princes and feudal lords. Before going off to war, troops from the area were instructed to place one stone each on a pile. Those who returned from battle had to move their stone to a different pile in order to count how many soldiers had been lost. 'If you did that with the runners, with a pile for those who made it and a pile for those that didn't, which would be bigger?' I ask. 'The pile of those that didn't would be a mountain,' Desaleyn says. I am reminded of famous American coach Jack Daniels' joke about the eggs against the wall theory of coaching, whereby if you get enough athletes training incredibly hard some of them will make it – or if you throw a basket of eggs against a wall, if you're lucky one of them won't break. I will learn, though, that life in the camp is less about training hard as it is about doing things right and waiting for progress to come gradually.

The three Moyo Sports athletes explain to me why they have come back to the club. 'We come here on the bus,' Selamyhun tells me, grinning, 'we spend two weeks collecting condition, and then we put it in our bags and take it back to Addis!' He is here because he is frustrated with himself after Istanbul. It makes sense for Birhanu and Abere to come here following a marathon, because they can get the same aerobic benefit at a slower pace while recovering from the battering their legs took in their marathons. 'You get into good shape just from running six minutes per kilometre in Kimir Dingay,' Birhanu assures me, which makes me feel better about my chances of running with them this week. They refer to it as 'taking the air', which makes it sound somewhat leisurely and Victorian, although I suspect it will be anything but.

Coming all the way up to the Guna camp is an extreme example of something all Ethiopian runners do – letting the environment shape the way they train. If you need to recuperate and save energy, you seek the terrain that will best allow you to do this, that will force you to run slowly. When we think of East African runners the assumption is that they simply *work harder* and push themselves to run faster than we do. There is, of course, an element of truth to this. Often, though, it is not hard work but cleverness that they emphasise – the ability to know when to push and to know when to take it easy. There is an obvious expertise in their speed, but there is also, at times, an expertise in their slowness.

* * *

The next morning we wake up at 5.50 a.m., and the temperature is barely above freezing. Selamyhun hurriedly changes into two tracksuits before getting back into bed for a few more minutes of warmth. I can hear people knocking on doors down the corridor. It is impossible to sleep in and miss training here. A group of about 30 of us shuffle outside to find coach Desaleyn in a thick tracksuit, top tucked into bottoms as usual, with a stopwatch round his neck. We walk a few hundred metres to the edge of the forest, where he surprises me by announcing that he is going to lead the run today himself. I can't imagine a coach in Addis doing this. As we start to jog slowly, in two single-file lines, he tells me that he ran 30.05 for 10 kilometres and 14.34 for 5 kilometres – at altitude – before concluding that he didn't have the ability to make it as a runner. I tell him that I have run two seconds slower than him for 10 kilometres and he asks me what altitude I ran my best time at. I tell him I'm not sure of the exact altitude of Leeds, but that it is probably around 50 metres.

'This place is perfect,' Desaleyn tells me as we run uphill into the forest. 'The air is clean and pure and free of pollution.' And oxygen, I think, as I will my lungs to work harder. We make our way up the slope in a gradual zigzag as he tells me how difficult it is to keep the best athletes in the camp. With so much more money available for running on the roads, and so few international opportunities on the track, this is becoming an increasing problem. Selamyhun, he says, is built for the 5000m. He can run under 14 minutes at high altitude and Desaleyn thinks he could get down to 13.30 in a couple of years. 'That means 12.50 outside of Ethiopia,' he says, 'but athletes are less interested in the track now. They are interested only in adjusting their life and to do that they have to run on the roads.' My instinct when talking about this is to blame the managers and I ask Desaleyn whether running a marathon so early was what Selamyhun had wanted. 'Selamyhun's idea?' he replies. 'Asphalt. Naturally he is built more for the track than asphalt, but there is no money, even if you run a lot of races.'

A couple of years previously, when he was just 17, Selamyhun won the Amhara region 5000m. He had never run on asphalt before in his life and the longest run he had ever done was one and a half hours of 'jogging' in the forest. A manager came to the race and asked him if he wanted to run a marathon in China. He jumped at the chance. 'He was just a little boy at that time,' Desaleyn says. 'He only weighed 49 kilos.' I've heard the story of his first marathon from Selamyhun before. He told me his legs were 'very loaded' after 15 kilometres, shocked by the hard surface. Somehow, he finished fifth in 2.15. To this day he hasn't seen the money from that first race. Selamyhun briefly moved to Addis assuming that now he had a manager he would train there, but they disappeared with his money and that of the first- and second-placed finishers. 'I don't like that guy,' Desaleyn says. 'Really I don't like him. Because I hate him actually.' I'm not surprised. Selamyhun had to return to the club, and several of the other runners at his club, and at other clubs I visit, have similar stories of unscrupulous and unregistered agents going directly to athletes in rural areas, who have little choice but to trust them in exchange for a chance. Rather than a straightforward trajectory from rural club to a club in Addis, and then a management group and opportunities to run abroad, this was often experienced as a cyclical process, characterised by ups and downs and frustration.

Given that Desaleyn was coaching Selamyhun for the 5000m at the time, he is relieved that Selamyhun wasn't injured by that first experience of the marathon and confident he can break 60 minutes for a half marathon. 'Athletics is like the terrain here, it has many ups and downs,' he says, echoing Fasil. I ask him about Abere, Birhanu and Selamyhun returning to the camp. 'All of the boys who go to Addis like to come back,' he says. 'Things are simpler here.' We run in silence for a few minutes, two abreast in a long train of athletes, heads down against the effort. Finally we emerge from the mist and the trees grow thin enough for Desaleyn to leave the narrow path we've been following and wind his way through them. We must have climbed a couple of hundred metres to around 3300 metres above sea level by now and conversation is beyond me as I slip down the train of athletes.

The runners in the group today specialise in distances ranging from 800m to 10,000m and even one of the javelin throwers has tagged along. To accommodate this range of ability, when we get to an open space Desaleyn quickens the pace, but runs long, gradual arcs around the fields, frequently turning back to allow the stragglers (myself included) to get back to the group. Some of the runners have been told to run for 50 minutes, some for 60 and some for 70, so small groups gradually peel off, and start doing drills and strides together. It is a great example of how to accommodate runners of varying ability and discipline while making the most of a group environment.

I stop with Desaleyn after an hour and we watch the athletes hurtling backwards and forwards running 150-metre sprints. This is how all runs end, he says. 'It doesn't matter how good your endurance is, raw speed is still the most important thing. They have to run together like this in order to adapt to the kick during competition.' Asres, who is going to the World Junior Championships in Poland in the 1500m, is slightly off the back as a group flashes past. '*Asres, gaba tempo!*' Literally this means, 'Enter the tempo.' The belief in improving *together* is incredibly strong here. Speed is something you can slip into, an adaptation to another person. As Abere runs past, Desaleyn shakes his head. 'When he runs on asphalt too much he tightens his body. He contracts his body more and more. Even his hands are tight. That influences his running return.' Abere has always run like this to my knowledge, hunched like he's trying to squeeze the last few drops out of an invisible, internal bag of energy. 'He has run a 2.08 marathon, though,' I point out. It seems to be working for him. 'To be honest, he should be running 2.06,' Desaleyn says.

In spite of his disapproval of athletes going abroad too young, when another athlete runs past he shouts, 'Telahun, what the hell? Your friend went all the way to Turkey to run and you're just sleeping here!' He knows that the lure of money on the roads is the easiest way to motivate people. After training, the athletes come together for a meeting. The farm kids rush around trying to find stones for them to sit on before retreating to a respectful distance and watching intently. Then we all join hands, stomp in time with each other and, preferring to associate the club with the mountain than the water company, chant, 'Our squad, Guna!'

* * *

The next morning we run in the forest on Mount Guna itself, Ethiopia's second highest mountain. By the time we walk to the edge of the forest we are all shivering violently. It is close to freezing again and pouring with icy rain. We run in a long single-file train behind Desaleyn. Tomorrow the athletes will start 'heavy' interval training, Desaleyn tells me, so today the aim is to run as slowly as possible. As I've learned, though, more often than not this means picking out terrain that is almost impossible to run on, in case they happen to feel good and push too hard by accident. Looking up at the mountain I suspect that today might be a textbook example of this approach.

We start very slowly and Desaleyn follows tiny mud-slicked paths running along the steep hillside, so that it takes all of my concentration just to stay upright. Every now and then we cross what looks to me like a perfect running trail, two metres wide and covered in gravel. I just have time to appreciate the infinitely more runnable surface before we're back in the forest again. Before long we meet a five-foot high stone wall, and Desaleyn scrambles over it on his hands and knees, followed by the athletes, a couple of whom have to help each other over. I feel like we're on some sort of army exercise, not a training run. 'Coach is crazy sometimes,' Birhanu whispers as he pushes me over the wall.

For the next 20 minutes the slope is so steep that we are walking more than we are running, using our hands to pull ourselves up using the tree roots and shouting to each other through the mist, which by this stage is so thick that we can scarcely see two feet in front of us. This is no exaggeration. I'm genuinely concerned that I'm going to get lost for ever on this mountain. Desaleyn is certainly achieving his goal of not having us run too fast, at least. When we reach the top of the slope we run across fields so rutted from ploughing that the only way to do a convincing imitation of running is to take exaggerated strides across the furrows. We run in this peculiar, plyometric-like way, stretching our muscles and then suddenly contracting them, for 10 minutes, before winding our way back down to where we started. We've been out for an hour and 10 minutes. My hands are covered in mud and scratched from hauling my way up the slope. I feel like I've been on a five-hour hike, not a run.

When we get back to the camp everyone strips down to their shorts for an outdoor shower. It can't be warmer than three degrees. I decide to skip this particular bit of masochism. 'Aren't you cold, Birhanu?' I ask as he throws a bucket of water over his head and exhales loudly. 'No, hot!' he shouts back in English. 'I am a very dangerous man!'

In the afternoon Abere invites me to visit his family, whose farm is only a short journey in a *bajaj* – auto rickshaw – away. When we arrive, having threaded our way across a *teff* field and fended off the neighbours' dogs, we find Abere's grandmother barefooted and perched on the top of an enormous pile of firewood, sorting through it. 'She's 83, but she's strong,' Abere says. She clambers down and immediately starts offering us a bewildering array of food and drinks: coffee, *beso* made from barley, local beer, fresh pancake-like *injera* and warm butter, bread and *kolo*, an assortment of roasted grains like chick peas, barley and sunflower seeds. We settle on local beer – *tella* – which is poured until it is flush with the top of the glass. She watches intently as I drink it and when I fail to finish it in one go she turns to Abere and asks, 'What's wrong with this guy?'

Abere is built like a top marathon runner; he usually weighs 55 kilos and he looks lighter than that after his recent race at the Zurich marathon, where he finished second in 2.13.08 in terrible conditions. It snowed during the race and he says he didn't warm up until he got back to Addis. He returned full of admiration for Japanese runner Yuki Kawauchi, who finally broke him at 39 kilometres to take the win. 'That guy just pushed and pushed and pushed,' he tells me, before showing his family a photo of Kawauchi waiting at the finish to give him his bunch of flowers, a mark of appreciation for a 'valiant' race. In the podium photo Abere stands hunched against the cold, still in his running shorts and a borrowed woollen jumper. A week later, he still looks like he could do with spending a bit of time in the company of his grandmother.

Various other family members arrive and we are offered even more food as Abere is quizzed about his diet in Addis. 'Is the food grown nearby?' they ask. 'Is it fresh?' He tells them he buys it from the market: he's not sure. Much shaking of heads. As we talk, his grandmother makes fresh *injera* using *teff* she ground into flour that morning. 'This is from the field right outside,' she tells us. Ten metres away; it doesn't get much more local than that. The *injera* is served with warm melted butter (from one of the cows milling around outside) and *berbere*, the spice mix made from their chilli plants. 'You need to stay away from any food that comes in packets,' Abere's aunt is telling him. Sound advice. 'And foreign bananas. They're made of chemicals.' They are as keen as everyone else to impress the importance of *beso* on me, as are most of the runners. Abere calls it 'cultural juice' in English and swears by it. The farmers can keep going out in the fields all day long fuelled on only the liquid carbs of *beso* and *tella*, both made from the grains they are harvesting.

The *injera* is cooked on a huge metal hotplate over an open fire and the smoke soon fills the room. 'Is he OK?' Abere's grandmother asks him. 'Do they have smoke in his country?' I assure her, my eyes watering, that we do, but she looks doubtful. 'It must be modern smoke that they have,' she decides. Various kids run in to scoop up handfuls of *injera*, point at me and then career out into the fields again, laughing. In his ethnography of the Amhara, Donald Levine writes that when asked about their ambitions, many farmers answered simply, '*Sarto meblat*' – 'Having worked, to eat.' A simple ambition, perhaps, but one I can relate to given how much running we've been doing. We return to the camp so stuffed we can barely speak.

When we get back coach Desaleyn announces that we will decamp to Debre Tabor, the nearest town, for 'condition time' ahead of the Amhara region athletics championship in 10 days. Selamyhun, Abere and Birhanu won't compete, but this is an opportunity for the other runners in the club, who hope to follow in their footsteps and move to Addis, to prove themselves. The competition will be held in Bahir Dar at lower altitude, so he wants them to train somewhere where they can do some 'intense running'. In fact, Debre Tabor is only a few hundred metres lower and is still higher than Addis, but 2700 metres above sea level is an awful lot easier than 3100 metres.

* * *

We stay the night in a noisy boarding house and I wonder about the logic of taking the athletes out of a familiar (and quiet) environment days before a race. Doing some training at lower altitude makes sense, but we are only an hour's drive from the camp: we could have just driven to the track every day. Perhaps coach Desaleyn wants people to adapt to the stress of travelling for competition early. Ask the athletes, though, and they tell me that the main reason for being here is juice. There is no juice in the camp, but here the athletes get a 200 birr (£6) per diem, allowing them to eat a special pre-race diet. Most of the money goes on meat and avocado juice, which are seen as vital for 'condition'.

Birhanu, Abere, Selamyhun, Telahun and I go out to a *sega bet* or 'meat house' for dinner. The walls are plastered with lurid yellow and red posters for Giorgis beer, with life-size images of St George slaying the dragon. Huge slabs of ox meat hang in the adjoining butcher, which is daubed with a big red-painted cross. Meat is ordered by the kilo and Birhanu orders two kilos between the four of us. We are given a small paper ticket and sit down, the only ones in the room not drinking beer. When the meat arrives, one kilo is raw, the other cooked and cut into chunks with garlic and chilli. We eat by tearing off strips of *injera*, scooping up chunks of meat and dipping it into a red-hot mixture of chilli powder and mustard which hits me right between the eyes. By the time they've stopped watering, the meat has more or less disappeared and I realise I'm going to have to speed up in more ways than one if I'm going to be able to keep up with them. Birhanu goes to order more, with he and Abere as the wealthier athletes footing the bill. The raw beef is delicious, but I'm slightly nervous about how my stomach will react. When Birhanu returns to the table he brings a small glass of *areke*, a kind of home-brewed vodka that is often over 70 per cent proof, and pushes it in front of me. 'Better drink this,' he says, 'in case you're not used to the meat.'

We eat the remaining meat and the runners are clearly in high spirits – as I am after the *areke*. '*And zur!*' – one lap – Telahun says as he mops up the remaining meat with the last piece of *injera* in a sweeping oval. 'Fifty-five!' This, I assume, is the pace he imagines himself running the last lap of his race at the weekend. The connection between food and performance is incredibly strong, as ever. 'The reason he's running so well,' Selamyhun says, poking Telahun's bulging cheek before pointing to his midriff, 'is that everyone else's stomach ends here, but his goes right down into his legs.' I tell him we have an expression for that in English too: hollow legs. Telahun weighs a mere 48 kilos. Birhanu sits back in his chair, clearly very full. His equation for running success is succinct: '*Rucha, sega, birr*' he says. 'Running, meat, money.'

* * *

We spend another night in the boarding house in town, which is filling up with other teams who are here to compete. The building is scarcely finished, the walls inside the rooms a cold and unplastered concrete. There is one toilet for our floor of 30 or so athletes, and athletics kit that has been washed in the sink proliferates on the washing lines strung in the courtyard. The next morning we go to Old Airport, another improvised grass track. To get there we trek across farmland for 40 minutes, fending off guard dogs and the entreaties of farmers to eat and drink *tella* with them. This takes a while – refusing food is about the most offensive thing you can do in rural Ethiopia. We follow a dried-up river bank and eventually emerge on a plateau. There is no landing strip, but it's easy to see why the Derg regime, the military junta that ruled Ethiopia from the mid-1970s to the late 1980s, used this as an airport. It's much flatter than the track at the training camp. A small hut is all that is left of the airport itself. 'Before there was a sort of airport,' Abere explains in English, 'but now deleted.'

I go for a run with Birhanu, tracing the outlines of fields and 'using the diagonals' as Birhanu puts it, to ensure we don't run too fast. He is still recovering from running the Rome marathon a few weeks previously and wants to maintain his aerobic fitness without putting too much strain on his legs. This means sticking to a sloping camber and not going much faster than five minutes per kilometre, which certainly feels fast enough for me. I try to keep conversation going but find, as is often the case, that Amharic is harder to come by with an oxygen-starved brain.

We return to the track in time to watch the group train. This, certainly, will be a lesson in speed. They are doing 'lap training' today, close to 10,000m race pace. The extra few molecules of oxygen here equate to three seconds per lap according to coach Desaleyn. Telahun, Selamyhun and Abere are running 69 seconds per lap rather than the 72 they would run at the camp, and Telahun is making the others hurt. Last year Selamyhun beat him to gold in the 10,000m at the Amhara championship. The year before that, Abere won it. Telahun is determined to win this time so that he can move to Addis and start competing abroad.

They are supposed to run 16 laps at this pace. Abere lasts eight, his legs still in pieces after Zurich. 'Breathing,' he starts to tell me, before raising a finger in matter-of-fact excuse and turning to quietly vomit on the grass, 'really burns here. It's not like in Addis.' Selamyhun lasts 12 before he too has to stop. The deal with this session is that if you fall off the pace, you're done. You're not allowed to keep running. It is a version of the session developed by renowned coach Woldemeskel Kostre and made famous by Kenenisa and Haile.

'Telahun's condition is full,' Selamyhun gasps. 'You can't compete with him after being in Addis.' Because Telahun has been in the camp for the previous year, he is better able to cope with the training. Having 'full condition' in Debre Tabor is different from having 'full condition' in Addis: with the altitude up at the camp you can simply fill the cup higher. Desaleyn blows his whistle on 69 seconds, echoed by the crack of a farmer's whip as he herds his cattle across the infield. He is the only one to make it to the 15th lap and when he reaches the start of his 16th and final lap Desaleyn shouts, 'OK, Telahun, let's see what you can do! Don't be scared!' Telahun takes off and runs the last lap in 59 seconds.

* * *

The next day he is even more impressive. Not only is he better acclimatised to the altitude, but he's now simply faster than Birhanu, Abere and Selamyhun – marathon training has deadened their speed. They are doing one-kilometre repetitions with three minutes recovery, enough time for Abere to come over and complain between each rep. He says, '2.45, 46 for me is simple. I can do that all day. But 2.38, 2.39 is horrible.' All morning there has been a joking exchange of 'prize money' for people finishing first on reps, usually in the form of a one-birr coin pressed to a sweaty forehead.

Once more, Abere has bailed out of this session early. Zurich was only two weeks ago and he can't get his legs going at this speed. Before the last kilometre, Telahun claims he's going to run under 2.35, which coach Desaleyn says has never been done by one of his athletes at this altitude. 'What will my prize money be if I do it?' Telahun asks. Abere says he'll give him 100 birr and Telahun jogs over for a quick handshake. The joking and laughing continues until they get to the line where Telahun crosses himself and takes off. He runs the first 200 metres in 28 seconds, a steely glint in his eye as cheers ring out across the plateau – 100 birr is no laughing matter, it's enough to eat out every day for a week. He reaches 400 metres in 59 seconds and 800 metres in 2.00, before fighting his way up the final home straight, utterly spent, to record 2.34. Abere is stunned. 'The boy can run,' he says, shaking his head as Telahun lies flat on his back offering weak high-fives to his teammates.

This is a rare instance of money directly influencing the way that people run at the camp, but it's an illustrative one. According to coach Desaleyn, track athletes face a stark choice between remaining in the camp and moving to the city. With ever-increasing frequency and at an ever-younger age, athletes move to the road and to the marathon, the lure of money simply too tempting. With the money he won for his eighth place finish in the Dubai marathon, Abere has just built a compound of houses, overlooking one of the fields they train on here, which he will rent out. It is a constant reminder of the potential riches on offer for abandoning the track and hitting the roads.

Visiting these remote camps, situated in rolling farmland, and sustained entirely with food grown in the surrounding fields and a desire to make Ethiopia proud, is a refreshing break from Addis. It feels like travelling to a more innocent time in athletics history. As Selamyhun and I pack to return I hope he's right about the 'condition' we'll be taking back with us. It would be nice for it to feel easy for once.

13

OF COURSE THEY ARE TRYING TO KILL EACH OTHER

It should be clear at this point that a main preoccupation of many of the runners I train with is ensuring they protect their energy levels. Training together in a way that is measured and controlled is seen as the best way to avoid 'burning themselves' up through excessive training. It should also be clear, though, that on occasion this general rule is flouted in a fairly extravagant way, by running for two and a half hours in the middle of the night for example, or by deliberately choosing particularly ridiculous training routes. In general, though, the emphasis is on improving *together* and on running in a way that allows the group to function as one intact unit, whether that is achieved through Meseret setting the pace of a run or by zigzag running allowing those at the back to catch up.

The underlying reality of the sport, though – that while runners train together they must eventually compete alone – is a tension that never completely goes away, as the previous chapter should have made clear. Sooner or later everyone has to face the reality that it is pure speed that will win most races, and they have had enough experience of watching the likes of Tirunesh Dibaba and Kenenisa Bekele unleash phenomenal last laps at major championships to know this. Our group works on speed specifically on a Wednesday, but we also work on it most days, finishing the majority of easy runs with a set of progressively faster strides which seem designed to instil a 'use it or lose it' mentality about speed.

In fact, one of the most striking differences between running in Ethiopia and the UK is the sheer range of paces and motion encompassed by most training sessions. In Edinburgh I would regularly head out of the door and run each kilometre of a run in around four minutes, and maybe do some cursory stretching outside the flat if I felt like it. In Ethiopia, an equivalent run is more likely to consist of an opening kilometre in eight minutes and a final kilometre well under four, followed by a series of strides culminating in a flat-out sprint and a set of increasingly ambitious plyometric exercises that left my hamstrings in pieces for days afterwards when I first arrived.

When I ask people to explain the importance of doing these every day they often struggle, usually resorting to rapid-fire clicks of the fingers to demonstrate that they are for training leg speed and for keeping a kind of snap in the legs even when we are running a lot of kilometres. We run as fast as we can taking tiny little steps or fling our legs up straight in front of us before snapping them back to the ground. Sometimes Fasil will even charge backwards as fast as he can, taking big exaggerated strides and imperilling anyone who happens to be in his way.

For the most part, though, the post-run strides are intended to stretch the legs and to work on form. We always do them on a Tuesday evening ahead of speed training on a Wednesday morning, so that our legs 'know what to expect' the next day, as Hailye puts it. Hailye especially encourages me to do the short-step, quick-feet drills, identifying my loping running style as a bit of a problem. 'Your legs kind of wait in the air,' he says. 'If your stride was narrower you could add more speed.' We run in time with one another, like we do on many of our other runs. Wednesday morning speed training, though, is often explicitly seen as an opportunity to train the competitive instincts and to let people see what they can do. These sessions are almost always on a forgiving surface, either on the grass in Sendafa or Sululta to the north of the city, on the dirt track of Legetafo or on *coroconch* in Akaki. With the exception of our excursions to the track, these sessions are relatively simple, consisting of unmeasured repetitions of one to six minutes, the idea being to 'free athletes' minds' from constraint and encourage them to really let fly.

This morning we are at Satellite in Sululta, about 20 kilometres due north of the city. A favourite haunt of Mo Farah when he is in Ethiopia, the field is so named for a huge satellite dish in one corner. I am not running today, having managed to step on a sea urchin on a 'writing retreat' in Zanzibar, but this is a good opportunity to watch training unfold with Hailye and Meseret. The training session is a simple one, consisting of 14 repetitions of two minutes of fast running, with a minute recovery between each interval and a five-minute break in the middle of the session.

When I've done training sessions like this in the UK, they have always been around a pre-determined lap. Here in Satellite, however, the field we are running on is a few kilometres around, with no defining features apart from the occasional rutted track where a horse-drawn cart has passed during rainy season. Meseret doesn't tell the group where to run or who should lead; this is expected to just emerge organically in the course of the session. They are expected to run the two-minute repetitions flat out, but we are at 2800 metres above sea level here. As the runners group together following their warm-up I catch Selamyhun's eye. '*Selam naw?*' I ask him: Is there peace? 'There is no peace on this field,' he says with a little smile.

When Meseret gives them the go-ahead they take off round the edge of the field, with Teklemariam in the lead initially. Hailye, Meseret and I jog vaguely towards the middle of the field with Birhanu the driver in tow. Birhanu knew nothing about running when he was hired to drive the team bus, but he has begun to really enjoy watching training sessions and looks forward to Wednesdays especially. Rather than keeping to the edge of the field, the runners play a kind of follow-the-leader where someone surges into the lead and then picks the direction. Tsedat takes off on a diagonal across the field and the others seamlessly change direction to follow him. 'Haha!' Birhanu says, clearly delighted, as the runners come careering past us. 'They are fighting each other today!'

Already, after three repetitions, there are gaps appearing and it takes a while for the runners to regroup in the rest periods. Tsedat is back at the front again on the fourth repetition and he makes a couple of abrupt changes of direction as he surges back across the field. 'Look at this little guy, zigzagging all over the place,' Birhanu comments, shaking his head.

'When they do intervals it has to be like this,' Meseret responds. 'They need to unleash their energy like this in turn. After a couple of minutes, Tsedat will be exhausted and someone else will be the leader at the front. The key for Tsedat is to learn to respond.' As he speaks, Tsedat relinquishes the lead and falls back into the group. '*Gaba!*' Meseret shouts – 'Enter the pace' – encouraging him to stay with them rather than fall behind.

I point out that this seems very different from training on other days of the week, when Meseret emphasises the importance of control and energy conservation. He laughs and gestures towards Tsedat, who is now desperately hanging on to the back of the group.

'Training like this is costly in terms of energy,' he says. 'But they have to do this in order to learn tactical efficiency.' This kind of training can upset some of the more senior runners, who feel that there are some who don't do their fair share at the front. 'You see there are athletes who stay most of the time behind the leaders and even drop behind the team completely,' he says, pointing out that Fasil is around 50 metres adrift. 'But then suddenly when they feel a bit more comfortable they will want to be the leader and kick beyond the capacity of the leaders, and that sometimes upsets Birhanu and Mekuant. They tell me, "You have to control those guys!" I say, "I don't want to control them. You have to respond to be efficient enough to go with them." Kenenisa is efficient. Why? Because he can respond to all different kinds of challenges. And then with 400 metres left,' he opens his arms in an expansive gesture, 'Kenenisa says, "Ciao," and he is gone.'

The runners stagger over to us for a drink during their five-minute rest and Hunegnaw is violently sick. When he is done he comes over to Hailye and I, and greets me by saying 'Farenji!' in a deep voice. With the sweat and spittle dripping off his chin, and the deep blue tattoo of a cross on his forehead, he is as close to threatening as a distance runner gets and the only member of the group who still insists on calling me 'Foreigner'. I respond how I always do, with 'Habesha!' 'They are trying to kill each other,' he says. 'This is speed training,' Hailye laughs. 'Of course they are trying to kill each other.'

The five minutes recovery is over sooner than Hunegnaw would have liked and they are off again, weaving around the field with a new leader every couple of hundred metres. 'There Mekuant goes again!' Birhanu exclaims gleefully, as he makes a move round the outside. We watch them go from the centre of the field, encouraging the stragglers to try to regain contact. Meseret is clearly enjoying watching the runners 'fight' with each other as he puts it. As they fly through the last repetition, with Fasil suddenly charging to the front like a sprinter, he slaps his rolled-up notebook in his palm. 'Today I am totally happy!' he exclaims. 'One hundred per cent happy! While they are kicking, somebody kicks, again somebody kicks, again somebody responds, again somebody kicks, again! That is what you call a speed session. With speed you have to push beyond your capacity if you want to improve it.'

The runners shuffle off at walking pace to warm down, before returning to the bus to get changed. Meseret asks them to come together in a huddle before they get on to the bus. 'Please make a circle,' he says, 'to encourage those who were sent back. On *coroconch* you go comfortably, on asphalt you go by the pace I give you, but when we come to speed training it is natural that everyone tries to prove their talent. When the lead exchanges you have to keep going with whoever takes over.' He calls Fasil and Teklemariam, the two least experienced runners, over to him and puts his arms around them before addressing the whole team again. 'You should not be afraid of each other, because if you fear each other you cannot bring change. So if there's someone pushing, praise him and go. Fasil was a hero today. I saw him send everyone back. Teklemariam too.'

While this is the most competitive session of the week, with the runners encouraged to try to 'send each other back', which is how

Meseret describes getting a gap on someone, competition and collaboration are still linked in Meseret's eyes, with each surge the runners make helping those behind them to improve in the long term. He asks Zeleke to get his phone from the bus. One of the biggest successes the group has had this year is his second-place finish at Fuzhou marathon in China, where he won the $15,000 with which he is now constructing a house in his home town of Debre Birhan. When he emerges from the bus, Meseret asks him to show us the footage of the last few hundred metres. We gather round the tiny screen. Five Ethiopians are hammering along on an empty six-lane highway, filmed from the front by a motorbike. Zeleke is on the left, straining towards the camera and starting his sprint. Even on the grainy phone screen you can see the whites of his eyes and how hard he is fighting to get to the line first.

The camera pans away to show the finishing line. Zeleke's arms start to whirl in the last few metres as he completely runs out of steam and he crashes through the tape alongside another runner, with the other three just behind them. 'Ooooeee,' Aseffa exclaims, in spite of having been shown this clip multiple times before. Zeleke shakes his head. 'One second only between all of us,' he says. 'One second and lots of dollars.' This is why they need to learn to kill each other in training, so that when it comes to the race they are able to learn to 'resist' the surges thrown in by the others and time their finishing sprint to perfection.

Meseret often presents this as more of a mental strength than a physical capacity, as less to do with fast-twitch muscle fibres and more to do with the fibre of the will, as though it is possible to just decide that you can run faster and it will happen. One of his favourite stories is about Haile Gebrselassie's win over 10,000m in the Atlanta Olympics. 'Before he left for Atlanta, he said, "I have to win gold or I will not marry my fiancée!" That was the promise he made. After he won, he took off his shoe and blood poured out on to the track. "Are you injured?" they asked him. "Didn't you feel it? Why did you keep going?" Haile said only, "I had to win." This is the power of a promise to do something.' Meseret doesn't mention how Haile's fiancée (now wife) felt about this, but it is clear that an absolute, all-or-nothing approach to life and competition is admired.

The objectivity of speed training and the necessity of holding your hand in the fire longer than everyone else gives those who are able to really embody speed an almost mythic status, which I find is guarded quite religiously. It is to Kenenisa that everyone looks as the embodiment of both speed and mental strength during races, and he is spoken about with an enormous amount of respect. I remember early on in my time in Ethiopia asking a young runner about him on our way back from a run in the forest. 'He is dangerous,' he says. 'You know, a lot of Kenyans who ran with Kenenisa, they are totally destroyed. I have a friend from Kenya, he told me that in the last 10 years every runner who has tried to compete with him is out of action now. They are damaged, he says. He is not… That guy, he is not human.'

Human or not, he proves impossible to interview, in spite of numerous attempts to contact him and visits to his hotels in the city. I do, however, manage to speak to Mersha, his coach. We meet at a noisy bar in Arat Kilo and order *malta*, a malt drink made in a similar way to beer but non-alcoholic. It tastes like something between a fizzy Horlicks and liquid Maltesers, and I've found it to be excellent fuel for running. He laughs when I tell him about my quest to meet Kenenisa himself. 'To interview him in Ethiopia when he is trying to focus on his training, it would be you who would have to become the record breaker,' is how he puts it.

Given the general attitude that anyone can make it as an elite runner as long as they approach their training with patience and have access to the right training environment, Mersha is surprisingly keen to stress that Kenenisa has something special. 'He is different,' he says, shaking his head. 'He is different. It is natural. If you show him one exercise, you see the first time it is perfect. Cognitively he is good. And his mentality is just different. He isn't afraid of anyone. Actually a lot of runners think like this when they are 12 or 13 – "I can be like that, I can be like this" – but he can actually do it.'

He tells me that he has collaborated with Renato Canova, the Italian who also coaches many of the top Kenyan runners, to devise Kenenisa's training programme, and I am keen to learn details. 'Oh no,' he says, 'I am a professional. Kenenisa is interested to publish it some day, but he says it is dangerous for anyone else to use it directly. Because actually Kenenisa's body is much different. Maybe you may need more intensive, more duration, more strength workout than Kenenisa. It is up to the coach to adjust.' I find this fascinating. I had expected him to say it would be too much for most runners to deal with, not that it wouldn't be enough.

He tells me that the biggest challenge he had in trying to turn Kenenisa into a marathon runner was slowing him down. Their first marathon-specific track session was 20 repetitions of 400 metres with one-minute recovery. 'The point of the session,' Mersha says, 'is to learn to run at a relaxed speed and to improve lactic tolerance. But on the first rep he comes back in 61 seconds. He is not interested to run so slowly on the track.' After three or four repetitions, Mersha was able to persuade him to run as 'slowly' as 63 seconds. 'But then he arrives on the line again after only 30 seconds' rest and he says, "I'm ready to go, coach." At that pace his body is barely producing lactic acid, this is the problem. So we had to adjust the session for shorter recovery.' He tells me that the trick was to keep things interesting, because Kenenisa could find some of the longer marathon sessions boring. 'So we let him add some one-minute intervals at the end of a long run, for example,' he says. As is often the case, making training as interesting and inspiring as possible is paramount.

'Kenenisa is a man not just to win but to break records. Coaching him, or an athlete like Tirunesh Dibaba, it is easy to make them winners. You have to think beyond, to try to break records. National records, course records, world records. Winning is… His grandfather can do the training for that.' I ask about Kenenisa's run in the London marathon in 2016, when he was third in 2.06.36. I had read that he was only able to train for six weeks before the race after struggling with injury, but I wanted to hear it directly from Mersha. 'That is true,' he says. 'You need to have a minimum of 13 weeks – one three. It depends on the athlete and their condition to begin with, but six weeks before he was still in the rehabilitation phase. We took a risk to bring him straight into specific marathon workouts instead of having him in a good transitional phase to bring him gradually. But we didn't have time, so we took risks. Before the race, I said, "What is your feeling?" He said "I am OK."'

There were two groups with separate pacemakers in London and Eliud Kipchoge wanted an incredibly fast pace for the first half. The second group would run more conservatively to halfway in 63 or 64 minutes. Renato Canova contacted Mersha to suggest that Kenenisa run with the second, slower group, given his limited preparation, and word of this got to Kenenisa. Having related this, Mersha throws up his hands and says, 'I said, "How could you suggest this?!" Kenenisa has a very strong mind, so he rejected it. It was a very silly suggestion. He was a hero for me at this time.' The leaders ended up running 4.30 for the first mile and 61.24 for the first half marathon, and for Kenenisa to do that and still hang on for a 2.06 finish after six weeks' training is quite astonishing.

Often if Hailye becomes frustrated with the athletes for failing to show mental strength, it is to Kenenisa that he turns as an example, often in stark terms. On one occasion, as we sit on the bus after training, he put it like this: 'If you do not give yourself completely to running and wish big things, you will not get what you want. Otherwise you will not be changed. This is the decision Kenenisa made. You know what happened, his wife collapsed while she was running in the forest and died of a heart attack. It was a tragedy. When Kenenisa was in mourning, he said to himself, "If running can kill, let it kill me." In the same year, he broke the world records for 5000m and 10,000m. His training from that time is difficult to even hear about. Does anyone go 16 laps in 61 seconds in Addis Ababa Stadium? He did that, and when the 17th lap was 63 seconds he stepped off the track and he knew he could break the record in Hengelo.'

This is a story I had heard before, and a training session I had witnessed Telahun, Birhanu and the others do as far away as Gondar. 'The sixteen laps session came from Woldemeskel Kostre,' Hailye says, 'and it was the session Haile Gebrselassie used as well. The point is that it helps you to send everyone back by going fast every lap.' Given that Addis Ababa Stadium is at 2500 metres above sea level, the training session Hailye describes above sounds impossible, but the runners I meet in Ethiopia believe that Kenenisa did it and he is revered to such an extent I'm almost inclined to believe it, too. For Hailye the simplest training sessions, requiring the most mental fortitude, are often the best ones. Woldemeskel Kostre coached both Haile Gebrselassie and Kenenisa to world records on the track, and as far as Hailye is concerned his methods were the best. 'These other young coaches have their science blah blah but they are not as successful,' is how he puts it.

While I'm not able to break a record of my own by meeting Kenenisa, I am fortunate that towards the end of my time in Ethiopia I am able to spend quite a lot of time with a young runner who will go on to break the Ethiopian half marathon record, running 58.33 in Valencia in 2018. We have some very talented athletes in our group – Hunegnaw has run a 59.42 half marathon, for instance, and the group features a few sub 2.10 marathon runners. Hailye is keen to stress, though, that Jemal Yimer is potentially capable of something very special at the shorter distances and, even two years before he makes his debut, at the half marathon distance.

When we first meet in a café near Megenagna roundabout, Jemal arrives wearing his national team vest and tracksuit top, and a faded pair of jeans, walking gingerly following a track session that morning. He has recently arrived in Addis following an impressive first race abroad, where he finished fourth in the 10,000m at the African Championships in Durban, and Hailye wants to meet him so that they can discuss the race and talk about the next few weeks' training. I expect him to be relatively pleased with his fourth-place finish, but he is clearly disappointed.

'I prepared really well for that race,' he says. 'And I was ready to go with five laps remaining, which is what I had visualised. The coach on the sidelines told me to wait and I was outsprinted. I was upset about that. I don't like to lose because of tactics.' In the camp of the Amhara Prisons Club, a lot of emphasis was placed on psychological preparation. Before travelling to competitions, the athletes would gather together for a special coffee ceremony. There, the athletes would get into groups according to discipline, and each group had to stand up and talk about what they had done in training, what they expected from the race and any worries they might have. 'For example,' Jemal tells us, 'someone might be worried about their speed at the end. They will talk about that and their friends will remind them of the training they have done for that specific thing. That way they can travel to the race without stress.'

That first race abroad in Durban was the culmination of a process that started a decade earlier. It was watching Kenenisa race that inspired Jemal, as it was for many of his contemporaries. The fourth of seven children, he was tasked with herding the cattle on the family farm. When he snuck off to watch the race, the cattle strayed on to a neighbour's land and were busy munching on their crops when Jemal returned. 'My mother was furious,' he laughs now, 'but that was the day I started with simple forest training.' He credits the strength he has now to another job, however. From a young age, he used to buy hundreds of eggs from the small market in his village and carry them to the town several kilometres away on a basket slung over his back to sell for a profit. He used the money he made to buy running kit and nutritious food, but he also ate any eggs that broke along the way. If there is ever a film about Jemal this will have to feature in a *Rocky*-esque training montage.

He tells us that his favourite sessions are those that develop the ability to run at a fast pace from the gun. The 16 laps of the track session above is a favourite, but also fast 2000-metre or

3000-metre repetitions run four or five times. And if those don't sound tough enough, he also mentions a session of 30 laps of continuous running at a steady pace, specifically designed to 'adapt' to the monotony of a 10,000m race on the track. It is this attitude – of embracing these kinds of ultra-objective, nowhere-to-hide training sessions – that makes Hailye think Jemal could turn into a record-breaker like Kenenisa and Haile.

It is a focus that permeates all aspects of his life. As we walk back towards the road Hailye says to me, 'Jemal is going to be a very special athlete. You saw what he was wearing. He told me he hasn't touched that money in his bank account.' To have lived for several years on the $50 per month salary of a member of the Amhara Prisons Club, training morning and evening, and eating a simple diet in the club canteen, and then to receive your first $6000 in prize money and leave it sitting in your account takes some discipline. 'He told me the money can wait, his running can't,' Hailye says. Hailye has a phrase in English for the distractions that can affect the preparations of even the strongest athletes – 'hodgepodge things'. Facebook Messenger is a 'hodgepodge thing', as is watching television and playing pool or sitting in a café.

* * *

I return to Ethiopia briefly in 2019, and I am curious to see how Jemal has got on with avoiding 'hodgepodge things' and to talk to him about how on earth he managed to run a half marathon in 58.33. Hailye and I go to Stadium to watch him train on the track and we are told to arrive at 7 a.m., which seems remarkably civilised compared to how we used to train. Jemal does a simple but extraordinarily hard session of fast 300-metre repetitions punctuated by a 100-metre jog. He runs the repetitions in around 43 seconds, with a revolving cast of three different pacemakers required to keep the tempo high enough for him. They sub in and out after two or three reps each, resting on the red, green and yellow-painted concrete steps of the stadium, sheltering from the sun underneath advertising hoardings for Giorgis beer. Jemal just keeps going, running chest-out and tall, his spikes barely seeming to peck at the track before he lifts into the next stride.

After a slow warm-down, Jemal offers me a lift to his house so that we can talk. The faded jeans from our first meeting are gone and he is now dressed from head to toe in the clothes of his sponsor, Nike, with a baby-blue t-shirt under a black gilet. He has just bought himself a new Toyota Corolla, which is seemingly the sedan of choice for successful Ethiopian runners. The seats are still shrink-wrapped and covered in 1970s-style beaded seat covers. As we get in, he tells me cheerfully that he finally passed his driving theory test the day before on his fourth attempt. I congratulate him nervously, but he drives well, with the right mix of caution and assertiveness needed to get anywhere in Addis, and well-timed bursts of acceleration when necessary.

We stop at a juice house round the corner from Jemal's place, which is to the north-west of Kotebe in a part of town called Farensay Legasione, near the French Embassy. It is a surprisingly built-up area, but the forest is tucked away behind Jemal's compound and he can run all the way to Entoto if he wants to. The juice house walls are covered in brightly coloured laminated posters of fruit and highland landscapes. I order some bread and a mango juice, but Jemal eats nothing. 'I just need juice,' he says. 'I'm number one when it comes to drinking juice.' He rather alarmingly drinks seven large glass tankards of juice, one after the other in quick succession – mango, avocado, pineapple and papaya – before declaring himself full and recovered from the morning's training. The waitress who comes to clear the table laughs and tells me, 'That's nothing, sometimes he drinks 10 or 11.' I ask him why he hasn't eaten and he says he often doesn't feel like it after a hard track session, and adds that he has a race coming up and he finds he sprints best when he is 46 kilos.

I wonder what it must feel like to run a half marathon in 58 minutes. It is very difficult to relate to someone who is one of the top-five performers ever at something, especially something as objective as running, and yet trying to do so compels us. David Foster Wallace puts it well when he writes that while the question of who is the best plumber or accountant is impossible to define, the rankings of top sportspeople are 'a matter of public statistical record' which appeals to 'our twin compulsions with competitive superiority and hard data'. They are also, he points out, beautiful. 'Great athletes are profundity in motion,' he writes. 'There is about world-class athletes carving out exemptions from physical laws a transcendent beauty that makes manifest God in man.' But are the performances of the likes of Jemal experienced in this way by the athletes themselves?

When I ask him about his training for the race in Valencia the word he uses to describe it is not 'impossible' or 'amazing' or even 'hard'. Rather, he says he trained 'properly' (*badenb* in Amharic). We walk into yard of his house and I am surprised to see an outdoor gym, complete with a rusting squat rack and weights – I have not seen this in Kotebe – with inspirational graffiti several layers deep painted on to the concrete ground. A series of interlocking Olympic rings are overlaid with text in English and Amharic. 'Push yourself' one slogan reads, another, 'Sport is my passion'. One simply says,

'Discipline'. I turn to see that at the top of the steps that Jemal walks up every morning to go to training the last thing he reads is 'No easy way out'. He tells me that he decided to live here, in a modest one-bedroom house, because of the gym and because the water in this part of town was renowned for its purity. We sit down on weights benches in the sun and he taps the weights affectionately. 'Every time I lower the bar on to my shoulders to do some squats it reminds me of the egg basket,' he says.

As he outlines the training he did before Valencia the main things that strike me are the focus on pure speed and the careful avoidance of running on the surface on which the race he was preparing for would take place. In the months leading up to the race Jemal ran on asphalt only twice, to do hill reps on a popular hill next to the Sheraton Hotel. He even avoided *coroconch*, going to Sendafa just for two of his longest runs, which I was surprised to hear were no longer than 90 minutes. He credits this with protecting the speed in his legs, which would have been deadened by too much running on asphalt. His training was simple but 'proper' he says, which means that he focused on resting as much as possible between sessions. He did two track sessions a week and a lot of easy running on the grass at Jan Meda and in the forest at Entoto.

On the mornings when he didn't have training on the track he ran for an hour and 20 minutes in the forest, and jogged a 'very slow' 40 minutes in the evenings. When I ask him to estimate how many kilometres he covered he does so based on times when he wore his GPS watch, but admits to rarely remembering to charge it up. We head into the house to find something to write on and there are six identical Nike kit bags stacked in the corner. 'They send a lot of kit,' he says. 'More than you can use. I will think of what to do with it when I finish running.' We scribble an estimate of the figures on the back of an old race number and come up with a weekly total of around 170 kilometres per week, which is a lot but nothing crazy.

The shoes he is using at the moment are drying outside in the sun, next to the plastic bucket he washed them in the previous afternoon. He says he usually comes home from training to eat and then sleeps for most of the afternoon before doing some weights and the customary 40-minute jog. It is perhaps the total lack of distractions or drains on his energy that is most significant about his preparations. With the possible exception of the long sessions of 3000-metre repetitions, the training he's doing could probably be managed by many of the more serious distance runners in the UK. People say, 'It doesn't get easier, you just get faster,' and I wonder whether perhaps that is true even for someone able to run as fast as Jemal. Perhaps it feels the same for him to run a half marathon in 58 minutes as it does for me to run one eight minutes slower. And I guess I'll never really know.

14

RUNNING IS LIFE

They walked up to the top of the mountain to make their decision. They knew their coaches wouldn't want to make the trek and they would be able to talk freely. With the January wind whipping around Arthur's Seat and through their thin Eritrea national team tracksuits, they formed a huddle to decide what to do. They had not performed as well as they had hoped in the 2008 World Cross Country Championships in Edinburgh the day before, although most of the men's team had finished in the top 30. They were delayed for a week in Egypt en route, and then further held up in Heathrow, and arrived in Edinburgh tired and stressed. Tewolde Mengisteab finished in 52nd place, ahead of the entire Great Britain team, but he was scared of the reactions of the coaches.

'We asked them what would happen to us when we got back to Eritrea,' he recalls, years later when I interview him. 'And they just said, "We'll see."' Athletes who were seen to have underperformed in the past had been forced into the army, he explains. 'And when you enter the Eritrean army you don't leave it.' Other punishments they had heard of included being locked in a metal storage container for several days to endure the merciless equatorial sun by day and the near-freezing temperatures at night. 'We stood on top of the mountain and we decided that at night we would head to the train station,' he says. They didn't have a great deal of money with them, so when they arrived at the train station they asked where the nearest big city was – and that is how they ended up in Glasgow.

John Mackay had stood in line for autographs from the Eritrean team at Holyrood Park and still has a signed race number in his house in Glasgow. When he received a call from the Scottish Refugee Council a week later asking him if his club, Shettleston Harriers, would accept some new athletes, he agreed at once, but didn't see the connection until he arrived at Crownpoint athletics track for training on Tuesday night, and saw a large group of men and women in full Eritrean national team tracksuits. 'It was a pretty amazing coincidence,' John tells me and one that shook up the Scottish athletics scene considerably, seeing a number of national titles go the way of Shettleston. Their arrival coincided with the rise to prominence of brothers Callum and Derek Hawkins, who run for Shettleston's west of Scotland rivals Kilbarchan AAC, and in fact the British Olympic marathon team in 2016 was made up of the Hawkins brothers and Tsegai Tewelde, one of the former Eritrean athletes who decided to stay in 2008. John credits the arrival of the Eritreans with raising the standards of Scottish distance running.

For my own part, I have finished second or third behind Eritrean, Ethiopian and Kenyan runners who are resident in the UK on countless occasions in road races in the north-east of England (including Ethiopians Tadele Geremew – many times – and Yared Hagos), in Scotland (mostly to Eritreans Tewolde and Weynay Gebrselassie) and Dublin (to the Kenyan Freddy Situkk). While I never actually won any of these head-to-heads, they are some of my most enjoyable running memories, of barrelling along country roads a couple of minutes ahead of the rest of the field, running stride for stride with Tadele or Tewolde. I owe my best half marathon time of 66.13 to a race at the Wilmslow half marathon where I traded surges with Ethiopian-born Thomas Abyu and Jordanian Mohammed Abu-Rezeq, before being convincingly outsprinted by both of them. Afterwards, Thomas told me it had been windy and that on a better day I would run 63 minutes. The mentality of these post-race conversations always motivated me, and I went away wanting to train harder and believing I could run quicker, even if I didn't.

Tewolde, Tsegai and the others arrived at Shettleston Harriers by chance, but they couldn't have happened upon a more supportive club. Shettleston has a deeply ingrained social conscience that can be traced back to the 1930s when the current club President Elaine Mackay's grandfather Alan Scally would use his race winnings to fund soup kitchens in the East End. The Eritrean runners' new homes were soon furnished with donations from fellow club members, but this was a proud working-class area of Glasgow. The runners received support from the club, but they were also expected to work alongside their running, which was something of a culture shock at first, as they took on shifts in factories and warehouses. Over time, some of them became important mentors to junior runners in the club, a role Tewolde still fulfils over a decade since he arrived for that first Tuesday night session.

The way in which runners from Ethiopia and Eritrea move around the world is brought home to me in full force when I arrive at the Shettleston 10km road race shortly after returning to Scotland from my time in Ethiopia. I last saw Eritrean Weynay Gebrselassie – who remained in the UK following the 2012 Olympic Games under similar circumstances to Tewolde and the others – in a juice bar in Addis Ababa. And yet here he was, about to have a crack at the £300 bonus on offer for running under 30 minutes. Eritrea fought a 30-year war of independence against Ethiopia, and peace between the two countries was only officially agreed to in 2018 following a border dispute that began 20 years earlier. In spite of this runners from the two countries are on good terms, and many Eritrean runners choose to train in Ethiopia. Weynay frequently travels to Addis for training trips and told me in the Kotebe juice bar that the training is very similar in the two countries, with the possible exception of the severity of coaches. Alternating periods of working and spending time with his family in Birmingham with periods of training in Ethiopia works better for him than trying to juggle the two.

I warm up for this Scottish 10k race with Weynay, Tewolde and two other Eritreans, Abraham and Amanuel. While our competitors head on to the roads or along the river, we begin at a barely perceptible jog on the grass and Weynay finds some trees to run around before zigzagging across a large field. We string out in a single-file line, the pace gradually and only just perceptibly increasing. It is just like being back in Ethiopia, following Weynay through the forest. We finish our warm-up with a couple of minutes approaching race pace, streaking back across the field to the sports centre in the familiar single-file train and earning curious glances from our competitors.

I am unable to follow Weynay when the gun goes. He flies off on a one-man mission to run under 30 minutes, ending up just short with 30.10. I finish second almost two minutes behind him, with Abraham third, Tewolde fifth and Amanuel sixth. We jog back across to the sports centre together, and catch up over tea and cake. There are quite a number of Ethiopian and Eritrean runners and ex-runners living in the UK, some like Tewolde and Weynay who are here for political reasons, and others for whom the decision is primarily an economic one. They have recently been at a reunion for Eritreans in Manchester that was attended by more than 60 athletes. Many have found the balance of running and work tipped firmly in the direction of work, however. Two members of the Eritrean team who arrived in 2008 are now taxi drivers. Tsegai, who represented Great Britain in the Rio Olympic Games, is a care worker in Cambridge. Tewolde has done a number of different jobs, but is currently using his significant endurance capacities to ride a bicycle for Deliveroo, which is especially incompatible with training.

Weynay reflects on his trips to Ethiopia. He still thinks, based on his training, that he is capable of running a 2.10 marathon, but the trips to Addis can be a rollercoaster of emotions. 'On the days when you feel good, you can finish a training session and feel euphoric, innit?' he says. 'But on the days it's not going so well, you think, I'm trying to focus on my running, but I lost my time, I lost my money, I miss my family to be here, you know?' His wife, who joined him in the UK from Eritrea, and young children live in Birmingham. I don't know what it's like to rely on running to pay the bills, but I understand Weynay's struggle to convince himself that it is worth it to try to train at that level. Most of the Eritreans and Ethiopians I have met at races in the UK approach their running with varying intensity depending upon their other commitments to work and family at particular times, just like any other runner.

Even when not making money from the sport, though, there are few who have given up running completely. It retains a hold on people, which reminds me of something Hailye said to me on the training bus in Sendafa at 6.30 a.m. one morning. He was injured and had been unable to run for a couple of weeks, but was still exhausted from watching the early-morning training sessions and standing in queues to apply for visas for athletes in his capacity as sub-agent. 'It is better, running and being tired, than not running and being tired.' He paused to peer out of the bus window, where the group were working their way towards the crest of a hill. 'Running is life,' he added.

I had struggled a little with running while in Ethiopia. I found it was hard to maintain the *illusio*, that meaning-making necessary to convince myself of the importance of my own running when surrounded by athletes who were so much better than I was. And as an anthropologist committed to observant participation it was necessary for me to try to accompany runners who were fitter than I was, more acclimatised to the altitude and more comfortable with the terrain, on runs that I found challenging in the extreme. It might make the insights in this book more interesting and contribute some new ideas to the anthropology of sport. It meant, though, that I was almost always overtraining and usually exhausted.

After more than 15 months in Ethiopia, back in Edinburgh Roslyn and I welcomed our daughter Madeleine (middle name Tirunesh) into the world, and worked on our PhD theses. For the first six months I ran to university through Holyrood Park, but struggled to motivate myself to get back into proper training. The fact of not having officially run a marathon still nagged at me, though. I didn't really want to walk away from the sport without a marathon time, but if I was going to run one I needed inspiration. I tried to think of what Hailye or Tsedat or Birhanu would do in this situation. Probably something a little crazy, like travelling hundreds of miles to train at extreme high altitude, or getting up at 3 a.m. to run up and down a hill. With a six-month-old, Roslyn and I were up at 3 a.m. a lot anyway, and travelling to altitude was out of the question. What I could do, though, was ask them to write me an Ethiopian-style training programme and try to follow it through an Edinburgh winter.

We don't have the altitude of the Ethiopian or Eritrean highlands in the UK, but Tewolde assures me over the phone that the climate (even in Glasgow) is perfect for running. It is also possible to mimic most of the surfaces quite well. I knew this from training with Tadele on Town Moor in Newcastle. The *coroconch* surface there is similar to Sendafa. And I knew it from the training Tewolde, Weynay and the others did in Glasgow. The Cathkin braes were a perfect substitute for the forests, and Strathclyde University playing fields could be used for long interval sessions (five laps, four laps, three laps, two laps, one lap). And if you felt the need to throw in a crazy session you could do something like run 40 x 400m on the track, as Tsegai did in his build-up to qualifying for the Olympic Team at the London Marathon.

In Edinburgh I turned to the various golf courses in the city centre to identify the correct terrain and found *coroconch* trails along the coast, sending photos for Hailye's approval. Duddingston golf course, which is on a long slope, he was especially keen on, assuming I could avoid the ire of the golfers. He approached the task of sending me training schedules with far more care than it deserved, enlisting the help of Getamasay Molla. He had taken over responsibility for coaching the Moyo Sports runners after Meseret went to work for the national team and also coached athletes from Global Sports Communications, the biggest sports management agency in Ethiopia, including 2.04 marathon runner Leul Gebrselassie. The schedules arrived neatly written out in biro on white paper, then photographed and sent via Whatsapp.

The priorities of the Ethiopian runner were clearly set out by the emphasis given to particular things. The entry for each day ran to at least a paragraph of text with a series of subheadings. 'Training Place' was the first. For easy running this read '*Chakka* [forest] or golf place'. Faster sessions were to be done on a combination of fields, *coroconch* and occasionally on the road. The second sub-heading was usually 'Training Type'. If a run was supposed to be really easy – something that Hailye knew I struggled with a little in Addis – the schedule read 'EASY pace', with the duration of the run specified in minutes. I tried as much as possible to mimic the forest runs in Ethiopia on the incline of the golf course, zigzagging backwards and forwards and running in the worst of the winter weather when there was no-one on the course. I put a head torch on and ran around at night, taking seriously the invocations to keep things interesting and feel a bit crazy sometimes.

Even these easier runs were mostly followed with '+ intervals' in brackets, reminding me of the importance of tapping into a little speed every day. The harder running days were on a combination of *coroconch* and grass for the most part, with the occasional foray on to the roads or a track. The importance of learning control and discipline was there in the very specific paces for many of the sessions, which included long track intervals of the kind favoured by Jemal, but watered down a little for me. Two repetitions of 4000 metres was an especially uncompromising one, the first repetition to be run in 12.36 and the second in 12.24. The road sessions were often acceleration runs like the ones we did in Sendafa, the pace increasing every 15 minutes by a few seconds per kilometre. I ran these out-and-back along the coast towards Musselburgh, inevitably ending up having to attempt to speed up into the wind on my return.

This block of training – and knowing that Hailye and Getamesay had put in the time and effort to write out the sessions – revitalised me and left me fit enough to contemplate marathon training. I targeted marathons in Edinburgh and Frankfurt by incorporating much of what I'd learned in Ethiopia – maintaining the golf course running and borrowing many of the longer road sessions we had done in Sendafa – with advice from my long-time coach Max in Durham, finding in the process that there are actually many overlaps between the running culture of the North East in the 1980s and Addis Ababa in the 2010s. In Edinburgh I finished third in 2.24.43, running primarily to ensure I actually finished a marathon and struggling with the final 10 kilometres into the wind. At the finish I celebrated finally having an official marathon finish time to my name with Roslyn and Madeleine, who was just about making her first steps. And then I set my sights on Frankfurt.

* * *

It is a few months short of two years since I left Ethiopia, and five months after the Edinburgh marathon. I sit in a hotel room in Frankfurt with Tsedat and his friend Kelkile Gezahegn. I am here to catch up with Tsedat and to try to run a marathon in under two hours and 20 minutes. Since I left Ethiopia Tsedat has improved to 2.09.26 and won the Riga marathon the week before I ran in Edinburgh. The room is strewn with empty bottles, and overflowing with plastic packets of *kolo* snacks and sachets of energy powder. Tsedat and Kelkile will mix the latter into eight bottles each, which will then be transported to the drinks tables positioned every five kilometres along the course in the morning. Tsedat keeps entreating me to eat more *kolo* and telling me to drink one of the bottles of water piled on the table to ensure I am ready to run in the morning.

Kelkile lies in bed under his duvet. He barely moves and says little, but he seems confident. Today is all about saving energy. I have transported a 19 kilo bag of Nike kit – which was sent to Malcolm in Edinburgh – to Frankfurt for Tsedat, one of two he will receive this year as part of his sponsorship deal with the company. He carefully inspects some of the shrink-wrapped items of clothing, and removes all 16 pairs of socks and lies them out on the floor. 'This one is nice,' he says, showing it to Kelkile. 'It is very thin and very light.' 'You should wear those tomorrow,' Kelkile says. Tsedat carefully pulls a sock on and tests the feel of it in his racing shoe. Satisfied, he puts the socks in the shoes for the morning and places them in a small bag.

He puts on a gilet and a broad-brimmed baseball cap from the bag, and tries on a few other items of clothing. Among them is a knee-length padded jacket of the kind a football manager in the English Premier League might wear, which he carefully lays on the bed, and about 10 pairs of trainers. 'You can sell those for a lot of money in Addis Ababa,' Kelkile points out. Tsedat nods, but he has told me his philosophy on running kit before. 'I never sell shoes like the others do,' he said. 'These shoes are my factories. I use them to produce dollars.' He takes a UK size six;

his racing shoes must be among the most efficient factories in the world.

At around 3 p.m. Tsedat climbs into bed and covers himself with the duvet. We have discussed his race strategy for the morning and decided that he should go with the second of four pacemakers and aim to run the first half marathon in 63.30. He keeps saying, 'I just want to run 2.07 – 2.07 would be a nice time, right?' I can tell he is tempted to try to run with the first group, who are aiming to be 45 seconds faster at the halfway point, but Malcolm has asked me to try to persuade him not to. 'It's a difficult one,' Malcolm said. 'He could have a huge breakthrough and run 2.05, but it's far more likely that he would completely blow up and run slower than 2.10 or fail to finish.' From Malcolm's perspective the priority is to aim for the comparative stability of a Nike contract, which will guarantee Tsedat an income for a couple of years. The idea is therefore to demonstrate forward progression to Nike, and other race organisers who might invite him to their events, by running at least 2.09 again. '2.07 would be great,' I tell him. 'It is within my capacity,' he replies.

As I line up the next morning I do what Hailye has taught me to do. I visualise the *coroconch* long runs and the big acceleration runs that I had done in my build-up – deemed necessary by both Hailye and Max. I remind myself of the 15-mile run where I averaged 5.28 per mile and of the session of 4 x 5km at faster than race pace with one kilometre in four minutes for 'recovery'. I tell myself that I have done enough two and a half hour long runs, and I remember Tsedat's simple but reassuring phrase. 'It is within my capacity,' I tell myself, before wishing Tsedat good luck.

I had done most of my training alone, running to and from my office on easy days and trying to minimise the time I spent on my running while Madeleine was little, so I had thus far failed to heed one bit of advice I always heard, and experienced, in Ethiopia: that running in a group is easier than running alone. In Frankfurt, though, the elite women's field were also aiming to run under 2.20, so I ended up in a kind of peloton. A screen mounted on the pace car alternated between showing us a split for the last kilometre and our projected finish time, which barely fluctuated between 2.19.40 and 2.19.50. Behind the pace car were three Ethiopian male pacemakers, running side by side, and behind them were about a dozen of the best female marathon runners in the world, followed by a couple of other hangers-on like myself. It was, I kept telling myself, like a Breaking2 attempt of my own: it couldn't be set up any better than this. My main memory of the race is actually of terror – especially around the drinks stations – of getting in the way of the real race going on around me. I found that the likes of Ethiopians Meskerem Aseffa and Haftamnesh Tesfaye (whose name means 'You are rich') have pretty sharp elbows, though, and were good at letting me know if I was too close.

Being in a group clearly makes a big difference, and one that runs deeper than the aerodynamics tested by Nike and Ineos for the various sub two-hour marathon attempts. I recall what Kipchoge said immediately after his run in Monza. 'I want to thank the pacers for bringing their energy,' he said. This is how it feels as we click off the kilometres in Frankfurt. The energy in the group is more than the sum of its parts and we flow along as one unit. In the end we all drop off the sub 2.20 pace slightly; the tall buildings in the last few kilometres in Frankfurt channel the wind in cruel ways and once the group breaks up there is no shelter to be had. It is a privilege to watch the crucial moment in the race from the best seat in the house on the heels of the lead group.

We go around a corner and Meskerem Aseffa ratchets up the pace big time, looking over her shoulder after a couple of hundred metres to see what kind of damage she has done. It is a sudden and clinical and brutal acceleration, and one that is rarely caught effectively by the race cameras. In barely a minute she has a winning lead. She goes on to win the race and break the course record with 2.20.36. The finish in Frankfurt is quite spectacular, with the final hundred metres or so run inside the Festhalle along a red carpet. I enter as she crosses the finish line, and the flashing lights and flying confetti are sensory overload after all those miles outside. I soak up the atmosphere and finish, lightheaded, in 2.20.53.

As soon as I am able to think straight, I head off to find Tsedat. The top runners are all sitting on folding plastic seats behind an advertising hoarding, waiting to be escorted back to the hotel or to drug testing. Tsedat and I share a brief and sweaty embrace before I ask him how it went. He shakes his head and keeps repeating, 'I couldn't do it today, I couldn't.' He points to his heel, which has been bothering him on and off for a while. I am not allowed to stay in the elite athlete area for long, so I leave assuming that he had to drop out and could not finish the race.

Later in the day, after a shower and a lie down, I look up the results to find that he finished eighth in 2.09.39, just slightly slower than his best time, which seems like a positive result. When I get back to the hotel he is in bed again, but seems a little happier than he had in the morning and asks me to look up whether there was any prize money for eighth place. With his 2000 euro appearance fee and 1500 euros for eighth he will take home 3500 euros. His roommate Kelkile won the race and with it 37,500 euros. He will probably receive a large bonus from Nike on top of that. 'Where is he?' I ask. 'I don't know,' Tsedat replies. 'Prize ceremony, drug testing, interviews. You do many things when you win.'

Tsedat and I limp over to the department store across the road to spend some of the cash he has brought with him from his win in Riga. As we are shopping a young Ethiopian man in a battered Levi's jacket sidles over to us to chat about the phones. He ends up spending an hour helping to discuss the various handsets in Amharic, English and German with the shop assistant, before Tsedat finally settles on a Samsung smartphone which he pays for with two 200 euro notes. We leave the shop and sit down on some benches to take the weight off our aching legs, where a few more elite runners, including someone of Ethiopian origin in a German national team tracksuit, join us. He explains that he had come to Germany for a race three years previously and decided to stay and try to make it as an athlete here. He now has eligibility to compete for Germany and clearly speaks excellent German. The young man whom we had met in the shop had also come to Germany as a runner, but with no intention of running once he arrived. 'I just want to work,' he says. 'Any work. But at the moment there is nothing.'

As Tsedat and I walk back over to the hotel, I ask him which race he is planning to run next and he is unsure. 'First I need to wait a month and recover. Then it will take two months to regain my condition.' For both of us, the previous three months have entailed carefully marshalling our resources in such a way that we were in the right 'condition' to run so hard for just over two hours, but we have just rendered ourselves incapable of regaining such fitness for weeks if not months hence. For both of us – or for anyone living on the edge of 'condition' – there could be no certainty that we would ever reach it again.

We sit in a café and trace where the runners whose stories feature most prominently in this book have ended up. Abere is now in Melbourne and, while he intends to find a club and become an athlete again, he is yet to run a race in Australia since he decided to 'disappear' there almost a year earlier and is working sporadically in a food processing factory. Birhanu is still in Addis Ababa working with a Dutch manager, but has been unable to regain the form he had when I knew him. Selamyhun is back with his club in Gondar and looking for an opportunity to race abroad. 'He is losing hope at the moment,' Tsedat says. Besides Tsedat, Aseffa, Mekuant and Jemal are the only one still working with Moyo Sports.

As we talk I keep refreshing my Twitter feed for news from Dublin, where Aseffa is also running today. Finally, we learn that Aseffa has won the race, after twice finishing second and once finishing third in previous years. With it, he wins the 12,000 euros which will allow him and his girlfriend Teje to get married and finally 'change their lives'. This transforms Tsedat's mood and he keeps saying, 'First place for Aseffa!' in obvious delight at his friend's success. As for the other athletes who had made up our group, however, he says he is no longer in contact with most of them. 'Athletes are moving here and there,' he says. 'They are not interested in staying still.'

At the beginning of 2020 Tsedat's best marathon time is 2.06.17, achieved in finishing two seconds behind the winner in third place at the Dubai marathon. He has added the Seville marathon title to his win in Riga. Mekuant has demonstrated the value of the patience he spoke to me about by running the 22nd marathon of his career in a PB of 2.04.46 to follow in Tsedat's footsteps and win in Seville. Jemal has probably been the most consistently amazing half marathon runner on the planet, running times of 59.00, 59.14, 58.33, 59.45, 59.09 and 59.25 in a two-year period, as well as finishing fourth in the World Championships. Moyo Sports has seen broader success too, with Callum Hawkins running phenomenally well in two World Championship marathons and Kenyan Timothy Cheruiyot becoming the best 1500m runner in the world. It is tempting to look for clues as to why Jemal, Tsedat and Mekuant have become world class while the fortunes of others have faded. If anything, consistency is the thing that stands out, with Jemal and Tsedat remaining part of the Moyo Sports set-up from the very beginning of their careers and Mekuant leaving only briefly. To apply such survivorship bias is not the intention of the book, however. The trajectories of the runners I got to know well ranged widely.

I recall the conversations we had in the bar when Birhanu decided to stop the bus on our way back from training. What stood out was the value of years spent dedicated to running that went beyond money. The value of having a goal to work towards, of having friends who share your desire to 'bring change' together, and of putting health and vitality first. The ways in which the runners sought to 'change their lives' – through making every run different, by seeking out adventure in what they did and by attaching value to particular environments around the city – were also ways of focusing on the process, and maintaining interest and enjoyment from day to day.

Much like the energy of the group being greater than the sum of its parts, the culture of Ethiopian running as a whole – the sheer number of people willing to live their athletic lives in such an all-encompassing and committed way – is what allows the individuals who emerge at the top of the sport in Ethiopia to be so

incredibly good at what they do. Through following each others'
feet and learning by example and experiment, sport at the highest
level can be driven by curiosity and adventure as well as measurement
and discipline. The day after Tsedat runs 2.06 Hailye calls me in
Edinburgh to ask how much running I'm doing. '*Tinish*,' I tell
him: a little. 'What about breaking 2.20?' he asks. I can hear him
smiling down the phone. 'Maybe I'll give it one more go,' I tell
him. 'Running *is* life, after all.'

ACKNOWLEDGEMENTS

The research that forms the basis of this book was funded by a studentship from the Economic and Social Research Council (ESRC), and the writing was supported by an ESRC Postdoctoral Fellowship. I am grateful for this generous support and expression of confidence in my work. Thank you to my agent Richard Pike for believing in the book, to Charlotte Croft and Zoë Blanc at Bloomsbury for improving it, and to Eliza Southwood and Owen Delaney for bringing it to life with the cover illustration and map.

In Ethiopia I am deeply grateful to Benoit Gaudin and his family for making me feel welcome for longer than they perhaps first anticipated, and to Benoit in particular for fascinating conversations about running and social science on his balcony. To Mimmi Demissie for endless hours of patient Amharic tuition in the cafes of Arat Kilo. To Ed and Rekik for wonderful and caring friendship.

Thank you to Fasil, Birhanu, Tsedat, Jemal, Aseffa and the many other runners who provided hours of laughs and company in pool halls and at football matches on top of all the hours of running on the trails. To Messeret for sharing his coaching wisdom with me. Finally and especially my thanks goes to Hailye Teshome, without whom this project would not have been possible. Hailye provided introductions, translation, patient explanations, incredible cooking and endless encouragement. I hope this book does justice to the running life that he and the other runners allowed me to share with them. Through encouraging me to train alongside the runners of *Moyo Sports,* Malcolm Anderson gave me a window into the world of Ethiopian running that would have been almost impossible to negotiate without his support.

Thanks to my PhD supervisors in Edinburgh, Neil Thin and Jamie Cross, whose ideas and support made all the difference. Jamie had faith in this project before I did, and encouraged me to apply for the funding that made it possible. Jeevan Sharma, Elliott Oakley, Tom Boylston, Juli Huang, Nick Long, Allysa Ghose, Dan Guiness, Niko Besnier, Leo Hopkinson, Felix Stein, Declan Murray and Tom Cunningham have all been generous readers of my writing. Diego Malara was an especially attentive reader and helped me enormously. The hours we have spent discussing Ethiopia have been extremely valuable.

Back at home I thank my own coaching duo, Max and Julie Coleby. They have invested countless hours in making me a better runner, and always tolerated my tendency to ruin all the training by taking off travelling. Without their encouragement I would have abandoned competitive running years ago and this book would never have been written. Thanks to my parents, for having a house full of books and for always encouraging my international adventures.

Most of all, to Roslyn, for turning the PhD into a joint adventure, and to little Maddy who turned up halfway through the writing of the book and put the whole thing in perspective.

ACKNOWLEDGEMENTS

Photo credits: All photographs © Michael Crawley except: page 3 all photographs © Getty Images; page 4, top © Getty Images; page 5 top left, photograph of the author by Marathon Photo; page 5, bottom right, photograph of the author and Roslyn Malcolm © Hailye Teshome; page 8, bottom, photograph of Tsedat used courtesy of Seville Marathon.

INDEX